PRAISE FOR *THE LAST PATRICIAN*

"Unorthodox and stimulating...[*The Last Patrician*] will force many to reevaluate the Kennedy they thought they knew."
—*Publishers Weekly*

"A lively, audacious argument."
—*The New York Times Book Review*

"*The Last Patrician* is likely to provoke and enlighten readers, regardless of their predispositions. As such, it is a rare work, well worth the read."
—*Mobile Register*

"A fascinating portrait of an American aristocracy that sought grandeur and importance in government service....*The Last Patrician* is both engaging and effective."
—*The Roanoke Times*

"Utterly convincing...[Beran] reminds us how much we lost when Bobby Kennedy fell to an assassin's bullet thirty years ago."
—*Kirkus Reviews*

"This stunning and most reflective of the current RFK books ponders the historical and intellectual roots of his political philosophy."
—*Library Journal*

"This is a book of wide breadth that questions many of our assumptions....Highly recommended."
—*Booklist*

"Fascinating...A truly exciting book, by a very young author, one of those all-too-rare experiences where the reader is drawn back again to rethink and reconsider what he thought he knew."
—*History Book Club*

"Beran writes so gracefully...."
—*Salon*

"Spirited and thoughtful..."
—*The Globe and Mail* (Canada)

"[A] remarkable book..."
—*The Boston Globe Magazine*

"A welcome rejoinder to the customary take on the Kennedy family...."
—*Tucson Weekly*

The Last Patrician

Bobby Kennedy and the End of
American Aristocracy

MICHAEL KNOX BERAN

ST. MARTIN'S GRIFFIN
NEW YORK

Design by Ellen R. Sasahara

Frontispiece: Bobby Kennedy on the Acropolis, mid-1960s (*AP/Wide World Photos*).

Part One, page 1: Mr. and Mrs. Joseph P. Kennedy posed with their nine children
for this photo in 1938 in Bronxville, New York. From left, seated, are Eunice, Jean,
Edward (on lap of his father), Kennedy, Patricia, and Kathleen, and standing,
Rosemary, Robert, John, Mrs. Kennedy, and Joseph Jr. (*AP/Wide World Photos*).

Part Two, page 85: Bobby Kennedy campaigns in Greenburg, Indiana, in May 1968
with a chipped tooth and a bruised lip. Bobby was pulled from his convertible in a
motorcade the night before by enthusiastic supporters (*AP/Wide World Photos*).

Library of Congress Cataloging-in-Publication Data

Beran, Michael Knox.
   The last patrician: Bobby Kennedy and the end of American
aristocracy / Michael Knox Beran.
      p. cm.
   ISBN 0-312-18625-8 (hc)
   ISBN 0-312-20659-3 (pbk)
   1. Kennedy, Robert F., 1925-1968. 2. Legislators—United States—
Biography. 3. United States. Congress. Senate—Biography.
I. Title.
E840.8.K4B46   1998
973.922'092—dc21
[B]

98-10200
CIP

First St. Martin's Griffin Edition: June 1999

10 9 8 7 6 5 4 3 2 1

*To my wife
and my parents*

Contents

Acknowledgments

I WISH TO thank the following people for their help in connection with the writing and publishing of this book: Mary Elizabeth Ward Beran, Denis Beran, Virginia Beran, Michael V. Carlisle, Henry P. Davis, Sarah Jeffries, Brian H. Johnson, Becky Koh, William W. Morton, Jr., Barbara J. Ward, Sedgwick A. Ward, and Robert Weil. I should also like to thank members of the staff of the John Fitzgerald Kennedy Library for permitting me to review documents in the library's archives. None of these individuals is, of course, responsible for such errors of fact or interpretation as the book may contain.

Note

HE DID NOT like the name "Bobby." He preferred that more grown-up, manly-sounding name "Bob." But just as his sister-in-law Jacqueline could not escape the intimacy of "Jackie," so he could not escape the diminutive boyishness of "Bobby." Jack Newfield, in his book *Robert Kennedy: A Memoir*, records the charming story of a ten- or twelve-year-old boy outside a Manhattan tenement who, when he was asked what all the fuss was about, replied that "Senator Javits and Bobby" were inside the building. It was as Bobby Kennedy that he was known to the world, and is now known to history, and I have therefore called him by that name in this book.

A man full of warm, speculative benevolence may wish his society otherwise constituted than he finds it; but a good patriot, and a true politician, always considers how he shall make the most of the existing materials of his country. A disposition to preserve, and an ability to improve, taken together, would be my standard of a statesman. Everything else is vulgar in the conception, perilous in the execution.

—EDMUND BURKE

INTRODUCTION

A Patrician in Pain

———❦❦❦———

THE WHITE HOUSE, JUNE 5, 1981. THE SURVIVORS OF Camelot have gathered in the Rose Garden to hear Ronald Reagan pay tribute to one of their own. Bobby Kennedy's widow is at last to receive the gold medal that Congress ordered to be struck in her husband's memory. Jimmy Carter, spiteful to the last, never found time to do it, and so it now falls to Carter's more magnanimous successor to present Ethel Kennedy with a token of the nation's gratitude.[1]

It is an exercise in irony, or rather in multiple ironies, this spectacle of a seventy-year-old President with a glistening black pompadour consecrating the memory of a tousled young martyr. Ronald Reagan was fourteen years old when Bobby Kennedy was born; he did not become President until twelve years after Bobby's death. In contrast to Reagan's long life, Bobby's was relatively brief: he was forty-two when he died in a Los Angeles hospital room in June 1968. Bobby's political career *ended* two years after Reagan's began. The younger man reached the summit of American politics half a decade before the older man started to climb. Bobby, in his thirties, was Attorney General of the United States when Reagan, in his fifties, was a faded actor working for the General Electric Corporation. Reagan privately blamed Bobby's Justice Department for costing him his job. Justice had long suspected that MCA—Jules Stein's company, the entertainment giant with which Reagan had formed close ties during his Hollywood career—was violating the antitrust laws.² When in 1962 Justice appeared ready to indict a number of MCA officials and others who had done them favors, GE panicked and fired the genial host of its popular television program—or so Ronald Reagan believed.³

Bobby died young, but now, as they gather at the White House to honor his memory, his disciples are old. The brilliant young lawyers who once brought the power of the federal government to bear on MCA are themselves out of power, and the fading actor whose ties to men like Jules Stein and Lew Wasserman once provoked their scrutiny is now the President of the United States. In the Rose Garden on this warm June day it is the aging Kennedy men, not the newly installed Republican President, who seem tired in spirit, worn out by the battles they have fought. Camelot is gone, and the faithful, bereft of their captains, are left to wander aimlessly in the diaspora. Ethel Kennedy, in her fifties, chats amiably with Nancy Reagan, but her good cheer cannot mask, quite, the sorrow written in the lines of her face.

The family's reigning prince, brother Edward, is also on hand. The handsome youth whom Bobby helped to win a Senate seat in 1962 has settled into an uncomfortable middle age.⁴ It has not been a good year for Teddy. Less than twelve months have passed since he was defeated by Jimmy Carter in his bid for the presidency. Six months ago he announced that his pro forma marriage to Joan Bennett was over.⁵ Gossips whisper about too much drinking; some talk of drugs.⁶ Suzannah Lessard has exposed his philandering; her article "Teddy's Women Problem / Women's Teddy Problem" caused a sensation when it appeared in *The Washington Monthly* at the end of 1979.⁷ But, beleaguered though he is, the prince can still summon his hundred knights. The geriatric Cavaliers have dutifully presented themselves at the palace: McNamara, Harriman, Alsop, a host of lesser figures. Unlike the heady days when they came here to stare down Khrushchev or sip champagne to the sound of Pablo Casals's cello, the old warriors are bent and gray, a shadow of their former selves. The strong and confident leaders of the sixties are themselves *in* their sixties. They were, of course, the best and the brightest of the new generation that Jack Kennedy summoned to power on a cold January afternoon in 1961, but today they are haunted by their former greatness, humiliated by the promise to which they failed to live up. There is a peculiar pathos in seeing *this*, of all political generations, in its dotage.

And yet there is no bitterness, no resentment, in these men, the decayed remnant of a generation that would have changed the world—had it but world enough and time—as they sip cold drinks served on silver trays in the summer afternoon.[8] *The New York Times* will report that "both Kennedy and Reagan loyalists" are using the word "graceful" to characterize the occasion.[9] The reporters want to play up the contrast between New England idealism and California conservatism, between patrician conscience and Hollywood glitter. The Kennedys aren't playing that game. Ethel Kennedy nods "approvingly" as President Reagan speaks.[10] Reagan may be the first movie-star President, but, after all, the Kennedys themselves made glamour an indispensable part of American politics long before the host of *Death Valley Days* and the *General Electric Theater* reached the White House. Joseph Kennedy was in Hollywood, learning its lessons, studying its methods, financing its movies, ten years before Ronald Reagan showed up at Jack Warner's studio in Burbank in 1937.[11]

Still, the occasion *is* strange. Why *is* Ronald Reagan paying elaborate—and apparently unfeigned—verbal homage to a man Alice Roosevelt Longworth likened to a "revolutionary priest"?[12] Is it mere politeness that leads him to celebrate the hero of the liberals and the left, the admirer of Che Guevara, the man whom Arthur Schlesinger called a "tribune of the underclass"?[13] Is it hypocrisy? It is as if Augustus, safely ensconced in the imperial palace, had celebrated the memory of good old Cato, or as if Charles II had praised the memory of Cromwell. It doesn't make sense.

The Liberal Icon

OR DOES IT? When Ronald Reagan claimed that Bobby Kennedy was critical of bloated bureaucratic government, *The New York Times* sneered: Reagan was playing politics with Bobby's reputation, turning him into an advocate of his own vision of smaller government.[14] The *Times* was subscribing to the conventional wisdom: that Bobby Kennedy was the antithesis of Ronald Reagan, a martyr to the cause of twentieth-century liberalism, an orthodox liberal figure who, if he was capable of flirting with the radical left, never strayed very far from the principles of Franklin Roosevelt, Adlai Stevenson, and his own older brother. To the extent that Bobby was moving "beyond" conventional liberalism, he was moving in a direction consistent with its larger purposes, its higher ends; in moving beyond it, he was not turning against it. This is the prevailing view of Bobby Kennedy, the view memorialized in Arthur Schlesinger's vast (and brilliant) tome and in Jack Newfield's slender memoir. Ronald Reagan might have had the audacity to challenge this view of Bobby; few others have. Unlike Jack Kennedy, Bobby has largely been spared the indignity of a critical reevaluation. The historians who are hardest on Jack Kennedy are surprisingly gentle in their treatment of Bobby, unwilling to disturb popular myths, hesitant to cast doubt upon the first principles of the man's contemporary cult. Garry Wills, who in *The Kennedy Imprisonment* depicted Jack Kennedy as one of the great frauds of all time, is surprisingly sympathetic to Bobby, a man who (as Wills sees it) was forced by the charismatic requirements of being a Kennedy to move to the left and create "a kind of revolution in the hills, his own personal Sierra Maestra."[15] Wills's Bobby is "radicalized" by the sixties; he "flirts with language that was framed in the hills of Cuba" and is in danger of becoming "a mini-Fidel."[16] This, of course, is nonsense; is as valuable a contribution to the Bobby literature as Frank Capell's right-wing polemic *Robert F. Kennedy, Emerging American Dictator*, with its picture of Bobby as a soul mate of Castro.[17] Neither Wills nor anyone else has succeeded in revising Schlesinger's picture of Bobby as the last great liberal. Is such a revision even possible? Will the sentimental defenders of the welfare state permit it? In his guise as the last great liberal, Bobby is a valuable commodity, a rare example of a liberal icon whose appeal remains undiminished today.[18] There has been no rush to tell the truth about Bobby Kennedy.

Reagan was nearer that truth than he—or his listeners—knew. Bobby *did* challenge the liberal orthodoxies of his day. If he was not a raging conservative trapped inside a liberal's body—a Bill Buckley waiting to be born—neither was he the gentle liberal whom Arthur Schlesinger depicted in his thousand pages.[19] According to the keepers of the liberal conscience, Bobby was, at the time of his death, poised to become the "Adlai Stevenson of the 1970s," the "torchbearer" of all that Eleanor Roosevelt stood for.[20] Eleanor Roosevelt herself was more canny; she "resisted" Bobby almost to the moment of her own death.[21] The liberals who canonized Bobby in death were suspicious of him in life—and for good reason. Newfield reluctantly conceded the existence of a conservative Bobby, a Bobby who "believed in the work ethic, family, and the rule of law."[22] The rigors of a liberal education and his own conscientious attempts at liberal piety never succeeded in eradicating the conservatism at his core. "He never lost," Newfield wrote, that "Puritan strain of moral conservatism" that made him despise *Playboy* magazine and movies that glorified sex and violence.[23] He "agreed with his wife that it was 'not right' when *Newsweek* published a nude photo of Jane Fonda on its cover," and he thought the decadence of Antonioni's film *Blowup* "immoral."[24] Bobby would have been the first to applaud the contemporary renewal of interest in the Victorian virtues. William Bennett's anthologies, with their Kiplingesque paeans to work, courage, loyalty, and faith, would have appealed to him.

The story I have to tell is not a simple one. Ronald Reagan grew to manhood in small Middle Western towns whose sunny verities he instinctively adopted as his own. Bobby's was, from the first, a more complicated existence. He was the son of an entrepreneurial father who believed that his sons could obtain power for themselves only if they forswore the role of entrepreneurial hero and allied themselves to a patrician elite. Bobby and his brothers would be raised not in the entrepreneurial tradition of Joseph P. Kennedy, but in the aristocratic tradition of patricians who, like Franklin Roosevelt and Adlai Stevenson, believed that the age of the entrepreneur was over and that America's continued progress depended on its creation of a government powerful enough to institute reform at home and guarantee peace abroad. These patrician statesmen were the architects of the twentieth-century welfare and administrative state; after World War II they helped to construct the twentieth-century national security state. The son of an entrepreneurial capitalist, Bobby became the proselyte of the tradition of grand government that Roosevelt and Stevenson championed. This tradition was, of course, at odds with his own deepest impulses, and he never ceased to admire brave, self-reliant, self-made men. But Bobby was a good boy and for the most part did as he was told. His rebellion came later, when he was on his own, when his older brothers were gone and his father lay crippled by a stroke.

This book tells the story of that rebellion. It was a rebellion that brought Bobby to question, as cogently and thoughtfully as any statesman of the postwar period, the orthodoxies upon which the welfare state and the national security state rested. The argument advanced in these pages is not that Bobby was a repressed conservative, patiently waiting for an opportunity to come out of the liberal closet. There was much in Ronald Reagan's policies that he would have abhorred. And yet he would, I think, have been no less troubled by his younger brother's defense of a welfare system that had manifestly failed. He would have thought it sad and perhaps tragic that Ted should have spent his career championing a welfare establishment that he himself despised. The New Deal, Bobby asserted, was over; it was time for Americans to "disenthrall" themselves, to find new solutions to old problems.[25] In looking for new solutions, Bobby became convinced of the value of old ones.

Toward a Post-Enlightenment Politics

THE THEME THAT gives his life its unity, its dramatic coherence, is his preoccupation with pain. Pain was for him a vocation of sorts; he would become, at the end of his life, a close student of Greek tragedy and an expert on the ways in which contemporary Americans suffer. When he came to write a foreword to the memorial edition of his brother's *Profiles in Courage*, pain was the first thing that came to his mind. "At least one half of the days he spent on this earth were days of intense physical pain," Bobby wrote of Jack Kennedy. "He was in Chelsea Naval Hospital for an extended period of time after the war, had a major and painful operation on his back in 1955, campaigned on crutches in 1958. In 1951 on a trip we took around the world he became ill. We flew to the military hospital in Okinawa and he had a temperature of over 106 degrees. They didn't think he would live."[26] But although Bobby grew up with pain, he did not immediately discover in it his life's work. One of the most vivid memories of his youth was the smell—putrid and horrible—of Lem Billings's burnt flesh when the two of them shared a room one summer after Billings had been scalded in the shower.[27] Much of Bobby's life was passed in the shadow of death; before he himself died, he would watch two brothers, a sister, and a brother-in-law die violent deaths. But it was not until middle age, long after he had first known the horror of charred and rotting flesh, that he discovered in human suffering his true métier.

If Bobby interests us today—and he should interest us today—it is because at some level his preoccupation with suffering was genuine, and not just a ploy to win over liberals and intellectuals.[28] At some level the anguish was real. Not simply his anguish over the sins of the nation, its manifold injustices to the poor, the blacks, the Indians. Not simply his anguish over his brother's death, his despair in the face of a world that could destroy a man like Jack Kennedy so casually, so carelessly, so capriciously. The tabloid histories that have appeared in recent years, so otherwise worthless, have this merit, a merit that goes beyond giving publishers an excuse to reprint old pictures of Marilyn Monroe: they have revealed to us the sordid places in Bobby's own soul, the shadowy depths to which Schlesinger and Newfield and the other hagiographers never dared to descend. A man with as finely developed a conscience as Bobby Kennedy's could not have been unaffected by the memory of his own less forgivable conduct. In this respect at least the anguish was real.

Hardly a day passes without our being introduced to some new and hitherto undiscovered aspect of the American agony. There is, of course, the physical pain of the inner-city slum, the deprivation described by Jonathan Kozol in his book about the Mott Haven section of the Bronx.[29] But this physical pain, Bobby knew, was a manifestation of a deeper pain, a pain that was not limited to the ghetto. This pain, a spiritual, or what we more often today call a psychological pain, is big business in America, one of our foremost growth industries. Evidences of this pain are ubiquitous in our culture: depression, anxiety, alcoholism, drug abuse, eating disorders, the pervasiveness of Prozac are among its more readily apparent symptoms. To escape the hurt, we spend billions of dollars in the pursuit of more or less counterfeit approximations of felicity. In the Old World, human suffering was a question for philosophers and theologians. Ordinary men and women were too busy *doing* the suffering to care much about why they suffered, or whether they should suffer. How different the case in America. In the second half of the twentieth century, the vast majority of Americans, free of the harsher forms of physical suffering, have become, if anything, even more conscious of the other agonies of human existence. They have become even more obsessed with the question of why they so often feel so bad. Depression, despair, frustration, alienation—whatever name we give the pain, it is there, defying the most ingenious attempts of the pharmaceutical industry to mitigate its deleterious effects.

The Enlightenment promised to end our pain. The *philosophes* promised to liberate us from our misery, to deliver us from the evil of suffering. It is in part because our pain was supposed to have

gone away—or greatly decreased in severity—that we are so morbidly conscious of its presence today. The free market, the welfare
state, the modern discipline of psychology, the modern pharmaceutical industry are among the more readily identifiable methods by
which the Enlightenment tried to put an end to human suffering.
Man's desire to escape from pain fueled the engines of Enlightenment, but in the end pain itself, our stubborn nemesis, revealed the
limits of Enlightenment. Pain is part of our destiny. Bobby, the first
post-Enlightenment American statesman, sought to make peace
with it. How, he wondered, can we learn to live with pain? How
can we profit from it? Bobby did not, in his attempt to fashion a
post-Enlightenment politics, come up with all the answers. But he
understood the problem; he grasped our predicament better than
most.

PART I

The Making of an Aristocrat

I

$$\text{—} \mathcal{O} \mathcal{O} \mathcal{O} \text{—}$$

H<small>E BECAME A QUESTIONER, A DOUBTER, BUT THAT IS</small> not how he began. It is an old story: before he rebels, the heretic is among the most pious of priests. Only those who have thoroughly understood a system can act decisively to change it. Augustine was a perfect pagan, Paul a perfect Jew, before each became a revolutionary Christian. Luther was a priest before he became a Protestant. It was only because he had embraced the orthodoxies of his age—embraced them with the passion of a believer—that Bobby Kennedy was able to become, at the end of his life, so constructive a critic of those orthodoxies.[1]

He grew up amid contradictions, a confusion of identities, a profusion of faiths. His life was grounded in Yankee realities: prep schools and Ivy League colleges, summers on the Cape. But he did not adjust to them in the ready and easy way his brothers did. He was shyer, quieter, more withdrawn. Vestiges of the old life, the life of his ancestors, so different from the secular Yankee world in which the father sought to envelop the children, perplexed him. Beside his father's worldliness there was his mother's piety, her daily attendance at Mass, her constant resort to prayer and contemplation. Her faith made a deep impression upon the young Bobby, deeper than the impression it made upon his brothers. For a time, it is said, he considered becoming a priest.[2] Who knows? He might have been a good one. But his father had different ideas.

The Meaning of the Malcolm Cottage

THE HOUSE ITSELF tells the story. In 1926 Joseph Kennedy turned thirty-eight. He was a stock speculator and millionaire who four years before had left the investment banking firm of Hayden, Stone & Company to play the bull market of the twenties on his own. More recently he had acquired a controlling interest in a motion picture company with operations in New York and California, and it is probable that he continued to derive profits from the illegal distribution of bootlegged liquor.[3] At all events, Joseph Kennedy had by 1926 become a rich man; in the spring of that year, when he moved from Boston to New York, he hired a private railroad car to take his family south. But Kennedy did not want his children to become New Yorkers, and in the summer of 1926 he returned to Massachusetts, took his family to the Cape, and there rented a house known as the Malcolm cottage at Hyannis Port.[4] Bobby Kennedy, who had been born the previous November, was not yet a year old.

Two years later Joseph Kennedy bought the Malcolm cottage outright for some $25,000.[5] It was not such a lot of money to a young millionaire who, like Kennedy, was fond of occasional extravagance. He claimed that he lost $1 million on the movie *Queen Kelly*, his failed attempt to showcase his sweetheart, Gloria Swanson.[6] And he agreed to put up a horse called Silver King, one of his studio's principal box-office attractions, in a stable that, at $25,000, cost as much as the Malcolm cottage itself.[7] The big spender in Hollywood was, however, curiously reticent when it came to throwing his money around on Cape Cod. Even after he enlarged it, the Malcolm cottage remained a conspicuously modest place, a New England summer house, spacious and comfortable, but not at all grand, a rambling, white-shingled, somewhat ordinary house, the chief distinction of which lay in the great swath of lawn that separated it from Nantucket Sound. It was the house of a successful lawyer, a well-off banker, not an American tycoon.

Later the family would acquire the neighboring houses: Bobby bought the adjacent property, and Jack bought the house next to that, a nondescript residence on Irving Avenue, some distance from the water.[8] Legend has exaggerated the glamour of the place; the very name the press gave the property—the Kennedy "compound," with its air of institutional, of vaguely military, dullness—proclaimed its plainness. Not even the most fanciful commentator could call it an estate. For Joseph Kennedy to have bought—and retained—so modest a property was out of character. It is almost a rule: the successful American—Vanderbilt, Frick, Rockefeller, Hearst, Gates—builds himself a house commensurate with his fortune. And yet Kennedy, though he was no less vain than the constructors of our various American Xanadus, refused to build himself a monument to his plutocratic pluck. Some would doubtless argue that the reason for such unwonted modesty lay in the fact that the Kennedy fortune was never as great as has been supposed, that misapprehensions of the extent of the family's wealth began in 1957 when *Fortune* magazine estimated the family's net worth at $250 million, roughly double the actual figure.[9] But even allowing for exaggeration, Kennedy's wealth would surely have permitted him to buy a bigger house than the one he did. Not Kykuit, perhaps, the Rockefeller mansion in Pocantico Hills, or Matinecock Point, the Morgan estate on the north shore of Long Island, but something more impressive than the Malcolm cottage. Why, then, did he buy it? Why did he choose Hyannis Port? His business ventures were taking him farther and farther afield, to Hollywood, to Chicago, to London; wouldn't a summer place closer to New York, his base of operations, make more sense? Wasn't Southampton, or Oyster Bay, or Glen Cove a more natural choice? Hyannis wasn't even *friendly* to the Kennedys when they arrived—or later. Watching the neighbors wave after her brother's election to the presidency, Eunice Shriver commented sourly, "They never showed such interest." The Kennedy "compound," however unglamorous that formulation sounds, was actually an improvement on the original name. For years the Kennedy property was known simply as the "Irish house."

He must initially have hoped for acceptance. He would not repeat the mistakes he had made in the Brahmin resort at Cohasset, where he and Rose had been blackballed at the country club.[10] By taking a modest house at Hyannis, Joseph Kennedy would impress his Protestant neighbors with his restraint, would convince them that he, too, despised vulgarity. Far from resembling the gaudy perfection of a Rockefeller residence, with Picassos and Mirós on the walls, Joseph Kennedy's houses tended toward a distinct shabbiness. Guests were surprised to discover that, despite the expense of their upkeep, the houses were never quite clean.[11] But the ingenious strategies failed; the modest houses, the modest sailboats, the modest cocktail hour (one drink before dinner) failed to convince the Yankees (and the Middle Western WASPs who were becoming increasingly prominent at Hyannis) that Joseph Kennedy was one of them.[12] "It was petty and cruel," one WASP recalled.[13] The women "looked down on the daughter of 'Honey Fitz'; and who was Joe Kennedy but the son of Pat, the barkeeper?"[14]

His money did not impress them, and neither did his genuine successes. Rose Kennedy spoke hopefully of a day when the "nice people" of Boston would accept her husband, but the day never came.[15] When Kennedy did an admirable job as the first chairman of the Securities and Exchange Commission, the "nice people" spoke darkly of his knowledge of the crooked and indirect ways of Wall Street; only a very corrupt man, they said, could have made the stock market honest. When he proved (at first) to be a popular ambassador to the Court of St. James's, the descendants of the Four Hundred (FDR among them) laughed at the spectacle of "a red-haired Irishman" being taken into the camp of the English.[16] "Do you know a better way to meet people like the Saltonstalls?" the young Joseph Kennedy asked, naively, after he had been appointed to the board of directors of the Massachusetts Electric Company.[17] But the Saltonstalls remained aloof; so, too, did the Harvard classmates who booed and jeered him at his twenty-fifth reunion; so, too, did the clubbable people who continued to refuse his applications for membership in their clubs.

Why then did he stay? Why did he not retire from the scene

of his disgrace, flee from the memory of his humiliation? It is true
that he moved out of Boston and took houses in New York, in
Riverdale and Bronxville (as well as in Palm Beach).[18] But he continued to maintain his principal residence at Hyannis, and he encouraged his children to think of Massachusetts as home.[19] His
decision to stay was, to say the least, out of character. Joseph Kennedy's inclination, when confronted with the possibility of failure
or rejection, was to cut his losses and get out: thus the ignominious
retreats from Hollywood in the thirties and from England and national politics in the forties. Failure of any kind reduced him to
almost pathological despair. Gloria Swanson recalled how Kennedy,
when he realized the full magnitude of the *Queen Kelly* disaster,
slumped in a chair and "held his head in his hands": "Little, high-
pitched sounds escaped from his rigid body, like those of a wounded
animal whimpering in a trap."[20] And yet, in spite of the proportions
of his social failure in Massachusetts, Kennedy determined to stay.
Stubbornness may have played a part in that decision, but it is not
the whole explanation. There was an element of calculation as well,
a hope of gratification generationally deferred. The establishment
oligarchs may have determined that *he* was unable to live up to the
standards of their civilization; it would be different with Bobby and
his brothers. It was for their sakes that he refused to give up, refused
to surrender his little toehold in New England, refused to become
an expatriate and join rich Europeans in a life of polo and purchased
titles. Massachusetts would be more than a political base for his
boys; it would enable them to become something he himself could
never hope to be. Joseph Kennedy could not have been elected to
the Board of Overseers at Harvard, but his son Jack could—and
ultimately did—obtain that high Brahmin honor. "If an Irish Catholic can get elected an Overseer at Harvard," Joseph Kennedy said,
"he can get elected to anything."[21] The elder Kennedy knew what
it was like to have the patent-leather jack-boot of class thrust in his
face; but not Bobby and his brothers. They would escape his fate.

Mastering the Mores of the Establishment

IT IS EASY to parody the more naive attempts of critics to describe the vast and secret powers of what used to be called the Protestant establishment in America, that shadowy preserve of old boys and DAR matrons that, according to E. Digby Baltzell, amounted to an indigenous aristocratic caste. In 1962 Richard Rovere published an essay that was perhaps just such a parody—a parody of the mixed sensation of delight and despair the paranoid prole feels when he thinks he has proved beyond all shadow of a doubt the existence of an elaborate conspiracy superintended by men like David Rockefeller and John J. McCloy with the assistance of the Council on Foreign Relations, Skull and Bones, J. P. Morgan & Co., and the Racquet Club.[22] Joseph Alsop, for his part, stated for the record that "there is no such thing" as an "American aristocrat," and that "anyone using that phrase" would have been "dismissed as 'common' " by those uncommon people who, although they might have acted like aristocrats (by, among other things, dismissing their fellow citizens as "common"), really weren't.[23]

Scoffers like Rovere might scoff, and covert snobs like Alsop might deny, but Joseph Kennedy never for a moment doubted the existence of an American aristocracy. He long remembered every snub, every rebuke, every cut he received from those who, he fancied, belonged to it. And how could he, the wunderkind of the Street, have forgotten the humiliation of sitting in the reception room at 23 Wall, waiting to see Mr. J. P. Morgan, Jr., and being informed that Mr. J. P. Morgan, Jr., was too busy to receive him?[24] Whether Kennedy ever admired the so-called "Protestant" or "Eastern" establishment will always be a question, but there can be no doubt that he had considerable respect for what he perceived to be its power. A mastery of its mores was, he was convinced, essential to anyone who wished to hold power in the republic beyond the next election or two. He had, in his own career, fatally misjudged the strength, the toughness, and the ruthlessness not only of such grandees as FDR and Averell Harriman but of their implacable capos, men like Hopkins, Frankfurter, and Ickes. His belief was not an unreasonable one: after the failure of his English embassy, the patricians turned on Kennedy savagely, turned on him in a way they never would have turned on one of their own.

His mistake might in other circumstances have seemed a venial one: he had, in an unguarded moment, offered a gloomy assessment of the future of democracy in England.[25] That was all, but that was enough. Kennedy had only to contrast the way the preppy oligarchs treated him with the way they treated Alger Hiss to see a genteel hypocrisy at work. Kennedy offered a gloomy prophecy of England's future; Hiss betrayed his country and engaged in treason. Hiss, however, was an insider, one who had distinguished himself at the Harvard Law School, clerked for Mr. Justice Holmes, and impressed Secretary Acheson. At the time of Hiss's indictment for perjury in 1948, David Rockefeller attempted to persuade his fellow trustees of the Carnegie Endowment to give the estimable but penurious young man a paid leave of absence (Hiss himself had offered to resign as president of the Endowment).[26] Adlai Stevenson and Felix Frankfurter testified to Hiss's good character at the trial, and so, too, did John W. Davis, the West Virginia lawyer whose service as Solicitor General, Ambassador to England, Democratic presidential candidate, founding member of the Council on Foreign Relations, and lawyer for the House of Morgan had made him into a pillar of the Eastern ascendancy.[27] The establishment that vilified Joseph Kennedy, and never forgave him, took pity on Alger Hiss and never forgave his accusers.

Seen from the perspective of his struggles with the grandees, Joseph Kennedy's choice of the unpretentious Malcolm cottage makes perfect sense. It is no wonder that he should have been anxious to ensure that Bobby and his brothers develop, through their experience of the Cape, New England manners, New England accents, a New England sensibility. It is no wonder that he should have desired them to attend not the Catholic prep schools (Canterbury, Portsmouth Priory) that Rose favored, but such quintessentially Protestant institutions as St. Paul's, Milton, and Choate.[28]

Joseph Kennedy had himself been educated at the Boston Latin School, but although this venerable institution had once graduated the cream of the Brahmin crop, by the time Kennedy entered it in 1901, it had lost much of its social cachet. As the nineteenth century drew to a close, the sons of Boston's Brahmin and New York's Four Hundred families were sent in greater numbers than ever before to be educated in the "English" fashion at boarding schools modeled on the great English public schools; it was to these schools that Kennedy sent his own sons to be educated.[29] There Bobby and his brothers would learn the secret language of the better sort of people, the code of the "nice people" of Boston, would learn about the things that the rest of the world didn't: "tennis, table manners, foreign and ancient languages, good pictures, fine music, French wines, the little harbors of Penobscot Bay" (so runs Nelson Aldrich's catalog of patrician esoterica in his book *Old Money*).[30] Their memories would be indistinguishable from those of their patrician peers, memories that together form a kind of collective unconscious of the preppy race: memories of "stumbling recitations of the *Anabasis*, the feel of grass tennis courts under bare feet, an embarrassing performance in the Tavern Club play, a coming-out party at Hammersmith Farm (*everybody* was there), the steamed mirrors at the Racquet Club . . ."[31]

The sons would gain more than memories at these Etons *manqué*; they would learn to compete with a grace, a humor, a nonchalance, that quite eluded the father. Joseph Kennedy impressed upon his sons the importance of excelling not only at tennis, but also at sailing and (mindful of Dink Stover, the hero of Owen Johnson's *Stover at Yale*) football.[32] (Kennedy drew the line at polo; when Teddy expressed an interest in the sport, his father informed him that Kennedys did not play polo.) The waters of Nantucket Sound and the playing fields of Milton and Choate would work their Anglo-Saxon magic and transform Bobby and his brothers into something Joseph Kennedy himself had never been able to become—competitors who not only won races, but who also won *over* the very opponents they bested. Christopher Matthews, in his study of the two men, has shown that even Richard Nixon, Jack's great rival, could not help but love and admire his adversary: Nixon burst into tears when it appeared likely that Kennedy would die in 1954 following back surgery, and he became "euphoric" when he learned that Kennedy wanted to visit him in Florida a few days after his defeat in the 1960 election.[33] The Kennedy siblings, George Plimpton observed, played touch football stylishly, with good humor and a ready wit, in contrast to the plodding Secret Service agents who sometimes joined in their games. Nice people played football one way, Secret Service agents—and the rest of the world—another. When "touch" was played on the lawns in front of the Ambassador's house at Hyannis Port, Plimpton recalled, "you had *them*"— the Secret Service men—"along with the dogs and the children and the sisters and the house guests . . . quite a mob of people." The numbers, however, were "cut down quite quickly," mostly, it seemed to Plimpton, "because of the hard-nosed play of the Secret Service people." "They'd been shut up in their sentry boxes or lurking about, whatever it is they do, and the touch football games gave them a chance to *star*, to perform." The agents played the game in a manner Plimpton thought "brutal and humorless":

> In the huddle they'd talk about running "post patterns," and they'd scrabble plays in the grass. The slightly hysterical and charming play of Jackie, say, which was full of little yells and darting, unpredictable runs in the wrong direction, wasn't quite suitable. So, by and by, people would drift away from the game—ostensibly, to get ready for dinner or . . . meet Uncle Ted coming in from his afternoon yacht race . . . and finally, in the dusk, there'd be four or five adults left, furious and panting, rushing quickly across the lawn and most of them were Secret Service people.[34]

Joseph Kennedy would never have understood why Plimpton thought the behavior of the Secret Service agents ("whatever it is they do") so lacking in charm, so lacking in grace—so appalling, in fact, that the nice people had to make up excuses to escape. When in the late forties Bobby and his Harvard friend Kenny O'Donnell "joked at dinner about finishing last in a sailing race," Joseph Kennedy was outraged. "What kind of guys are you to think that's funny?" the Ambassador demanded before quitting the table in disgust.[35] Like the Secret Service agents who spoke of "post patterns" and scrabbled plays in the grass, like Richard Nixon himself, Joseph Kennedy had not been educated at Milton or Choate; he was quite as incapable as the most graceless of the agents, with their "brutal" and "humorless" approach to competition, of speaking a language with which George Plimpton could have sympathized, of emitting the numerous little "recognition signals" (Joseph Alsop's phrase) that taken together indicate that one belongs, that one understands the rules, that one appreciates good form, that one knows how to dress for dinner or enjoy a postrace drink with Uncle Ted.[36]

Joseph Kennedy did not speak George Plimpton's language, but the result of his efforts at assimilation was that his sons *did* speak it, and as fluently as Plimpton himself. He did not understand what his sons had become, but at some level he was glad they had become it. Joseph Kennedy was not what the preppies called a clubbable man. Bobby, Jack, and Teddy were. They were initiated into the rituals of the preppy elite, made friends with the George Plimptons, the Ben Bradlees, the Joe Alsops of the world, were invited to join all the clubs from which the father had been excluded. Kenny O'Donnell said that Bobby had been invited to join "almost all" the best clubs at Harvard.[37] (In 1950, alas, not even a Kennedy could aspire to Porcellian.) The brothers became masters of the "New England manner," in Arthur Schlesinger's words, and so consummate was their mastery that some critics were incapable of distinguishing them from the genuine article.[38] Teddy White's evocations of the Kennedys read at times like an Emily Post text designed to instruct duller Americans in the fine points of patrician etiquette. White was amazed that Jack Kennedy, sipping a daiquiri on election night in 1960, should have had the presence of mind to talk about art, not politics, with his friend Bill Walton. This suitably highbrow topic was discussed, White tells us, in a "large white room furnished to Mrs. Kennedy's taste in antiques" without any interruption from "radio, TV, or the communications center." Jack's ruminations on the nature of art ended only when, "promptly at eight," dinner was announced and he and Walton went into the "elegantly different" dining room of Kennedy's Hyannis Port house.[39] Take note, America: when Jack Kennedy finally did settle down to watch the returns that would determine his fate, he watched them "on a small leather-covered TV set that his wife manipulated to bring into focus."[40] The smallness and scarcity of television sets in Kennedy residences are a favorite theme of Kennedy aficionados like White; television might have helped make Jack Kennedy President, but he himself, we are assured, watched the vulgar medium as little as possible.

The unrefined air of East Boston hung about Joseph Kennedy, an offense to Brahmin and Four Hundred sensibilities; Bobby and his brothers would grow up in a more suitable environment, would progress, as naturally and inevitably as the Stimsons and Achesons of the world, from sailboats and prep-school playing fields to the highest affairs of state. Jack Newfield was wrong to call Bobby a quintessential Boston Catholic.[41] Bobby and his brothers may have gone to college in Cambridge, but they never went to Boston for any reason other than to solicit votes. By the time they reached manhood, they were closer to the world of the *Social Register* than they were to the world of Honey Fitz.

Toward the Vineyard

LIKE SO MANY of their triumphs, the Kennedys' achievement in mastering the code of the Brahmins looks different in retrospect. Sailing off the Vineyard with *Social Register* swells appears a less enviable experience in the context of Chappaquiddick. Like the Harvard-Yale game or the first sail of the summer, the Edgartown Regatta was a Kennedy family tradition, one of those ritual events that mark the passing seasons. It offered the Kennedys a chance to catch up with old friends who summered on the island—the McNamaras, the Bundys, the Katzenbachs—and to burnish the family's intellectual credentials by cultivating literary preppies like John Marquand, Bill Styron, and their protégés. (Bobby met the young

Philip Roth on the Vineyard in the middle sixties.) But the regatta also offered the Kennedys a chance to let go, to find relatively anonymous release in a crowd of lawyers and stockbrokers dazed by sun and drink. In the thirties an "overly boisterous celebration" of a regatta victory in an Edgartown hotel resulted in Joe Junior and Jack spending a night in the Edgartown jail.[42] The Kennedy regatta parties in 1966 and 1967 were memorable affairs—happy occasions, if a trifle wild; the Kennedy brothers were able to relax on the Vineyard in a way they couldn't at Hyannis Port, where Mother and Dad frowned upon excess.[43]

Islands like Martha's Vineyard and Nantucket are extraordinarily illuminating guides to the social history of Protestant New England. This history is nowhere more evident than in the evolution of the islands' architecture; to go from the Vincent House in Edgartown to Captain Lawrence's house or Dr. Fisher's house there is to see how the harsh and unforgiving life of the early settlers gave way to the more opulent civilization of the great sea captains and rich merchants who succeeded them. More opulent, but hardly less severe. The old Federal houses of Edgartown and Nantucket, for all their elegance of design and splendor of proportion, retain still the memory of the austere God-fearing men who built them, men who in the midst of wealth deplored the corruption of their souls, and who in the apogee of prosperity looked into their Bibles to ponder the lesson of Job. In time, however, the gloomy introspection of old New England gave way to the masques and revels of its foppish descendants, and a once-formidable race of Brahmins degenerated into a supine tribe of mere preppies. The Kennedys had the misfortune to infiltrate the old Protestant aristocracy at the height of its decadence. They came too late, and mastered its customs too well.

Teddy himself competed in the 1969 Edgartown Regatta; he apparently enjoyed himself as he drank beer and sailed his boat, the *Victura*, in the sultry afternoon. The race itself was something of a disappointment: the *Victura* finished in ninth place.[44] No matter: the Kennedys had won the *real* race. They now "owned" a Senate seat that the Brahmins had once considered almost as their personal property. Ted could look on with serene magnanimity as the preppies made off with a sailing trophy. After the customary drink (rum and Coke) with the other sailors on the victor's boat, Ted was driven over to Chappaquiddick Island by his chauffeur for a party in honor of the "boiler room" girls who had worked for Bobby in his 1968 presidential campaign.[45] Garry Wills has said that Ted's presence at the party was itself an act of noblesse oblige, the honorable deed of a sad-eyed man who, haunted by his brothers' ghosts, felt it his duty to comfort the peasants who had plowed his family's fields. And yet it is difficult to believe that the party was simply a chore for Teddy; on the contrary, it seems to have been precisely the kind of preppy blowout he enjoyed. The guests at the Lawrence cottage drank deeply that night, but not, in the context of the moment, outrageously.[46] Nor was Ted the only preppy on the Vineyard to have a good time on the Friday night of regatta weekend. When, after the accident, he attempted to construct an alibi, he did so by appearing in the lobby of his Edgartown hotel—at half past two in the morning—to complain about the noise *other* revelers were making.[47] The alibi was never used; in 1969 not even the most fastidious old boy felt a need to put on a blazer to go into a deserted hotel lobby in the middle of the night. The sad attempt to construct an exculpatory chronology, if it did nothing to prove Ted's innocence, does reveal something of the overheated atmosphere of Edgartown on regatta weekend. The behavior that led up to the accident at Chappaquiddick was not anomalous; it was indeed perfectly explicable in terms of the mores of a preppy watering hole in the middle of the twentieth century. "Oh my God, what has happened?" Teddy is said to have exclaimed several times as he was driven to the Vineyard's airstrip the next day for the flight back to Hyannis Port. A short time earlier he had, at the Edgartown police station, given an account of the accident the night before in which he admitted that he had been the driver of the 1967 Oldsmobile that had careened off Dike Bridge and plunged into the dark waters below.[48] What had happened? The Kennedys had at last fulfilled the patriarch's dream; they had arrived, but had arrived only to discover that the promised land of the patricians was not an altogether happy one.

2

JOSEPH KENNEDY MOVED BOBBY AWAY FROM THE FAITH
and traditions of the Old World, the world of Honey Fitz and his
daughter Rose, the world of Sunday Mass and rosary beads, of lace
curtains and St. Patrick's Day parades. But he did not introduce
Bobby to the New World in which he himself had flourished, a
world where entrepreneurial energy and a fierce belief in the power
of individual effort brought him astonishing success. Joseph Kennedy was an archetypical New World character, a loner in all his
business activities, one who, operating with a small staff and few
institutional connections, raided promising markets, took his profits, and got out—a Natty Bumppo of Wall Street, one who eschewed affiliation with the established firms, one who was unwilling
to be tied down by the obligations of partnership and institutional
allegiance. For Bobby and his brothers, however, Joseph Kennedy
wanted a different life, a life lived not on the fringes of power, but
at the center. Bobby and his brothers would become not entrepreneurial improvisers on the frontiers of markets and communities,
but men who conformed to established codes and reverenced established institutions. Joseph Kennedy sent Bobby and his brothers
back to the Old World—not the world of the Boston Irish, to be
sure, but the world of what is sometimes called the Eastern establishment, that curious monument to the labors of a generation of
patricians eager to preserve, in America, those aristocratical privi-

leges that a rising tide of democratic entrepreneurialism threatened to destroy.[1]

Up from Individualism

JOSEPH KENNEDY'S EAGERNESS to connect Bobby and his brothers to a tradition of Eastern aristocracy stemmed in part from the extraordinary revival of patrician energy and talent that occurred in the United States in the first half of the twentieth century. This risorgimento of the well-to-do not only reversed a hundred years of aristocratic decline, it profoundly influenced the careers of Bobby and his brothers. The mastery of the aristocratic gesture that they eventually attained might have moved even FDR to envy. The Kennedys came in time to embody the idea of aristocracy in America; in some ways they were its fulfillment. But this aristocratic destiny was not as inevitable as might be supposed. Had Joseph Kennedy come of age a quarter of a century earlier, before the renaissance of the ruling class, it is unlikely that he would have *wanted* his sons to emulate the patricians. If there is splendor in the grandees who stare out at us from the canvases of Sargent, that splendor is diminished by a certain vacuousness in their expressions, a certain emptiness in their eyes. Sargent captured, in oil, not merely the elegance of the fin-de-siècle American aristocracy, but its impotence as well. Aristocracy in late-nineteenth-century America meant weakness; it meant effeminacy; it meant Henry James. Like the effete male protagonists of Edith Wharton's novels, the American aristocrats of the fin de siècle had surrendered to the charms of neurasthenic indolence; snobbery and tradition had insulated them from the larger life of the country. For the nation's first families the years between 1870 and 1900 really *were* the "Brown Decades," as Lewis Mumford called them, gloomy years of stagnation and (in spite of great wealth) decline. The patricians of the period counted Virginia dynasts, Hudson River patroons, pious New England clergymen, and rich New England merchants among their ancestors, but the ancient families were unable to exercise any real degree of political or economic power in the republic. They had ceased to be a governing class and were now merely a privileged one.[2] In Boston the Brahmins surrendered political control to the Irish in 1885, when Hugh O'Brien became the city's first Irish Catholic mayor.[3] Bobby's maternal grandfather, John F. "Honey Fitz" Fitzgerald, was one of a long line of Irish political leaders who followed in O'Brien's footsteps.[4] The soft young aristocrats who came of age at the end of the century were no match for the likes even of Honey Fitz; against such a lean and hungry competitor as Joseph Kennedy they had no chance whatever. The patricians had to contend, Edmund Wilson wrote,

> with a world that broke most of them. . . . They could no longer play the rôle . . . of a trained and public-spirited caste; the new society did not recognize them. The rate of failure and suicide in some of the college "classes" of the 'eighties shows an appalling demoralization.[5]

The patricians retired to the club or the sanitarium, read Walter Pater, and attempted—usually unsuccessfully—to cure themselves of their neurasthenic symptoms.[6] Although they retained all the outward show of aristocracy—the high ideals, the heavy pride, the intense conviction of their own superiority—the substance of aristocracy was gone. The greater number of America's snobbish hereditary organizations (Daughters of the American Revolution, Mayflower Descendants, etc.) were founded during this period, a sure sign, Richard Hofstadter observed, of patrician insecurity.[7] (The first Social Registers appeared, in Boston and New York, around 1890.[8]) A man like Henry Adams would doubtless have despised such pathetic attempts to recapture lost grandeur, but in spending his own life lamenting the demise of the eighteenth-century republic his ancestors had ruled, Adams himself, though in a more sophisticated and literary way, did much the same thing. Had the patrician order continued, in the twentieth century, to produce men like Henry James and Henry Adams, had these men continued to embody the highest qualities of the breed, it is doubtful whether

Joseph Kennedy would have wanted any part of it. He would never have coveted the Court of St. James's, the most aristocratic of the diplomatic posts, in the shameless way he did.[9] He would never have established a household at Hyannis Port. He would have kept Bobby and his brothers away from the Brahmins, lest the Brahmins corrupt their masculine virtue. Milton and Harvard were worse than useless, if in the end they produced T. S. Eliot.

But Joseph Kennedy *did* covet a place in the aristocratic firmament, for by the time he entered Harvard College in 1908, the character of the aristocracy had greatly changed. The origins of the change can be dated with some precision. The revolt of the blue-bloods against their consignment to an historical oblivion of poetry and country houses began on the day when the young Teddy Roosevelt, bullied "almost beyond endurance" by two boys whom he had neither the strength nor the skill to subdue, decided to take up boxing and learn how to fight back. Roosevelt's struggle to overcome his own tendencies toward dandyism was by no means an easy one; when he first took his seat in the New York State Assembly, the newspapermen, amused by his foppish apparel and shrill aristocratic accent, cried, "Oscar Wilde!" and hailed the arrival of a disciple of Walter Pater in Albany.[10] But Roosevelt persevered, and eventually purged the last remnant of sissiness from his character. It was the first indication of a new spirit at work in the descendants of America's most respectable families. Roosevelt—who was to become one of Bobby Kennedy's greatest heroes—was the embodiment of a patrician generation that could not be content with the passivity of its fathers.[11] Where the previous generation had luxuriated in its pain, its "obscure hurt," or transformed the pain into art, the new generation turned away from its suffering; it lost itself in action. "Get action, do things; be sane," Roosevelt once said, "don't fritter away your time; create, act, take a place wherever you are and be somebody: get action."[12] Roosevelt had injected a dose of testosterone into the feckless aristocracy, and the Four Hundred would never afterward be the same.

Roosevelt's conception of an aristocracy of action and power was one with which Joseph Kennedy could sympathize. But there was irony in Kennedy's adoration of the reinvigorated aristocracy, for Roosevelt and the preppy junta over which he presided despised men of Kennedy's type. Like all classes of people who have been deprived of influence by revolutionary transformations in the organization of society, America's patrician classes resented the economic changes that had, during the course of the nineteenth century, rendered their own position in society a so much more inferior one. Commerce had destroyed their claims to preeminence. The patricians lamented the economic "anarchy" of a free market that elevated such crude, raw-mannered men as Jim Fisk, Daniel Drew, Henry Clay Frick, and Joseph Kennedy himself to prominence.[13] Richard Hofstadter observed that, while in the 1840s "there were not twenty millionaires" in the United States, by 1910 "there were probably more than twenty millionaires sitting in the United States Senate."[14] Henry Adams, that brilliant snob, looking out of the window of his club at the "turmoil of Fifth Avenue" in the nineties, felt himself at Rome, under Diocletian, a witness to civic anarchy, the triumph of barbarism:

> The city [Adams wrote] had the air and movement of hysteria. . . . Prosperity never before imagined, power never yet wielded by man, speed never reached by anything but a meteor, had made the world irritable, nervous, querulous, unreasonable and afraid. All New York was demanding new men, and all the new forces, condensed into corporations, were demanding a new type of man,—a man with ten times the endurance, energy, will and mind of the old type,—for whom they were willing to pay millions at sight.[15]

The corporations, of course, were only the apparent villains; the real villains were the "new type of men," the men who, like Joseph Kennedy, stood at the head of the corporations, or who controlled their capital stock.[16] The politics of both of the Roosevelt cousins, Theodore and Franklin, were in part a reaction against Adams's "new type of man." Implicit in the political programs of the two Roosevelts was the idea that, if Americans were to continue to make progress, if they were to continue their marvelous ascent from pain and privation to ever loftier heights of prosperity, they would have to put their fate once again into the hands of the *aristoi*, into the hands of Enlightened statesmen who, through a rational application of modern theories of economic planning and control, could mitigate the more pernicious effects of a market economy—and not incidentally frustrate the ambitions of the tycoons and stock speculators (Joseph Kennedy among them) who were trying to take over the country.[17] Drawing on novel theories of economic regulation and European ideas of social reform, America's twentieth-century patrician reformers discovered a new means of enjoying the old feudal pleasures, and they found in the Creed of the Expert a way to effect their salvation as a class. They claimed a mandate for a new and Enlightened approach to the problem of human pain and human suffering, but beneath the trappings of science and economic sophistication lurked the familiar paternalistic ideas of the past.[18] The patricians succeeded in creating a grand seigneurial role, not indeed for themselves, but for the state, which in their theory was to function like a benevolent paterfamilias, helping people who (it was argued) could not help themselves. When he declared that he was going to be "President of all the people," Edmund Wilson observed, Franklin Roosevelt "meant that, as lord of the nation, he was going to take responsibility for seeing that all the various ranks of people, as far as was in his power, were going to be given what was good for them."[19]

The Idea of a Capitalist Villain

JOSEPH KENNEDY, THE Irish Catholic boy who dreamed of one day attaching his family to the aristocracy, was, of course, precisely the kind of interloper the patricians most feared when they denounced the "anarchy" of the free market. Kennedy was precisely the kind of capitalist predator whom the patricians believed effective government regulation would eliminate. Thirty years after his death, this picture of Joseph Kennedy as unprincipled capitalist villain continues to be a seductive one. To us no less than to his patrician contemporaries he appears crude, unscrupulous, untrustworthy. We picture him crossing the Atlantic (with Gloria Swanson in tow) or sitting amid the ticker-tape machines on the veranda of his house in Palm Beach, the very embodiment of a certain type of tycoon, a type that flourished in the twenties and thirties. To us he figures almost as a caricature, the Sinister Capitalist in a Graham Greene novel (cf. Lord Benditch in *The Confidential Agent*), a vulgar philistine who, if he enjoyed classical music, rarely read a serious book.[20] We put him in the same class with Max Beaverbrook and Waugh's Rex Mottram: a transatlantic adventurer, a cad, floating above the world on his own little cushion of capital, beholden to no one, selling short stocks and governments with equal ease, ready to do business with whoever made him the highest bid. Waugh's Charles Ryder says of Rex Mottram:

> One quickly learned all that he wished to know about him, that he was a lucky man with money, a member of Parliament, a gambler, a good fellow; that he played golf regularly with the Prince of Wales and was on easy terms with "Max" and "F.E."[21]

For the patrician, however, revenge is always sweet, and in the literature of aristocratic elegy the philistine stockjobber always gets his comeuppance. The "world was an older and better place" than men like Joseph Kennedy and Rex Mottram knew, and it soon enough saw through them. Like Joseph Kennedy's, Rex Mottram's ambition is frustrated by the orthodox patricians:

> Things had not gone as smoothly with him as he had planned. I knew nothing of finance, but I heard it said that his dealings were badly looked on by orthodox Conservatives. . . . There was always too much about him in the papers; he was one with the Press lords and their sad-eyed, smiling hangers-on; in his speeches he said the sort of thing

which "made a story" in Fleet Street, and that did him no good with his party chiefs.[22]

Waugh's Rex Mottram is a caricature; Joseph Kennedy was not. Like Mottram, Kennedy, too, was a friend of Beaverbrook and Luce and the other "Press lords"; he, too, got his name in the newspapers and used public relations men to "make a story" in the press; he, too, was accused of irregular business dealings and did things that got him into trouble with his party's chiefs. Joseph Kennedy might not have "played golf regularly" with the Prince of Wales, but long before his English embassy he succeeded, through a combination of brash and charm, in meeting the prince at a fashionable Paris restaurant and persuading him to give him letters of introduction to influential London businessmen.[23] And yet the picture of Joseph Kennedy that the patricians have left us is a deceptive one; the relevant evidence has been arranged to show him in the worst possible light. His mistakes are magnified, and his virtues are ignored or, worse, made to seem like vices. Shrewdness and entrepreneurial spirit become synonymous with dishonesty and treachery. Financial success becomes indistinguishable from moral corruption. Did Kennedy urge FDR to make a deal with Hitler? If he did, it was an unforgivable mistake. Did this mistake mean that he was rotten to the core?[24] It depends on the standard against which he is judged. Neville Chamberlain, after all, tried to make a deal with Hitler; but while we—very properly—censure Chamberlain's judgment, we do not question his integrity. Joseph Kennedy, however, is held to a different standard, for he was a Sinister Capitalist, unlike Chamberlain, who was merely descended from Sinister Capitalists. We are unable to resist the patrician interpretation of Joseph Kennedy precisely because we have been so powerfully influenced by it ourselves; we, too, tend instinctively to confound new money and entrepreneurial energy with lack of moral scruple. Even today we are quick to perceive villainy in the capitalist and the entrepreneur: Bill Gates, we are sure, must be violating the antitrust laws; Joseph Kennedy must have been a crook.

The elder Kennedy was shrewder, tougher, quicker than most of his patrician contemporaries; FDR alone, whom Kennedy called "the hardest trader I'd ever run up against," was a match for him.[25] In the relatively unfettered markets of the twenties Kennedy laid the foundations of a fortune that would in time dwarf the inherited wealth of most of his Harvard classmates. But although he had benefited greatly from the very opportunities the aristocrats sought to foreclose, Kennedy was nonetheless determined to ally, first himself, and later his sons, with a patrician caste eager to avenge the insults of the nouveaux riches by getting its hands on virgin markets as yet innocent of the government's suffocating embrace. Kennedy himself became the first full-time federal regulator of capital markets in the United States.[26] His Securities and Exchange Commission did not, it is true, have the cachet of Jerome Frank's Agricultural Adjustment Administration, the Mecca of the new regulatory state, the place to which bright young men like Adlai Stevenson, Telford Taylor, and the most talented of Frankfurter's "hot dogs" went to be confirmed in the New Deal faith, but the SEC could nonetheless boast of talented regulators like William O. Douglas of Yale and James Landis of Harvard.[27] Whatever doubts Kennedy might have had about the aristocratic program of federally sponsored paternalism, he eventually embraced it, and with some fervor. "An organized functioning society," he wrote in his 1936 book, *I'm for Roosevelt*, "requires a planned economy." The "more complex the society," he declared, "the greater the demand for planning." Certain "things have to be done," he concluded, "which no one but government can do."[28]

Half a century earlier, when the power of the patricians was at its lowest ebb, a tycoon such as Joseph Kennedy might have eschewed an alliance with the aristocracy, might have balked at the feudal sentimentality of the grand seigneurs, might have insisted on the critical role that unconstrained private initiative must always play in increasing a nation's prosperity. By the thirties, however, the idea of private initiative, the grand idea of Adam Smith and the Anglo-Scottish Enlightenment, was thought to be passé; the patrician reformers with whom Joseph Kennedy cast his lot drew instead on French theories of Enlightenment and Fabian notions of an elite class of "capable men."[29] Only a people who have been guided by wise and prescient leaders could ever hope to see the light, or know the truth. If Kennedy's decision to embrace FDR's theories of grand government was in part an act of prudence—he was afraid that if FDR failed, a purer form of socialism might triumph in America—it also represented a calculated gamble for power.[30] He had made his millions; he could afford to embrace the generous politics of noblesse oblige. "The boys might as well work for the government," he said of Bobby and his brothers, "because politics will control the business of the country in the future."[31]

The Traitor to His Class

IN SELLING OUT to the aristocrats, Joseph Kennedy, the self-made man, the brilliant entrepreneur, was a much more genuine "traitor to his class" than Franklin Roosevelt ever was. It is sometimes said that Roosevelt betrayed his class when he exacted his pound of flesh from the "economic royalists" during the New Deal. But in doing this, Roosevelt was not betraying his class, he was *avenging* it, avenging it against a class of new men, a class composed of the Wall Street speculators and big businessmen and great industrialists who had overthrown the old nobility. A few patricians, like Dick Whitney, the New York Stock Exchange president from whose gold watch chain dangled a little Porcellian pig, might have consented to join this aspiring class, and others, like the Morgans, might have helped to sustain it by raising capital for its ventures.[32] Many more patricians were compelled by financial necessity to act as lawyers for it.[33] But it was never Franklin Roosevelt's class; Roosevelt belonged to a family whose mercantile success had long before permitted its scions to set themselves up as country gentry.[34] The Roosevelts had once occupied the highest places in society, but in the second half of the nineteenth century the family came to be overshadowed by the magnificoes of the new plutocracy.[35] Roosevelt himself practiced law in a Wall Street firm after studying the profession at Columbia, but he quit in disgust after a few years. It was not a Roosevelt's job to do a Rockefeller's bidding.[36] Franklin Roosevelt did not belong to the aspiring class of plutocrats and would-be plutocrats that came into being after the Civil War. But Joseph Kennedy *did* belong to that class, and in rallying to Roosevelt's standard he betrayed it.

It is not difficult to see why Joseph Kennedy should have succumbed to the charms of the rejuvenated aristocracy. The risorgimento of the patricians represented one of the more astonishing comebacks in the history of American political power. Thrown out by Jefferson at the beginning of the nineteenth century, the patricians returned to power at the beginning of the twentieth, and the second time they did not make the mistake of alienating the common man. On the contrary, the patricians assiduously courted the people and, following the example of Caesar, promised no end of federally sponsored bread and shows. In the first half of the twentieth century the seemingly moribund aristocracy to which the Roosevelts belonged produced a succession of brilliant statesmen, administrators, and jurists; men like Elihu Root, Gifford Pinchot, Henry Stimson, Learned Hand, Averell Harriman, Dean Acheson, Sumner Welles, Francis Biddle, James V. Forrestal, Robert Lovett, Jack McCloy, Adlai Stevenson, Desmond FitzGerald, Richard Bissell, and the Alsop and the Bundy brothers represented a formidable collection of talent, of energy, of social and intellectual distinction. These statesmen were educated at the same schools; they belonged to the same clubs; they worked in the same law firms; they summered beside the same New England harbors. Their careers were advanced by the same Roosevelt patronage. In my own mind I call them Stimsonian statesmen, for Colonel Stimson, although he was not the most distinguished, was perhaps the most representative of the breed.[37] He was given his first government job by Theodore Roosevelt (as United States Attorney in New York) and his last by Franklin Roosevelt (as Secretary of War), and his public career coincided with the golden age of patrician governance. Like Franklin Roosevelt, Stimson (Andover '84, Yale '88, Harvard Law '90) practiced law on Wall Street, and though he was a much greater success at the bar than FDR ever was, he never liked being a corporate lawyer; it was a living, he said, and nothing more. It was not until he became a federal prosecutor that he felt himself "out of the dark places" where he had been "wandering all his life" and in a place where he "could see the stars."[38]

The men who followed in Stimson's footsteps to a large extent shaped the great public debates of the first half of the twentieth century. If this has been the "American century," it is because they made it so. Other groups besides their own, and other leaders besides themselves, were committed to many of the same ends, but none was as successful in articulating the new theory of government, and none was as effective in translating theory into practice. Their belief that a government composed of dedicated and Enlightened public servants could remake the world did more than give new purpose to a disaffected social class; it gave the nation a new sense of direction and aspiration, a new conception of its destiny.

The Stimsonians came to define twentieth-century American liberalism—a very different kind of liberalism from the nineteenth-century free-market liberalism they questioned. Their belief in the beneficent power of a government directed by brilliant Stimsonian illuminati received its most enduring expression, in domestic affairs, in Franklin Roosevelt's New Deal, with its insistence that government, not private enterprise, could best improve the conditions that had left a third of the nation ill-housed, ill-clothed, and ill-fed. It received its most enduring expression, in foreign affairs, in the Pax Americana advocated by Dean Acheson, General Marshall, and Joseph Alsop after the war, a policy whereby the American government, like the Roman one in a previous age, took upon its shoulders the burden of governing the world, of resisting, with the assistance of a vast military and intelligence establishment, the great heresies, and of improving, through lavish grants of money and matériel, the conditions of life in those countries that had been admitted to the American imperium.[39]

The twin orthodoxies of the New Deal and the Pax Americana were the foundations upon which both the twentieth-century welfare state and the twentieth-century national security state were constructed.[40] The molders of these orthodoxies were themselves members of one of the most extraordinary clubs the world has known, a national aristocracy which, with its belief that there were few problems an aggressive, conscientious cadre of public servants could not solve, and through its control of a complex web of bureaucratic and administrative machinery, influenced the life of the nation and the world to a degree unprecedented in the history of the United States. It was into this tradition of aristocracy and Enlightened liberalism that Bobby Kennedy and his brothers were eventually inducted; they would become, indeed, the last American statesmen to campaign, openly and unapologetically, as heirs to the Stimsonian conception of progressive aristocracy.

They were the last of the old, but they were also the first of the new. The last of the great aristocratic families in twentieth-century American politics, the Kennedys produced the first mainstream critic of the orthodoxies on which the old Stimsonian arrangements rested. Bobby Kennedy, who in the first phase of his career was almost a parody of a young Stimsonian statesman eager to make his mark in the world, would emerge, in the last years of his life, as a great though reluctant critic of the world the Stimsonians wrought.

3

THE DESIRE TO POSSESS A PARAMOUNT PURPOSE IN LIFE, more pronounced in some men than in others, is probably innate, but the form which that purpose assumes, in the life of a particular man, must depend upon the man's education. Of the nine children born to Joseph and Rose Kennedy, Bobby had perhaps the greatest need of a grand and overarching purpose in life; men who are indifferent to this need do not consider becoming priests. Left to its own devices, Bobby's hunger for purpose might have found expression in a life in the Church, in a life of piety and contemplation. But his father had determined that he would have a secular career, and as a matter of course Bobby adopted as his own those secular purposes that were held up to him at St. Paul's, at Milton, and at Harvard as being the most noble and fulfilling a man could have.

The ease with which he was converted to the creed of Stimson and the two Roosevelts is striking evidence of how skillful the New England academies had become, since Henry Adams's time, in producing pious ephebes eager to devote themselves to the cause of grand government. In his first months at Milton, Bobby attempted to lead "an underground movement" to convert his Protestant form-mates to the Roman Church, but his religious zeal quickly subsided, and his Roman Catholic faith became, in time, a merely secondary one, a Sunday faith. The achievement of secular power replaced the hope of eternal salvation as the principal object of his daily devotions, and he was soon writing home that the Protestant ministers who visited Milton, schooled in the ethic of public service propounded by Dr. Peabody and Dr. Drury, were more intellectually impressive than the Catholic priests who spoke of St. Augustine and St. Paul.[1]

The exercise of political power is, of course, as gratifying a form of egotism as any, but in the New England academies in which he passed his youth, Bobby learned to think of it as a selfless and even a noble activity, an obligation that, under the more pleasing appellation of "public service," the graduates of the New England schools had a sacred duty to discharge. Ever since Endicott Peabody had modeled Groton (founded in 1884) along the lines of Dr. Arnold's Rugby, the New England academies had attempted to imitate the English public schools in their mission of transforming well-born and not infrequently rich young gentlemen into conscientious wielders of political and administrative power. It was at these schools that patrician youths were initiated into the grand tradition of politics that men like Stimson and Theodore Roosevelt had recently revived. (Roosevelt sent his sons to be educated by Peabody at Groton; their Hyde Park cousin, Franklin Roosevelt, was also a Grotonian.[2]) It was in these schools that young men learned to look upon engagement in private business as a selfish and spiritually unrewarding activity; it was here that they learned to look upon government service as superior to those careers that existed only because a market had need of them.[3] (Bobby's own aversion to business, Schlesinger says, was confirmed during a summer he spent working in a Boston bank: it was "as close to business as he ever got".[4]) A collection of authorities, beginning with Aristotle, was cited as evidence of the proposition that a public career was the noblest of all, and a strict regimen of athletic competition was instituted in order to prepare the budding young statesman for the rigors of political life.

The Exorcism of the Playing Field

IT WAS NOT enough simply to instill in young men a taste for the delights of power; for after all, even Henry Adams, who, his brother Brooks said, would not have "touched" public office in any form under any circumstances, was fully aware of how charming power can be.[5] The New England academies had the additional duty of preventing young men from developing those intellectual interests that would have been fatal to any attempt at a career in democratic politics. Central to Peabody's educational theories was a belief that too much brilliance, too much wit, too high a standard of scholarship, too fastidious a sense of taste, would inevitably corrupt and enervate the classes that were meant to rule. "I am not sure I like boys to think too much," Peabody once said. "A lot of people think a lot of things we could do without."[6] Walter Hinchman, a Groton master, observed that Peabody "wasn't really interested in education of the mind."[7] "Intellectual curiosity," Hinchman said, "simply did not interest him, and a boy . . . who had such curiosity in abundance, was almost suspect."[8]

Henry Adams records in the *Education* that in his day scholars were taught practically nothing at Harvard College. It is difficult to conceive of a more effective method of stimulating the development of an original and undogmatic mind, or a poorer one of producing a mind capable of acquiescing in the platitudes and prevarications of modern democratic politics. In the same way that Gibbon despised the languid learning of Oxford a century earlier, Adams resented—or affected to resent—the nonchalance of Harvard in the fifties.[9] A more objective observer, however, is likely to be struck not by the failures of antebellum Harvard, but by its successes. The university then encouraged, what perhaps the English universities still do, an intellectual curiosity, a free play of mind, which, no doubt because it occurred in a place where old libraries were well stocked with classic books, produced a happier result than any number of more up-to-date methods. By Bobby's time, however, the New England academies had eliminated much of the element of free intellectual play from their curricula, and had implemented the program of conscious philistinism that men like Peabody had devised in the hope of producing patricians capable of succeeding in modern politics. (The philistinism came naturally enough to a man who believed, as Peabody did, that Theodore Roosevelt was "America's greatest statesman and *In Memoriam* England's finest poem."[10]) The New England academies taught a good deal more in Bobby's day than they had taught in Adams's, and taught it in such a way as to make it as dull and uninteresting as possible. Any genuine love of learning a boy might possess was almost certain to be extinguished in the drudgery of the classroom; nor was there, outside of the classroom, sufficient time for the kind of desultory reading that is indispensable to the creation of a vital and imaginative intellect.[11] In Peabody's scheme of education, a boy's leisure hours were to be given over to games, especially to football. Whatever romantic vapors, whatever traces of imaginative passion, still floated in a boy's mind, in defiance of the regime of the lecture hall, were certain to be eliminated in the great exorcism of the playing field. "Don't worry, Corinne, we'll soon knock all that out of him," Peabody told Joseph Alsop's mother when she boasted of her son's love of reading.[12]

What Groton knocked out of little Joseph Alsop, Milton just as efficaciously knocked out of little Bobby Kennedy. Bobby threw himself into football and made friends with the greatest athlete in the school. Dave Hackett was, a contemporary recalled, "the hero of our school, captain of teams and those things."[13] It was upon this golden boy that the character of Phineas in *A Separate Peace* was apparently modeled.[14] It is said that the author of that morbid little volume encountered Hackett one summer at Exeter, where Hackett had been enrolled in the summer school. Hackett possessed such glamour that the smallest boys in the school followed him everywhere he went. And yet this magnanimous Steerforth was not as confident as everyone supposed him to be. He was tormented by feelings of worthlessness, and inexplicably believed himself to be a misfit. In Bobby he perceived a kindred spirit. Bobby was, Hackett said, "neither a natural athlete nor a natural student nor a natural success with girls and had no gift for popularity." As Steerforth had taken the sympathetic young Copperfield under his wing, so Hackett took the sympathetic young Bobby under his. "They spent a lot of time wrestling," one schoolmate remembered, "and going in each other's room and throwing things out the window and wearing each other's clothes and generally horseplaying around." Bobby eventually became known around the school as Hackett's friend, his *best* friend.[15] (The friendship was to be an enduring one, even as the balance of power between the two shifted; many years after their graduation from Milton, Bobby, riding with Hackett in one of those long black limousines that are made available to the Attorney General, looked at his old friend, laughed, and said, "Dave can't remember when it was I got ahead of him."[16]) Though far from being a natural athlete like Hackett, Bobby persevered in his pursuit of football immortality, and eventually achieved it when, unlike his older brothers, he made the varsity squad at Harvard.[17] It was a dubious victory. For the first time in his life, classmates began to remark not on Bobby's sensitivity or his shyness, but on his brusqueness, his coldness, his insolence. One Harvard classmate recalled him as a "nasty, brutal, humorless little fellow." Another described him as "callow and tough," a "remote figure," a "sort of a football player."[18]

Scholarship, predictably enough, was a purely secondary matter. If Bobby professed concern about his poor grades—lamented the fact that he was not "hitting the honors" the way his older brothers had—he wasn't *that* concerned; the Stimsonian aristocracy winked at poor scholarship.[19] Even Jack Kennedy, the most intellectual of the Kennedy children, lacked the discipline to put his senior thesis into a coherent form; it was Arthur Krock who transformed that piece into the book *Why England Slept*.[20] A college essay on the French king Francis I makes it clear that the future Pulitzer Prize winner was no Gibbon.[21] If Jack's scholarship left something to be desired, Bobby's was still more primitive. He was a thoroughgoing C student, one whose intellectual horizons were correspondingly limited. For years his reading was confined largely to books on the best-seller lists.[22] Bobby's college grades were not good enough for admission to Harvard Law School; for a time there was some doubt as to whether Virginia would have him.[23]

It was not his mind alone that suffered. The spirit showed signs of atrophy as well. Whatever depths of feeling had existed within him—whatever passions had inspired thoughts of a life of religious contemplation—they were suppressed, forgotten, ignored. Though Bobby was in some ways the most interesting—the most imaginative, the most passionate, the most questioning—of the Kennedy siblings, he emerged from Milton and Harvard an orthodox and, if the truth be told, an uninteresting figure. The romantic young Irishman whom Schlesinger gives us, lost in a Yeatsian melancholy, is largely a creature of fiction.[24] The young Bobby differed hardly at all from those of his contemporaries who left school, in E. M. Forster's words, possessed of "well-developed bodies, fairly developed minds, and undeveloped hearts."[25] A distinguishing feature of the Stimsonian aristocracy was its hostility to reflection, self-examination, the cultivation of the imagination. For years Bobby shared this hostility. His greatest admirers admit that he was "a man unprepared for introspection."[26] The Stimsonian creed was a formula for practical, not spiritual, success; it taught its disciples not to come to better terms with the root agony of existence, or to gain some new insight into its causes, but to lose sight of it in the press of affairs. As might be expected, the Stimsonians left behind them a tremendous legacy of practical achievement, but little of intellectual or imaginative excellence. They produced a vast quantity of legislation, but little literature. Other great political aristocracies had produced statesmen who excelled, not only in practical business, but in intellectual and imaginative endeavors as well. The Victorians had Disraeli to their credit, and the Georgians Edmund Burke and Charles James Fox. The founders of the American republic, with whom the Stimsonians are sometimes compared, included men (like Hamilton and Jefferson) whose intellectual achievements were no less memorable than their political activities. The intellectual and imaginative achievement of the Stimsonians was more slender. It is only because Bobby broke with their faith that he has any claim upon our attention today.

4

Eᴀsᴛ Hᴀᴍᴘᴛᴏɴ ᴀɪʀᴘᴏʀᴛ, Lᴀʙᴏʀ Dᴀʏ ᴡᴇᴇᴋᴇɴᴅ, ᴛʜᴇ middle nineties. Waiting for friends, I happen by chance to encounter members of the golden family itself. Caroline Kennedy Schlossberg and her husband, Ed, have arrived, together with assorted children, and are stepping out of a single-engine plane. I fail to recognize them; my eyes are fixed on the sleek jet that has just landed, bearing who knows what contemporary American eminence. Would the not particularly tall woman wearing a broad-brimmed straw hat, sunglasses, and a red-and-white-striped shirt please get out of the way, that I might witness the triumphant disembarkation of Mr. Geffen or Mr. Spielberg or Mr. and Mrs. Alec Baldwin? My wife gently gives me to understand that I have failed to recognize the real aristocrats in my midst; they have walked past me and are now struggling with their luggage. Someone has come to greet them: he is dressed in jeans and a black T-shirt; the face is youthful but the hair thick and gray, a look that President Clinton and Richard Gere have apparently made popular. Is he famous, too? To my wife's displeasure I stare at the progeny of the exalted dynasty. It is, of course, a really shameless thing to do, but I comfort myself with the thought that Pepys himself used to go and stare at the Queen while she dined at Greenwich.

I stare, but in truth I am disappointed. It might be too much to expect the pomp of a Veronese, but Kodachrome alone could do justice to this. Was there anything in the least aristocratic about the rather ordinary people who had just passed by me? Were *they* patricians? And if they were not, was there any point in my trying to demonstrate that the founder of their family's fortunes had sold out to an aristocracy that never ceased to regard his entrepreneurial successes as the dishonest achievement of a common thief? Perhaps Caroline Kennedy's father, or even one of her uncles, would have made a more dramatic entrance; they, after all, avidly *sought* the fame from which she so instinctively shrinks. Jack Kennedy's comings and goings, by all accounts, possessed a certain splendor even before he dragged a presidential entourage. But must one endow his glamour with a political meaning? Must one call it an *aristocratic* glamour? It is true that, in our loose and casual talk, we speak of the Kennedys as being America's "royal" family, and of its scions as being our "princes." But this is the frippery of conversation; we do not really mean to imply that the country has abandoned its republican forms, that there has been a violation of the constitutional injunction against titles of nobility.[1] Do we not let our imaginations outstrip the reality when we speak of the existence of an American aristocracy, or of the Kennedys and the Roosevelts as constituting an indigenous American nobility? Do we not deceive ourselves when we pretend to discover, in our public life, the elaborate forms of the Old World, when in reality there is nothing but the prosaic republican reality of the New?

"In all ages," the great historian Ronald Syme wrote, "whatever the form and name of government, be it monarchy, republic, or democracy, an oligarchy lurks behind the façade."[2] What distinguished the twentieth-century Stimsonian oligarchy from those that came before and those that came after it was the sheer audacity of its aristocratic pretensions. The Stimsonians could never get away with it today, could never have gotten away with it even in the era of Jackson and Lincoln. The two Roosevelts made a great show of trying to help the Common Man, the Forgotten Man, the Average Man, but they never made any pretension to being, like Jackson and Lincoln, like Eisenhower and Reagan, common men themselves. They were gentlemen, not common men. They were fascinated by

European nobility (Franklin Roosevelt was particularly fond of royalty). Not since the days of Hamilton had American statesmen been
so ready to acknowledge a debt to England and her aristocratic
system. The Stimsonians attended faux English public schools and
studied at real English universities; they belonged to English clubs
and corresponded with English peers. Oliver Wendell Holmes, who
owed his Supreme Court seat to Theodore Roosevelt's love of in-
telligent preppies (he "is just our type," Roosevelt would gush when
he singled out such a preppy for preferment), counted his trips to
England among the great blessings of his life.[3] Holmes liked to say
that "nature was an aristocrat, or at least makes aristocrats," and
once complained that he had to go to England for proper appreciation of his scholarship: the American mind was too "lax" to comprehend it. Decades before Ralph Lauren made a fortune selling
Americans on a New Yorker's vision of the life of the English gentry, the Stimsonians reverenced the quintessentially English institutions of the country house and the gentlemen's club. Until
relatively recently the interiors of respectable Wall Street firms,
though tucked away in modern skyscrapers, bore an uncanny re-
semblance to Brooks's or White's or the Carlton Club, replete with
wood paneling, oil paintings, and working fireplaces.

English Suits and Garden Parties

THAT BOBBY WAS influenced by the aristocratic ethos of the Stimsonians is difficult to deny. Simply look at his house. Rhetoric may
deceive; bricks and mortar do not. Joseph Kennedy, fearful of being
labeled a parvenu, might have shunned baronial splendor in favor
of New England simplicity. Not Bobby. In 1957 he moved his family to the Virginia estate known as Hickory Hill, a large Georgian
manor house set on half a dozen acres of landscaped grounds.[4] It
was horse country, and the Kennedys soon added new stables (as
well as a tennis court and the now-celebrated swimming pool).[5] Far
more than the cold perfection of Jack and Jacqueline's Georgetown
showpiece, with its eighteenth-century antiques and tastefully se-

lected art, Hickory Hill was an aristocratic establishment, tended by more than a dozen servants, and alive with the careless exuberance of a prosperous young noble couple.[6] It was a house filled with children, animals, and a constant stream of distinguished visitors. Jack Kennedy loved David Cecil's evocations of the country houses of the eighteenth-century Whig nobility, but he was not fated to live in such a house himself.[7] Jacqueline Kennedy's exquisitely furnished, beautifully arranged, and coldly classical interiors made a visitor instantly aware of the chatelaine's icy reserve; breaches of decorum—such as Gore Vidal's drunken behavior at a White House dinner party in 1961—were swiftly and effectively punished.[8] It was Bobby, not Jack, who realized Cecil's splendid vision in his own life, in a house "alive with the effort and hurry of politics," a house that resembled, in its energy and unrehearsed elegance, the great Whig establishments that Jack adored. Cecil's evocation of the "splendid naturalness" of those houses still beguiles. Though they are "among the most conspicuous monuments of English history," the Whig houses "are not palaces." There is

> something easygoing and unofficial about them. Between the library and the saloon one comes on little rooms, full of sporting prints and comfortable untidiness; . . . less designed for state occasions than for private life—for leisure and lounging, for intimate talk and desultory reading. . . . The Whig lord was as often as not a minister, his eldest son an M.P., his second son attached to a foreign embassy. . . . Red Foreign Office boxes strewed the library tables; at any time of day or night a courier might come galloping up with critical news, and the minister must post off to London to attend a Cabinet meeting.[9]

When Bobby himself was not forced to post off to Cabinet meetings in Washington, he and Ethel threw lavish parties at Hickory Hill. Those soirées have since become the stuff of legend: the masquerade party in celebration of Averell Harriman's seventy-fifth birthday in November 1966; the famous pet shows over which Bobby's court jester, Art Buchwald, presided; the epochal fete at which Arthur Schlesinger went shooting over Alice Roosevelt Longworth's shoulder into the swimming pool. "Ethel was so naughty for doing it," Mrs. Longworth said.[10] "How sweet the occasions were!" Teddy White exclaimed.[11] One never knew whom to expect; one might come upon Bob McNamara and Byron White playing hide-and-seek in the big house, or Chip Bohlen and Georgei Bolshakov sitting in a quiet corner discussing Russian politics, or Bobby himself, in the library, deep in conversation with Gene Kelly, the actor.[12] How different, the columnist Joseph Kraft thought, were these chaotic and "mixed up" affairs from the "layered and structured" parties Jack and Jacqueline gave at the White House.[13] At Hickory Hill one encountered such dissimilar personages as George Plimpton, Colonel Glenn, André Malraux, and Lord and Lady Harlech.[14] It was not, of course, all fun and games, mornings on horseback and evenings beside the pool. Aristocracy had not merely its privileges but its duties as well, and ever mindful of these, Bobby asked Arthur Schlesinger to arrange a series of educational seminars at Hickory Hill and the White House. Hardly less glamorous than the Kennedy pool parties, the seminars were all-star intellectual galas, and featured such academic luminaries as Sir Isaiah Berlin, then the Chichele professor of social and political theory at Oxford and a fellow of All Soul's, A. J. Ayer, another Oxford philosopher, and John Kenneth Galbraith, the Harvard economist who'd helped administer FDR's system of wartime price controls and who in the early sixties was representing Camelot in India.

Bobby's Stimsonianism was not limited to English suits and garden parties (yes, Bobby *did* wear English suits).[15] It was more than a matter of skiing in Sun Valley and dining at Le Pavillon (his favorite New York restaurant).[16] It went beyond honoring the English tradition of the long weekend at the country house. (Bobby's staff, although they loved their master, resented his "habit of taking off on a Thursday for a long weekend of fun and games, leaving them with lengthy assignments" to be completed before his return to the office on Monday morning.)[17] The patrician ethos had penetrated to the core of his consciousness. He was, in his relations with those whose circumstances were less splendid than his own, a model of sympathy, of generosity, of kindness—although one is forced to note Richard Nixon's assertion that when Bobby disliked his food, he was in the habit of throwing it on the floor.[18] Angie Novello, his secretary, was devoted to him. Able lieutenants, men like Pierre Salinger, Burke Marshall, John Seigenthaler, and Ed Guthman, loved him. And yet—it is impossible to deny it—there was an element of condescension in his dealings with social inferiors. Jimmy Hoffa did not fail to perceive it. "I can tell by how he shakes hands what kind of fellow I got," Hoffa said. When, in 1957, Bobby was investigating the Teamsters, the two men dined together at the house of Eddie Cheyfitz, an associate of the criminal defense lawyer Edward Bennett Williams. The encounter was not a success; Hoffa thought Bobby patronizing, a "damn spoiled jerk." "Here's a fella," Hoffa said, who "thinks he's doing me a favor by talking to me."[19] Bobby's condescending questions about the nature of union leadership offended Hoffa. "It was as though he was asking, with my limited education, what right did I have to run a union like this?"[20]

Bobby once said that for members of the American middle class life was reasonably comfortable. Perhaps; but how did *he* know? Nelson Rockefeller's ignorance of the New York subways is celebrated (Rocky thought each car had its own toilet; hi ya, fella).[21] On the single occasion on which Winston Churchill reportedly ventured into the London Underground he "got on the Circle Line and went helplessly round and round on it until, several hours later, a friend rescued him from the ordeal."[22] Bobby's own ignorance of this elementary aspect of modern urban life was no less mindboggling. On his first encounter with the New York subway, in the 1960s, he slammed into the turnstile, receiving "a jolt that caused him to double up" in pain.[23] "You can really lose your life that way," he said in a startled tone as an aide deposited a token for him. The gulf that separated him from the hopelessly non-U of the world, from those who composed what Vita Sackville-West called the "bedint" classes, was nowhere more evident than in his relations with J. Edgar Hoover.[24] Bobby is said to have wanted good relations with the FBI director, but in his attempts to establish them, he failed miserably, in part because Hoover resented his breezy patrician nonchalance.[25] Bobby made no effort to restrain himself in Hoover's presence; he might have been back in his Milton dorm, chewing the fat with Dave Hackett. Hoover was, in spite of the unconventional arrangements of his domestic life, the incarnation of the pieties and prejudices of middle America, and he was appalled by Bobby's behavior. During one of their conferences Bobby "idly tossed darts at a board on the wall."[26] Hoover, angered by this insouciance, "became even more upset when Kennedy missed the board, and the dart lodged in the paneling." "It was pure desecration," Hoover said. "Desecration of government property." It "was the most deplorably undignified conduct" he had "ever witnessed on the part of a Cabinet member."[27] Hoover was undoubtedly an unpleasant character, a bureaucratic tyrant, one who had carved out of the vast territory of the national security state his own little fiefdom. The fact remains, however, that Bobby and his brother had determined to keep him on as director, and having done so, they were bound to treat him with the civility due a man who had first entered the Justice Department eight years before Bobby himself was born. And yet Bobby seemed almost to enjoy subjecting the old man to the petty humiliations of office hierarchy. Contrary to all departmental precedent, Bobby would summon Hoover to his office by means of a buzzer.[28] Others were startled. "Nobody ever buzzed Hoover," Walter Sheridan, a former FBI agent and the head of the "Get-Hoffa Squad" in Bobby's Justice Department, said.[29] But "within sixty seconds" of Bobby's having pressed the buzzer, the old man came in "with a red face," though "it griped him very much" to do so.[30]

However careless Bobby was of other people's dignity, he insisted on his own and was zealous of the least punctilio of his family's honor. The director of the FBI could be ordered about like a common lackey; members of the Kennedy family were to be treated in a way that accorded with their rank and dignity in life. High government officials, whom Bobby received while sitting with his feet up on his desk chewing gum, could be chastised like schoolboys; the Kennedys themselves were to be treated with becoming deference.[31] When Jack's friend Paul "Redhead" Fay sought to publish a memoir of the late President, Bobby was angered by Fay's failure to adhere rigidly to the canons of diplomatic etiquette. "Mr. Kennedy," Bobby noted on a draft of the book submitted for his review, "should not be called 'Joe' [or] 'Big Joe,' but 'Ambassador' or 'Mr. Kennedy.' "[32] This lordly arrogance was not only startling, it was also easily provoked, as a hapless equestrian judge discovered during a contretemps involving Bobby's dog, Brumus, at a Virginia horse show. LaDonna Harris, the wife of Bobby's friend Senator Fred Harris of Oklahoma, recalled how Brumus,

> the lumbering ox, went out and sat right in the middle of the show! He was just sitting there! The ringmaster—or whatever his title is—said, "Would somebody kindly get their dog out of here? The dog is disturbing the horses. Would you get the dog . . . ?" And he nudged the dog with his foot. The Senator leaned over the rail and said, "Don't kick my dog." The ringmaster . . . well, it kind of took him aback. He said, "Senator, I didn't kick . . ." The Senator said, "I saw you! Don't ever kick my dog again."[33]

Bobby's insistence on the dignity and prerogatives of "the family" and all those connected to it seemed to England's *Sunday Telegraph* closer to the spirit of the eighteenth-century Whig aristocracy than the democratic spirit of twentieth-century America.[34] And why ever not? The Kennedys had, after all, married into one of the greatest Whig families in England. Rose Kennedy might have abhorred the prospect of her daughter Kathleen being taken to wife by Billy Hartington, the eldest son of the Duke of Devonshire, in a marriage performed outside of the Church, but Joseph Kennedy must secretly have been delighted by the idea of a union between the Kennedys and the Cavendishes. No matter that the splendor of the Devonshires' fortune derived largely from the first earl's traffic in abbey lands, in the despoiled property of the monasteries, in the sacred chattels of the Church: everybody loves a lord, and the Stimsonians loved them better than most. A man who hoped to see his children grow up to be Stimsonians could only have rejoiced to see his family contract an alliance that even the proudest patricians must have approved and even envied. Just as he wanted Jacqueline Bouvier for a daughter-in-law because she had more "class" than any of Jack's other girlfriends, so also must he have gloried in the idea of being the father-in-law of a genuine Whig aristocrat, one whose "class" made even Roosevelts and Astors look somehow shabby in comparison. Like his father, Bobby never forgot the family's aristocratic connection. When, in July 1951, his first child was born, he and his wife named the baby Kathleen Hartington.

5

S TIMSONIANS WERE NOT BROUGHT UP, THEY WERE NOT
trained, they were not equipped, to regard their fellowmen as
equals; Bobby was as little capable as FDR or Nelson Rockefeller
or Averell Harriman of viewing the "little people" of the world as
anything other than weak, helpless, and in need of patrician protection. The little people could not protect themselves; only statesmen possessed of an aristocratic sense of honor and noblesse oblige
could be relied upon to treat them fairly. Noblesse oblige must not,
however, be mistaken for a pure and unselfish form of charity; like
Thackeray's Miss Crawley, who, although she professes to love
equality, makes her "equal" Becky Sharp "run her errands, execute
her millinery, and read her to sleep with French novels," the Stimsonians, too, professed to love equality, but at the same time expected their social inferiors to defer to them in questions of
government.[1] FDR's own ambivalent attitude toward the lower orders—his ability to sympathize with them and at the same time be
made acutely uncomfortable by them—was perfectly captured by
his wife when she observed that "Franklin is not at ease with people
not of his own class."[2] Roosevelt ruled over the nation's "forgotten"
men, but he was not obliged to dine with them, or take tea with
them at Hyde Park.

Although Bobby had been brought up to regard this Stimsonian
paternalism as part of the natural order of things, it represented a

radical departure from the aspirations of the past. In the vision of Emerson and Lincoln, the common man, shrewd and self-reliant, was a heroic figure, endowed with more promise and potential than those Old World characters who were laden with the baggage of the past. It is the democratic Hawk-eye, not the aristocratic Major Heyward, who knows how to protect himself and his friends in Fenimore Cooper's tale. Lincoln similarly celebrated the promise of "the prudent, penniless beginner in the world" who in time becomes a capitalist himself:

> A young man finds himself of an age to be dismissed from parental control; he has for his capital nothing save two strong hands that God has given him, a heart willing to labor, and a freedom to choose the mode of his work and the manner of his employer . . . he avails himself of the opportunity of hiring himself to some man who has capital to pay him a fair day's wages for a fair day's work. . . . He works industriously, behaves soberly, and the result of a year or two's labor is a surplus capital. Now he buys land on his own hook; he settles, marries, begets sons and daughters, and in the course of time has enough capital to hire some new beginner.[3]

The Stimsonians stood Cooper and Lincoln on their heads; the common man became, in the Stimsonian vision, an utterly unheroic soul, one who was forced to look to a gentle patrician knight—an elegant Major Heyward, a smiling FDR—for protection against the evils of a marketplace he lacked the strength to master himself. For all its notions of progress and possibility, the American liberalism that grew out of the Stimsonian philosophy was a curiously regressive phenomenon: though it ostensibly celebrated the Forgotten Man, it in fact trivialized and diminished him. Where compassion had once consisted of giving a man the tools and the opportunity, as well as the self-confidence, to forge his own destiny, it now consisted of making him more comfortable in his mediocrity. For a time Bobby shared this way of thinking; he aspired to be what

Schlesinger called a "tribune of the underclass," a defender of those who were unable to defend themselves.

Franklin Roosevelt perfected the technique of enveloping the lower classes in a warm rhetorical bath of patrician solicitude. The embodiment of twentieth-century paternalistic aristocracy, the second Roosevelt raised noblesse oblige to the level of high political art. Cousin Teddy's career was but a foreshadowing, a prefiguration, of the master's.* FDR has a better claim than either Theodore Roosevelt or Woodrow Wilson to the title of founder of the twentieth-century regulatory and administrative state; it was FDR who, more than anyone else, succeeded in replacing the nineteenth-century tradition of liberal individualism with his own brand of welfare state liberalism. Scholars have for the most part failed to understand just how radical this break with the past was, and have tended to portray Roosevelt as a pragmatic improviser, one who carefully adjusted the machinery of American capitalism in order to preserve it. Richard Hofstadter was perhaps the first serious historian to argue that the New Deal was more than an act of splendid improvisation, that it represented a bold and comprehensive remodeling of the nation's economy and its socioeconomic ideals, a "drastic new departure" that was "different from anything that had yet happened in the United States."[4] Though Hofstadter had himself, in his earliest study of Roosevelt, depicted the great man as a patrician pragmatist who had largely failed to make the nation over in his own New Deal image, he later revised this estimate of FDR, and concluded that the New Deal represented one of the great sea changes in American history.[5] True, much of the early New Deal legislation was patently amateurish, and the Supreme Court made short work of the worst of it, striking down, for example, the system of little industrial communes envisioned by the National Industrial Recovery Act.[6] Later legislation—the Social Security Act, the Wagner Act, the punitive wealth tax—was better drafted and more far-reaching in its effects. The welfare state was born; henceforth, Hof-

---

* "One mightier than I cometh, the latchet of whose shoes I am not worthy to unloose."

stadter wrote, the federal government would "take responsibility on a large scale for social security, unemployment insurance, wages and hours, and housing."[7] Still more imposing, Hofstadter noted, was the "new fiscal role of the federal government" contemplated by the New Deal. By the end of the thirties, Roosevelt had fully embraced Lord Keynes's belief that a large and activist government could ameliorate the fluctuations of the business cycle, and it was during Roosevelt's presidency that the federal government became what it remains to this day—the force that "more than anything else determines the course of the economy" and the direction of national life.[8]

Jack and Bobby profited from FDR's example as best they could. During the 1960 campaign they shrewdly exploited Roosevelt's memory in places like West Virginia, and they made valiant attempts to overcome his widow's hostility to their cause. But although they studied Roosevelt's career, and copied his techniques whenever they found it useful to do so, they never idolized the man; indeed, they may never even have liked him. Roosevelt was adored by millions who never met him, who knew him only through his radio broadcasts; those who were more intimately acquainted with him—as the Kennedys were—had a different impression of his character. The men who were close to Franklin Roosevelt, Joseph Alsop observed, did not love him.[9] They did not weep when he died.[10]

How, the Kennedys wondered, had Roosevelt done it? During the 1960 campaign Jack asked Richard Neustadt to prepare a series of memoranda on FDR's approach to the presidency. "That Roosevelt stuff is fascinating," Kennedy exclaimed after reading it.[11] The brothers admired the great man's achievement, but the admiration was tinged with envy, and when they dealt with the Roosevelt children there was an unmistakable sense of scores to be settled.[12] "She hated my father," Jack said of Eleanor Roosevelt in 1960, "and she can't stand it that his children turned out so much better than hers." The brothers resented the way Franklin Roosevelt had toyed with their father, resented the fact that he had given the Treasury to William Woodin and Henry Morgenthau but never to Dad.

They were still more piqued by the fact that history would remember Roosevelt as the heroic founder of a state (albeit the welfare one); theirs would be the distinctly lesser glory of adding to another man's monument.

Did they ever understand the secret of Roosevelt's success? Did they ever glimpse the subtle bitterness that poisoned his mind and stimulated his genius? There is no bitterness like that of the fallen patrician; the resentment of the social climber is not nearly so great. Although Jack and Bobby could recall, with remarkable clarity, the insults their family had endured at the hands of the WASPs, neither of them was, at heart, a bitter man.[13] Roosevelt was. The popular conception of the happy warrior, the spontaneous, great-hearted, and generous leader, the infectiously optimistic statesman who, after contracting polio, resisted the temptation to indulge in self-pity, is not entirely wrong. There is truth enough in this picture, but it is not the whole truth.[14] Beneath the ebullient patrician facade lay a more vulnerable man than was apparent on the surface, a man who possessed a full array of human weaknesses, a smaller and less attractive man than the larger-than-life figure the crowds adored, a man who was not free from bitterness.[15]

The Kennedys, so lacking in bitterness themselves, could never comprehend the extent to which bitterness underlay Roosevelt's achievements. Their world was too different from his. The young Roosevelt grew up not in the rough-and-tumble atmosphere of a household like the Kennedys', but in the splendid isolation of a Hudson River estate. The only child of a protective mother, little Franklin had grown up in a universe that revolved around him, and he could never afterward be comfortable in that larger, colder world which refused at first to pay homage to his ordinary and at the time rather trivial self. He was a Roosevelt, of course, but not an Oyster Bay Roosevelt, and as a young man he soon discovered that the world was no longer impressed by Hyde Park Roosevelts.[16] (Joseph Alsop said that the Hyde Park Roosevelts' place in New York society "might well have been less than middling" at the end of the nineteenth century."[17]) In youth Roosevelt was never as popular as he wanted to be—not at Groton, not at Harvard, not in his early career. His wife said that his Groton years may "even have left scars," which is odd, because he was not *un*popular at Groton.[18] But he was not the most popular boy in his form, either, and he found this circumstance painful. Thirty years later he was still smarting over his failure to have been elected a class marshal at Harvard and to have been invited to join Porcellian.[19] He was a handsome young man, but according to Joseph Alsop, whose mother had known the gossip of the day, he was handsome in a "rather awful" sort of way, and had been given the nickname "Feather Duster" by the girls.[20] His reputation for shallowness led many discerning men to look upon him with disdain, to dismiss him as a "well-born, polite, not particularly gifted young man, something of a prig."[21] Henry Adams patronized him; Walter Lippmann thought him amiable and stupid; Oliver Wendell Holmes pronounced his intellect second-rate; Learned Hand thought him "nearly devoid of critical faculty."[22] The young Kennedys were similarly patronized, but they had *expected* to be patronized, had thought it inevitable that they would be patronized. Roosevelt had not expected it; he was not prepared for it.

Roosevelt's later successes never completely assuaged the humiliations of his early years, when first he had gone into a world that was indifferent to him. This residual bitterness manifested itself most signally in the quite unmistakable cruelty with which he treated others. It revealed itself in what Learned Hand called his vindictiveness, his "willingness to fan incendiary animosities" in ways Hand said he could "never forgive."[23] It revealed itself in the way he manipulated his subordinates, and in the way he dropped them after they ceased to be useful to him.[24] Marguerite "Missy" Le Hand, his secretary, devoted her life to him, but when she lay dying, Roosevelt did not bother to call her.[25] Cruelty showed itself, too, in the way he played his aides against one another, and in the heavy sarcasm, the petty humiliations, the demeaning nicknames, the relentless teasing to which he subjected them.[26] Sometimes this cruelty took the form of a playful, catlike malice, as when Roosevelt asked Joseph Kennedy to drop his trousers in the White House, to see whether it was true that Kennedy was bow-legged (it *was* true).[27]

Sometimes it was more brutally blunt, as when once he said to his wife, who was attempting to give her opinion of a pending bill, "Oh, Eleanor, shut up. You never understand these things anyway."[28] Dean Acheson resigned rather than submit to Roosevelt's daily calisthenics of cruelty. Roosevelt, Acheson said, not only "condescended" to his subordinates, he did so in a particularly "humiliating" way. It was not easy, Acheson wrote, for a person who had done his best to serve the President to receive in return "the easy greeting which milord might give a promising stableboy."[29] Roosevelt was a charming man, the most charming man she had ever known, Rose Kennedy said.[30] Winston Churchill compared meeting him to opening his first bottle of champagne. But Roosevelt's was the charm of Dickens's Chester, a superficial smoothness that was not in the least incompatible with great personal cruelty.

The adolescent behavior, the love of sophomoric practical jokes, the delight with which he called Corcoran "Tommy the Cork" and Morgenthau "Henry the Morgue" revealed not merely a man who was capable of a cruelty that was all the more devastating because it was so casual, so careless, so thoughtless, but a curiously underdeveloped man, one who was strong enough to overcome his crippled legs but who never succeeded in overcoming the barriers that had prevented the full maturation of his mind, a man who seemed content with the rather stunted emotional existence to which he was confined.[31] There was—everyone who knew him noticed it—a certain dullness in the great man's conversation and character. There was an air of youthful self-satisfaction about him, the complacent attitude of a flippant schoolboy.[32] The President's table talk, Alsop observed, was remarkably "stale."[33] His sense of fun, Gore Vidal said, was "heavy."[34] The beautiful Dorothy Schiff, to whom for a time the President turned regularly for female companionship, was surprised to find herself growing bored in his company. She listened "over and over again to the same stories—how once when he was going past the Vanderbilt mansion he saw on a clothesline some black chiffon underwear," and so on and so forth.[35] He was incapable, Missy Le Hand believed, of "personal friendship with anyone."[36] And yet Roosevelt was, in spite of his coldness and his cruelty, able to achieve things that the Kennedys, for all their superior warmth and greater personal loyalty, could not. The Kennedys lacked the deep bitterness, what Learned Hand called the "venom," that gave Roosevelt's ambition its edge, that made it possible for him to lead an ideological revolution. The unagitated mind does not propose the overthrow of an established order; it may rebel, but it hesitates to destroy. Roosevelt's bitterness supplied him with the animus he needed to create a system of his own, one in which he would again be the center of the universe, the sun around which everything else revolved.

Bobby would later question the wisdom of Roosevelt's revolution, but he would do so only with reluctance, with an ambivalence he did not bother to conceal. He could never have brought himself to denounce the philosophy of the New Deal completely. Bobby may have been, as his enemies said, "ruthless," but he lacked the capacity for quiet cunning that, far more than energy or intellect, accomplishes the reorganization of a nation, the reformation of a creed. A passage that Bobby quoted in one of his own speeches is revealing: " 'There is,' said an Italian philosopher, 'nothing more difficult to take in hand, more perilous to conduct, or more uncertain in its success than to take the lead in the introduction of a new order of things.' "[37] Bobby no doubt thought it prudent to refer to Machiavelli as "an Italian philosopher"; burdened as he was by a reputation for "ruthlessness," he could hardly afford to be revealed as a careful student of *The Prince*.[38] And yet the Machiavellian aperçu that attracted Bobby's eye was a cautionary, not a ruthless one, one that emphasized how difficult and how dangerous revolutions are. Real revolutionaries do not dwell on this fact; only ambivalent ones do. Bobby was not a Machiavellian prince; Franklin Roosevelt was in many ways much closer to being that. Roosevelt, less sensitive than Bobby, was more subtle. Roosevelt did not dwell on the dangers and perplexities of revolution; he would doubtless have denied that the New Deal was a revolutionary program at all. Certainly he never came clean as to the *nature* of the revolution he was leading; he was not about to alienate his fellow citizens by insisting openly, as the Federalists had done before him, on the virtues of aristocratic governance. Roosevelt instead appealed to the people and, in the temperate language of reform and Enlightened economic policy, denounced the new men, the plutocrats, the representatives of the vulgar "business interests," the "economic royalists" who had supplanted the ancient gentry. According to Roosevelt, they, and not he, were the real revolutionaries, the real villains.[39] Bobby talked of revolution and even fantasized about it, but he was not a genuine revolutionary. Franklin Roosevelt was. Roosevelt was the Moses, the Solon, the Lycurgus of the welfare state, and for a time Bobby could but piously follow in his footsteps.

The Significance of the Frontier in Patrician History

BOBBY'S AND JACK'S progressive and idealistic rhetoric, set off by toothy smiles and carefully maintained suntans, did more for the cause of Roosevelt's paternalistic federal establishment than anything since the great man himself. The brothers' decision to embrace the cause was not, however, the easy, obvious one it might seem, for by the time Jack and Bobby came of political age, the Stimsonian path had ceased to be a sure way to power. It is true that, in the quarter-century between 1940 and 1965, four brilliant aristocrats were at or near the head of affairs—FDR, Dean Acheson, Adlai Stevenson, and Jack Kennedy himself. But after all, Acheson's administration could not have survived without the plebeian beard that Truman supplied; Stevenson lost (twice) to the decidedly less Stimsonian Ike, and Kennedy's own margin of victory over the "classless" Nixon was slim. The paternalistic mentality that had proved popular in the first half of the century, during the climax of immigration in the early years of the century and at the height of the Depression in the thirties, produced far less enthusiasm in the electorate in the postwar years, years in which a booming economy proved that the United States remained a land of opportunity for individuals. In the postwar period Americans regained confidence in their ability to improve their lives through their own individual efforts, without the assistance of the welfare and administrative state. The legacy of that renewed confidence is with us still, in the millions of baby boomers who were born in the prosperous decades that followed the war, a testament to a generation's faith in its future. That confidence portended ill for the Stimsonians, portended, indeed, their demise as a governing class. Looking from the lofty heights of the presidency on a Massachusetts state Democratic convention in the early sixties, Jack Kennedy was scornful of Irish machine politicians like Edward J. "Knocko" McCormack, Sr., Patrick J. "Sonny" McDonough, and Peter "Leather Lungs" Clougherty. "Their day is gone," the President told Ben Bradlee, who was covering the convention for *Newsweek*, "and they don't know it."[40] Perhaps their day *was* gone, but so was the Stimsonians' own. Thirty years later characters like Dean Acheson, Averell Harriman, and Adlai Stevenson seem hardly less exotic than the Carmine De Sapios and Knocko McCormacks of the period; it is difficult to conceive of a patrician statesman displaying a similarly splendid plumage on the national political stage today. Contemporary patricians in public office, such as former Governor Weld, are reduced to melancholy stunts like jumping into Boston Harbor fully clothed. Jack Kennedy accurately foretold the demise of the machine politicians, the politicians who carried on the tradition of his own grandfather Honey Fitz, the politicians whose style he himself so emphatically rejected, but he seems not to have foreseen the death of the Stimsonian tradition he had struggled to make his own.

It was not simply their inability to foresee the Stimsonians' demise that caused Jack and Bobby to adopt the Stimsonian pose, to imitate the old Rooseveltian gestures. Their upbringing had not really prepared them to play any other part. Bred up from birth to aspire to the curule chair, they naturally adopted, when they came of political age, the forms and manners of the patricians. So convincing was their performance that for a moment they revived the enthusiasm for grand government, the high rhetoric of the state, that had flourished during FDR's administration. Politics, they said, was an "honorable profession," as though the other ones were less so. When Teddy, running for his first political office in 1962, asked his brother how he should explain why he wanted to be in the Senate, Bobby, tossing a football on the lawn in front of the Ambassador's house at Hyannis Port, replied: "If you get that question, tell them about public service. Tell them why you don't want to be sitting on your ass in some office in New York"—as though the work of men sitting in offices in New York was inherently less worthy than the work of Enlightened mandarins sitting in offices in Washington.[41] But the Kennedys' bold language and striking gestures concealed a cautious and pragmatic policy. As President, Jack Kennedy was reluctant to increase the size of the federal establishment to any great degree; in 1962 he actually proposed tax *cuts*.[42] Lyndon Johnson, it is true, knew no such restraint: he shrewdly exploited the idealistic impulses his predecessor had aroused, and drew on them to build the great legislative mausoleum he conceived as a monument to his fame. But the national mood that made the Great Society possible proved ephemeral. Johnson's successors in the White House shunned the Stimsonian school of statesmanship; Presidents Reagan and Bush sought to demonstrate their closeness not to the Eastern establishment that had built up the paternalistic state, but to the West, the mythical land of rugged individualism and frontier democracy.[43] Richard Nixon, at the time of the Manson murders, went so far as to pay tribute to the virtues of a John Wayne movie, *Chisum*, and suggested that America would be a better place if it revived the harsher code of the lone Western hero whom Wayne played.[44] (It is one of the curious ironies of history that Johnson, although he was a far more genuine Westerner than the Illinois-born Reagan, the Massachusetts-born Bush, or even Nixon himself, the product of Southern California suburbia, should have been far less self-consciously Western in his politics than they. Like so many Westerners who come to the East, Johnson was fascinated by Eastern standards; his Great Society was the ultimate homage a Westerner could pay to the Stimsonian ideal of grand government.)

This preoccupation with Western individualism was nothing new; before the advent of the Stimsonians, American statesmen had, in more and less contrived ways, attempted to identify themselves with the West and the opportunities it represented for individuals in search of freedom and independence. The more memorable presidents before FDR had closely associated themselves with the frontier, had determined to prove themselves Hawk-eyes, not Major Heywards. Washington had been deeply involved in the settlement and colonization of the West and had traveled extensively in the Virginia and Ohio wilderness. Jefferson, in addition to being a backwoods land lawyer, had spoken eloquently of Western lands "with room enough for our descendants to the hundredth and thousandth generation." Jackson and Lincoln were both men of the frontier, and even Teddy Roosevelt, the cowboy of Harvard Yard, felt a need to grab a gun and roam about the Badlands in search of big game and dangerous men. Franklin Roosevelt broke with this tradition; he made no pretense to being a cowboy, to being anything other than a twentieth-century Major Heyward. Unashamed of his pinstripes, he possessed the easy manners of the faded gentry, and he felt no urge to don denim. Americans ceased, during the heyday of the Stimsonians, to demand in their politics the same Western motifs they enjoyed in their novels and their movies. But the Stimsonian interlude could not last forever; Bobby and Jack might well have been the last major American statesmen to get away with an overtly patrician style, a well-tailored manner, a Harvard accent. In the thirty-five years since President Kennedy's death, only one genuine patrician has occupied the White House, and George Bush, the second son of a Brown Brothers Harriman partner who for a time represented Greenwich in the Senate, was at pains throughout his career to prove that he *wasn't* a patrician, that he was really a Texan, a lover of country music and pork rinds. In his eagerness to repudiate his Stimsonian heritage, President Bush outdid St. Peter, and denied his faith, not three, but countless times.

For a time Bobby himself considered moving out West and running for office. Dissatisfied with his work as a young lawyer on Joseph McCarthy's Permanent Subcommittee on Investigations, Bobby decided to quit when McCarthy passed him over and named Roy Cohn to the position of chief counsel instead. Bobby told J. B. Matthews, an investigator with whom he worked on the committee, that "some hard work" and "a lot of hand-shaking" could get him the Democratic nomination for Senator in a state like Nevada.[45] The example of Teddy Roosevelt perhaps inspired him, and he no doubt genuinely loved the open spaces and severe freedom of the West. But as his brother's career gained momentum, it became obvious that the family needed him in the East, and the idea of a Western career was quietly dropped. Joseph Kennedy, though he himself had gone West, to Hollywood, to further his own career, would never have permitted Bobby to stray so far from the Stimsonian establishment over which he and his brother were (in the father's grand scheme) meant to preside. Bobby never became a Western Senator; if he had, he might have learned earlier those lessons he was fated to learn only at the end of his life.

6

━◯⦋◯⦌◯━

THE STIMSONIANS WERE SUCCESSFUL IN PART BECAUSE
they combined two distinct sets of qualities and skills. First, they
were intensely practical. "It is common sense," Franklin Roosevelt
declared in 1932, "to take a method and try it. If it fails, admit it
frankly and try another. But above all, try *something*." Though he
might have lacked intellectual depth or ideological conviction, the
Stimsonian statesman excelled at doing things, at setting up commissions, building bureaus, devising programs, processing paper, all
of which tended to create the illusion (if not the reality) of progress.
McGeorge Bundy, for example, was believed by many of his Stimsonian peers to possess the most brilliant mind of his generation,
and yet when Jack Kennedy made him his National Security Adviser
in 1961 (Kennedy considered making him Secretary of State),
Bundy had, David Halberstam observed, almost no scholarship, no
serious intellectual work, to his name.[1] His reputation was based
solely on the great practical ability he had demonstrated as a Harvard dean. Bundy proved his bureaucratic genius in Washington by
setting up what amounted to a second State Department, an enlarged National Security Council that duplicated the work of the
actual State Department.

It was not practical ability alone, however, that distinguished
the Stimsonian statesman; he possessed other qualities as well, qualities that were less easy to define but no less readily apparent in his

makeup, qualities vaguely allied to birth or class. Bundy himself possessed these qualities to an exceptional degree, as befitted one who was descended from the Lowells and the Putnams of Boston and who had been educated at Groton, where he won all the prizes, at Yale, where he was tapped for Skull and Bones, and at Harvard, where he was awarded a Junior Fellowship.[2] The holy trinity of Eastern universities—Harvard, Princeton, and Yale—played an important role in creating and consolidating the Stimsonians' sense of themselves as an elite; it took no less than two of the three to create the kind of man that Mac Bundy became. The Stimsonians had the confidence of a caste, a confidence that enabled them to overcome the skepticism of many who would otherwise have been hostile to the kind of privilege they represented. So deeply had the Stimsonian mystique penetrated the American consciousness by the middle of the twentieth century that even a Middle Westerner like Theodore Sorensen could write that a "Harvard diploma is considered by most Massachusetts voters to be evidence of devotion to the public."[3] Jack Kennedy, who was more familiar with the situation, corrected Sorensen's sentence to read: "A Harvard diploma is considered by many Massachusetts voters, although not all I hasten to add, to be evidence of some talent and ability."[4] The ingenuousness with which Sorensen associated Harvard with an ideal of public service was perfectly understandable. Whether as the result of birth or education, or both, the Stimsonian gentlemen who passed through the halls of Harvard, Princeton, and Yale in the first half of this century were in the eyes of many Americans eminently respectable characters, devoted to the common good and in love with civic virtue. The nature of their background, the polish of their diction, the very fact that they had been to Harvard, Yale, or Princeton, all seemed a guarantee of probity and integrity: one might call it the Elliot Richardson syndrome. The Stimsonian statesman might have been a manipulative man (FDR was among the most manipulative of democratic leaders), but he didn't *seem* like a manipulative man; he seemed like a man you could trust.

The Division of Labor

IF BOBBY AND Jack were among the most adept Stimsonians of their generation, this was due in part to the artful division of labor upon which the two settled early in their careers. Jack was the reassuring Brahmin figure, quoting poetry and imitating English statesmen; Bobby was the Stimsonian fixer, ready to do battle in the wards, to prod the bureaucracies, to tell a man he had to work harder, to tell a man he was fired. The older brother's style, "reticent, patrician, bookish, urbane," in Arthur Schlesinger's words, seduced a nation; the younger brother became one of the great raw *doers* in twentieth-century American politics.[5] Each had mastered a part of the Stimsonian equation; acting together they seemed unstoppable. Jack, if anything, played his chosen role *too* well. Schlesinger might have been thrilled by "our Harvard and Massachusetts Senator" (note the order) whose "perfect manners" and "Brahmin taste" reminded him of "a young Lord Salisbury," but after the young lord became President, there was grumbling on Capitol Hill about too much Mozart and fox-trotting at the other end of Pennsylvania Avenue.[6] Could Bobby have been any less baffled himself by his brother's fondness for aristocratic high culture, for the poetry of Byron and the music of Pablo Casals?[7] Ethel Kennedy frankly admitted that she and her husband did "not feel easy in the company of highbrows."[8] They liked what she called "happy, jolly things," not Sartre and Stravinsky.[9] With his hair perpetually askew, his necktie loosened, his shirtsleeves rolled up, and his horn-rimmed glasses pushed high up on his head, Bobby was as natural and unselfconscious an aristocrat as his brother was a studied one. Bobby took for his models the men he saw around him; Jack took for his the men he read about in books. Jack adored the Englishmen—and Englishwomen—who formed his sister Kick's set in London; Bobby, after meeting a number of them in the late forties, confided to his sister Patricia that between "you & me except for a few individuals you can have the bunch."[10] As President, Jack relished the diplomatic cables and dispatches that chronicled aristocratic high jinks like the Profumo affair; it is difficult to imagine Bobby taking a similar pleasure in such things.[11] Bobby did not revel in the novels of Scott or the prose of Burke and Churchill the way his brother did; he was as little capable of understanding his brother's fascination with the English aristocracy as Cato the Younger was of understanding his brother Caepio's addiction to jewelry and perfume.[12]

To Bobby fell the more prosaic tasks of counting delegates, shaking up bureaucracies, administering committees, and humiliating enemies. Bobby's early career was devoted to learning the details of how the system worked. He learned how to use the tax code against criminals and enemies (during a stint at the Criminal Division of the Justice Department), how to conduct an investigation (the McCarthy apprenticeship, in which Bobby's efforts to expose profiteering by Western shipping interests eager to make deals with Red China represented one of the few constructive things McCarthy's subcommittee did), and how to manage a bureaucracy (the investigations of organized labor in the second half of the fifties, in which Bobby presided over a small army of lawyers, investigators, and accountants). He learned how to run a Senate campaign (his brother's in 1952) and how *not* to run a presidential campaign (Adlai Stevenson's in 1956). Bobby's increasing technical mastery of the system was not, to be sure, at odds with his deepest convictions; his commitments in the fifties generally reflected his conservative moral core, his belief that bad men (Communists, criminals) should be punished and that weak men could not be trusted (he voted for Eisenhower rather than Stevenson in 1956). If he was not the reactionary McCarthyite some have made him out to be, neither had he yet adopted the spacious liberalism he would embrace (reluctantly) in the middle sixties.

His bond with his brother, a bond that began to grow during Jack's 1952 campaign for the Senate, did not mature until later in the decade, when the two worked closely together to make Jack President. It was a bond grounded less in personal affinity than in personal need. "All this business about Jack and Bobby being blood brothers," their sister Eunice said, "has been exaggerated." Jack was a statesman on the English model; politics was for him a grand game, to be played with ironic detachment.[13] He loved a first-rate political performance—Churchill's, for example, or Melbourne's— but loved it as much for its aesthetic excellence, its dramatic appeal, as for anything else. Bobby, with his earnestness, his passion, and his zeal, was a very different kind of man. The two brothers had, Eunice observed, "different tastes in men, different tastes in women."[14] Bobby married a simple, pious, athletic girl; Jack married a woman of exquisite cultivation, a lover of literature and art, the essence of sophistication and poise. Eunice lamented the fact that Bobby should have chosen friends who were, well, so *different* from Jack's. Jack was drawn to self-confident preppies, to men who were "smooth and assured and adept with girls and parties."[15] Bobby, however, was made uncomfortable by the George Plimptons and Ben Bradlees of the world; he did not begin to take pleasure in the company of such men until much later in his life. At Harvard he found excuses for staying away from the snobbish Spee Club; a classmate recalled that he "just wasn't particularly happy around those guys; he was rather uncomfortable."[16] He made friends instead with oddballs and outcasts, with "big and bulky and very unsophisticated" types who "weren't in the usual social stream at all."[17] Jack was a fashion plate, impeccably tailored and groomed; his hatless style and two-button suits set a new standard in men's fashion. Bobby dressed, in Ben Bradlee's apt description, like a "Brooks Brothers beatnik"; nobody, Ethel Kennedy said, would "confuse him with Dean Acheson."[18] As Attorney General he still wore the Brooks Brothers button-down shirts that his older brother considered hopelessly passé. "Bobby doesn't know any better," Jack Kennedy concluded.[19] Bradlee said that the closest Jack Kennedy liked to come to the great outdoors was a well-manicured lawn; white-water rafting, mountain climbing, and swimming in the Amazon River could never have appealed to him in the way they so obviously did to Bobby. Jack's idea of a fun vacation in the fifties was to rent a yacht with friends and sail around the Mediterranean. Bobby's was to trek through Soviet Central Asia with Justice Douglas, trying to persuade Communists of the error of their ways.[20]

In the end politics brought these two very different men together.[21] Without "the common link of Jack's destiny," David Halberstam wrote, the two brothers "might have gone quite different ways, with different friends, different wives, different tastes."[22] Jack Kennedy, who for all his energy and purpose had certain of the habits of a dilettante, needed an enforcer. And Bobby, who for all his talk of running for various offices himself was at heart a manager, needed a candidate. As a Stimsonian Bobby wished, of course, to make a contribution in public life, but in the late fifties he came to realize that the best way he could do this was by getting his brother Jack elected President.

The Ascent

THE BROTHERS' ASCENT to the top of the Stimsonian hierarchy was so rapid and so apparently smooth as to seem, in retrospect, inevitable. In reality it was neither inevitable nor smooth. Dean Acheson was dubious about the "unformed young man" he took Jack Kennedy to be.[23] Adlai Stevenson was equally skeptical. "That young man," Stevenson said, "he never says please, he never says thank you, he never asks for things, he demands them."[24] Truman, the Middle American face of a patrician administration, was openly disparaging of "the boy." Bobby, by turns sullen and rude, was even less popular with the grandees. For all the skill with which they played their Stimsonian roles, Jack and Bobby could not escape their father's past. The Stimsonians looked upon the sons with the same wariness with which they regarded the father. The elder Kennedy blamed the Stimsonians for ruining his political career, and in retirement from public life he had become openly contemptuous of their most cherished dogmas. He was critical of the Truman Doctrine and the various policy decisions that flowed from it—the decisions to intervene in Greece, in Turkey, and in Korea.[25] America's postwar foreign policy, Joseph Kennedy declared, amounted to a "grandiose subsidization of the world," an undertaking of commitments abroad that America could not possibly fulfill.[26] It was a formula, he said, "for minding other people's business on a global scale," an "imperialism of mind," an arrogant effort to "make every state into a copy of America."[27] The Ambassador was no less caustic in his criticism of proposals to expand the welfare state. A greatly enlarged federal establishment, he believed, would become a tyrannical subverter of traditional American liberties, the "beginning of some form of socialism in this country," with the government "mixing itself more and more into everybody's lives."[28]

Jack and Bobby were careful to demonstrate their independence of their father's heretical views. During his years in the House and Senate, Jack was an altogether orthodox supporter of the national security state and the welfare state.[29] And yet there was something not entirely convincing in his protestations of fidelity to the Stimsonian ethos; the right wing of the Stimsonian establishment, led by Acheson, and the left wing, led by Stevenson and Mrs. Roosevelt, continued to be skeptical. It was not so much Kennedy's 1957 speech calling for Algerian independence that troubled the Stimsonians, although that speech, the only controversial one Kennedy made during his eight years in the Senate, troubled both the Achesonian and the Stevensonian factions a great deal. Their skepticism seemed rather directed at the lightness of his manner, the irreverence of his wit, perhaps even the freedom with which he conducted his personal affairs; Jack Kennedy seemed to them too glib, too flippant, too in love with pleasure to be a really serious public servant. He had written a book about political courage, and yet in 1954 he had cravenly abstained from voting to censure Senator McCarthy, Bobby's old boss and the nemesis of the Acheson administration. When Arthur Schlesinger suggested to him that he "had paid a heavy price" for giving his book the title *Profiles in Courage*, Jack could only smile and reply, "Yes, but I didn't have a chapter in it on myself."[30] Jack, if he never rebelled against the orthodoxies of the day, never gave the impression that he took those orthodoxies— or anything else—altogether seriously. Bobby could have admired a man like Henry Stimson, a stoic plodder for whom life consisted of work, duty, and occasional riding and shooting at Highhold, his Long Island estate, or on extended visits to Scotland. Jack would have found Stimson lacking in the brightness, the mandarin charm, the high and vivid powers of imagination that he found so compelling in the historical characters he admired, in Fox, in Melbourne, in Winston Churchill. Jack would have been bored by Stimson, just as he was later to be bored by Stimson's spiritual descendant, Dean Rusk. The Stimsonians sensed Jack's fascination with color and romance, his love of style, the ironic detachment with which he viewed matters of substance, and they wondered if these were not the qualities of a frivolous man.

Converting the Stimsonians

BOBBY, WITH HIS as yet pious and conventional nature, was in some ways a truer Stimsonian than his older brother, but in the end it was Jack who, with a seductive combination of charm and intellect, succeeded in converting important Stimsonian statesmen, intellectuals, and journalists to the Kennedy cause. Schlesinger, the unofficial historian of the liberal wing of the Stimsonian establishment, proved, after his conversion, to be a particularly valuable ally, one who could put urbane prose (which he was able to produce on demand) at the Kennedys' disposal. He was more worldly than the other intellectuals to whom Bobby and Jack looked for advice and counsel, more intellectually elegant than Sorensen or Landis; he spoke the Stimsonian language more fluently than they; he was at home, in a way the other Kennedy intellectuals were not, at Hickory Hill and Hyannis. Except for the time he spent at Phillips Exeter Academy, in England (at Cambridge), and with the OSS during the war, Schlesinger had passed his entire life at Harvard, where his father had been a professor before him. At the age of twenty-eight he had published *The Age of Jackson* (it won a Pulitzer Prize), the first in a series of books that together form a kind of history of the Stimsonian point of view. In Schlesinger's brilliant but ahistorical account of Jacksonian America, Jefferson's overthrow of the villainous Federalists proved to be in vain, for a no less pernicious "business community" rose up in place of the evil Hamiltonians.[31] This "business community," predictably enough, abused its power and oppressed the laboring classes, whose humble members were forced to turn to a hero (General Jackson) to save them, much as their descendants would one day turn to the Roosevelts and the Kennedys. (Of Jackson Schlesinger wrote that the "people called him, and he came, like the great folk heroes, to lead them out of captivity and bondage."[32]) In a sequel, *The Age of Roosevelt*, Schlesinger chronicled the Golden Age itself. His Decline and Fall came later, in the magisterial studies of the Kennedys.

Schlesinger's first encounter with Bobby Kennedy was not auspicious. In 1954 the young professor was provoked by a letter of Bobby's that appeared in *The New York Times* condemning Franklin Roosevelt's actions at Yalta. The disgrace of Yalta was a favorite theme of the hard-line anticommunist Bobby of the late forties and early fifties; in an essay he wrote while at the University of Virginia Law School Bobby condemned FDR's "amoral" concessions to the Soviets at the Crimean conference.[33] Schlesinger responded to Bobby's anti-Roosevelt invective with a letter of his own to the *Times:* Bobby's right-wing views, Schlesinger said, represented "an astonishing mixture of distortion and error."[34] But Bobby, contrary to much that has been written about him, readily forgave his adversaries (he was less forgiving of his brother's opponents), and he soon enough perceived Schlesinger's value. Schlesinger knew everyone, from Mary McCarthy to Reinhold Niebuhr, but he was particularly valuable to the Kennedys because he knew—and was able to act as an emissary to—the liberal Stimsonians, the Stimsonians who worshiped Mrs. Roosevelt and thought Adlai Stevenson an oracle whose public utterances ranked with those of Plato. Schlesinger was never admitted, it is true, to the real penetralia of Jack's and Bobby's political councils, and he was always regarded by the Sorensens and O'Donnells of the world as an "impractical liberal."[35] But the foggy platitudes of Stevensonian liberalism had not prevented him from perceiving, in the late fifties, that Adlai Stevenson was too indolent, too effete, too intellectually delicate, to be President of the United States. Schlesinger wrote in his journal:

> I have come, I think, to the private conclusion that I would rather have [Kennedy] as President than [Stevenson]. [Stevenson] is a much richer, more thoughtful, more creative person; but he has been away from power too long; he gives me an odd sense of unreality. . . . I find it hard to define this feeling—a certain frivolity, distractedness, overinterest in words and phrases? I don't know; but in contrast [Kennedy] gives a sense of cool, measured, intelligent concern with action and power.[36]

And so in 1960 Schlesinger abandoned Stevenson and went to work for Jack and Bobby Kennedy.

Joseph Alsop was an even greater prize. In the late fifties Alsop began spreading the word at Georgetown dinner parties that Jack Kennedy, unlike his father, was one of them, that he was safe, that he spoke their language, that he was "just their type." Pronouncing Jack a "Stevenson with balls," Alsop was as responsible as anyone for inducting the young Senator into the Stimsonian fold.[37] In return Jack spoke of him affectionately as "that old thing" and flattered him constantly. It was one of the odder spectacles in the annals of the Eastern aristocracy, the anointing of the handsome young prince by the ugly old columnist, and yet it was also somehow fitting, for Alsop himself was one of the odder Stimsonians. An influential newspaper columnist, an art collector, a Georgetown savant, and a (relatively) discreet homosexual, Alsop was also the self-appointed judge of the moral and intellectual fitness of the leaders of the postwar American empire. Jack was okay in Alsop's view: He had "balls." Chester Bowles was not: Bowles was a "eunuch" because he didn't know when he'd been fired.[38] Adlai Stevenson, whom Alsop for a time admired extravagantly, disappointed him by turning out to be a wimp; Alsop noted that the Sage of Libertyville had a distressing tendency to invoke Abraham Lincoln's name in his miscellaneous table talk—a sure sign, Alsop said, that Stevenson was a case for the psychiatrist, a man who could not be depended upon to uphold those standards of unsentimental Cold War machismo that fat little Joe had himself helped to fashion.[39]

Alsop's epicene tastes, his sinuous prose, his devotion to the rarest and most beautiful forms of art, would seem to have fitted him for nothing more than the life of a leisured aesthete, unsuited to an active role in the world. He lived out his long life amid rare plants and exotic Oriental art, amid lacquer and porcelain and jade; nothing but silk, he liked to say, was permitted to touch his body (his shirts, his underclothes, and his pajamas were made of imported Chinese silk).[40] But this aestheticism was deceptive, for Alsop had, at a tender age, been exposed to the charms of power, and he who has tasted those charms once will never again be content merely with books and pictures. At the age of twenty-five he had been made Washington correspondent to the New York *Herald Tribune*, and he had soon afterward found himself on close terms with Senators and Cabinet Secretaries. Alsop's conspicuous position and respectable connections made him a welcome guest in the grandest houses in the capital. He lunched regularly with Alice Roosevelt Longworth, to whom he was related through his mother's family, and he was frequently invited by his mother's first cousin, Eleanor Roosevelt, to intimate little suppers at the White House itself. He knew *everybody* who mattered, from Duff and Diana Cooper to Phil and Kay Graham, and to record the many and various acquaintances he accumulated over the years, from Mme. Chiang to General Marshall, from Harry Hopkins to Colonel Lansdale, would be to write a portion of the history of the empire to which he devoted his career. He who was by nature an arbiter of taste became a connoisseur of power, and the author of *The Rare Art Traditions* was not ashamed to acknowledge that he had occasionally encountered, in the coarser realm of politics, instances of beauty quite as wonderful as any that he had discovered in the realm of art. In his pantheon of beautiful people the Kennedys were soon to occupy the most exalted places.[41]

Alsop's power derived from his newspaper column, a column that owed much of its interest to its author's Stimsonian connections. During the Truman and Eisenhower years Alsop became an influential figure in a powerful preppy coterie known as the Sunday-night supper club, so called because of the potluck dinners its members attended on their maids' night off.[42] Georgetown had only recently been discovered by fashionable people, and it was to one or another charming eighteenth-century town house that Alsop repaired each week with friends like Chip Bohlen, Paul Nitze, Richard Bissell, George Kennan, Desmond FitzGerald, Tracy Barnes, and their wives.[43] (It was at a Sunday-night supper that Averell Harriman famously switched off his hearing aid to avoid having to make conversation with Richard Nixon.)[44] Alsop himself became one of Georgetown's most conspicuously successful hosts; so packed with power and celebrity were the parties he gave with Susan Mary Alsop, with whom for a time he had a marriage of convenience, that they amounted almost to an unofficial policymaking arm of the United States government.[45] It is no wonder that the Soviets should have attempted (unsuccessfully) to blackmail Alsop with compromising photographs depicting him in the arms of a KGB agent during a visit to Moscow in the late fifties. In the years since George Kennan had sent his Long Telegram outlining the strategy of containment and Paul Nitze had drafted his blueprint for the national security state—the NSC-68—Alsop had become giddy with the responsibilities of empire. By the time the Soviets tried to snare him he had been among the nation's most influential Cold Warriors for at least a decade.[46]

Alsop spoke for only one of the Stimsonian factions: the diplomatic schemers and intriguers who, filled with the insolence of empire, had in the years since 1945 become accustomed to the exercise of proconsular power around the globe. He spoke, in other words, for the Achesonian wing of the establishment, the wing that descended directly from Stimson himself, an internationalist, a diplomat, a soldier, a man who, though he was skeptical of certain aspects of the New Deal, had played an important role in creating the American empire and the national security state.[47] Alsop did not speak for the more aggressively liberal Stimsonians, for Adlai Stevenson, for Chester Bowles, for Mrs. Roosevelt, for those who were less interested in raw imperial power than in principled reform at home and abroad. Bowles and Mrs. Roosevelt, although their outlook was no less global than Alsop's or Acheson's, were critical of America's lack of sympathy for the democratic yearnings of emerging nations around the world. The gulf between Stimsonian bleeding hearts and Stimsonian Cold Warriors should not, however, be exaggerated; there was a great deal of common ground. One faction was enthralled by the Wilsonian vision of an America good enough to make the world safe for democracy, the other by an Achesonian vision of an America strong enough to make the world *un*safe for communism. In the area of domestic policy there was an even greater degree of unanimity. If different factions within the establishment disagreed about the pace of reform, none disagreed about the need for it. By 1960 there was a consensus among the Stimsonians in favor of preserving and indeed expanding the welfare and administrative state. Reformers like Mrs. Roosevelt preferred Stevenson to Jack Kennedy in part because they believed Stevenson to be the more faithful proselyte of the welfare state. The Cold Warriors (like Alsop) and the old imperial proconsuls (like Harriman) came to prefer the leadership of Jack Kennedy, and so did the most influential member of the "Groton clique" in intelligence, Richard Bissell.[48] To these men Kennedy was indeed a "Stevenson with balls," a man who would make foreign policy exciting again. In supporting him they had nothing to lose but their places in a Stevenson administration, and as 1960 began many even of Adlai's supporters doubted that there would ever be a Stevenson administration.

7

U NLIKE HIS OLDER BROTHER, BOBBY WAS FROM THE
first impatient of the Stimsonians. The duller specimens of the
breed might have bored Jack Kennedy; the more stylish ones intrigued him. Men like Bob Lovett, Chip Bohlen, and Averell Harriman possessed a combination of charm and cunning, of perfect
manners and worldly shrewdness, that appealed to the man who
admired—or affected to admire—Ian Fleming's James Bond novels.
The Stimsonians of Jack and Bobby's day were less fastidious, less
stuffy, less stiff, than they had been in the past, when Henry Stimson had felt compelled to sever personal relations with those of his
friends who divorced their wives. The new generation drank more
often, fornicated more freely, divorced more readily, than their fathers had done; work appeared at times to be a mere interlude
between Georgetown cocktail parties, a way to pass the time until
the next Sunday-night drunk—Joseph Alsop's name for the Sunday-
night supper—where the martinis were passed around like so many
glasses of water.[1] In the pulpit at Groton, Endicott Peabody had
preached incessantly of the dangers of loose morals and marital
infidelity, but the moral of his sermons was lost not only on many
of the boys who graduated from his school, but even on the members of his own family. In 1947 Peabody's granddaughter Marietta
divorced Stimsonian spymaster Desmond FitzGerald to marry Ronald Tree, a rich Tory politician. Could the Rector have foreseen

the fate of his daughter's niece Edie Sedgwick, he would doubtless have given up altogether.[2]

It was not, however, the Stimsonians' standard of private morality that bothered Bobby Kennedy, it was their standard of professional competence. The Stimsonians piqued themselves on their tough, efficient, pragmatic conduct of public business, but even in the earliest period of his career, Bobby seems to have detected those qualities of seigneurial sentimentality, that love of lordly ease, that fatally undermined the Stimsonians' efforts at efficient administration. The liberal Stimsonians—Adlai Stevenson, Chester Bowles, and Mrs. Roosevelt—were in Bobby's view completely useless: they did not understand political power. Stevenson was, of course, the very model of a Stimsonian statesman. His grandfather, the first Adlai Ewing Stevenson, had been Vice President during Grover Cleveland's second administration; his grandmother, Letitia, had been three times the president of the Daughters of the American Revolution.[3] Educated at Choate, Princeton, and Harvard (where he failed out of the law school), the young Stevenson married an heiress before going on to work in FDR's Washington, where he held a variety of New Deal and national security posts in between intervals of legal work at what is now the Sidley & Austin firm in Chicago.[4] Stevenson's patrician languor appalled Bobby; the man was all but incapable of making decisions. Bored with his law practice, Stevenson was intrigued when his Lake Forest friends suggested that he run for the Senate in 1948. But if the prospect of a Senate race thrilled him, it also, he said, "troubled" and even "frightened" him.[5] It was the great theme of his career; he could not make an important decision without agonizing for days or sometimes weeks over its possible consequences. The prospect of running for office in Illinois in the late forties (he eventually became governor of the state) excited and repelled him in precisely the way the prospect of running for President would excite and repel him in the fifties. Although Bobby worked on Stevenson's 1956 presidential campaign, he was disgusted by Stevenson's laziness and seemed out of place among the candidate's passionate admirers. Looking back on Bobby's role in the '56 campaign, Arthur Schlesinger, who had not yet become friends with his hero, could recall only "an alien presence, sullen and rather ominous, saying little, looking grim, and exuding an atmosphere of bleak disapproval."[6] On election day Bobby voted for Eisenhower.

The Stimsonians were supposed to be master administrators, but they were never able to move fast enough for Bobby. He did not bother to conceal his exasperation with, for example, the preppy clique at the CIA; he is said at one point to have told Richard Bissell, who had dropped the ball on a plan to eliminate Castro, to "get off his ass" and get a plan off the ground.[7] Even those Stimsonians who were undeniably energetic often angered Bobby with their ostentatious displays of antiquated honor. No one could accuse Chester Bowles, the Yale man who made a fortune on Madison Avenue before going to Washington to run the Office of Price Administration, of being lazy, but if Bowles displayed a fanatical zeal in working to set the nation's prices, he was curiously reticent when it came to practical politics.[8] Although Bowles thought nothing of incurring the wrath of Senator Taft, a staunch opponent of price controls, during his stint at the OPA, the fastidious Connecticut Yankee could not bring himself to campaign for Jack Kennedy in Wisconsin in 1960, even though he was, at the time, one of the candidate's principal foreign policy advisers.[9] His friendship with Hubert Humphrey, Bowles said, meant too much to him.[10] (Bowles was equally reluctant to campaign against Stevenson, an old friend from his Choate days.) Bobby was not impressed.

Establishment Theory

WHY DID JACK and Bobby *want* the support of the Stimsonians? Jack could have gotten the nomination in 1960 without it. The Stimsonians had, as a rule, very little power at the polls or in the primary contests. Particular Stimsonian candidates might, with their eloquence and their grace, possess exceptional vote-getting ability, but as often as not their aristocratic demeanor worked against them on Election Day, made voters uneasy, made them sympathetic to the plainer candidate, the Everyman who reminded them of themselves. Whatever the strength of such individual candidates as Roosevelt and Rockefeller, the Stimsonians as a group had neither a political base nor even a political party to which to look for consistent support (some Stimsonians were Republicans, others were Democrats). The great majority of those statesmen we might classify as "Stimsonian" were not politicians at all; they were administrators, mandarins who relied for their immense authority on the patronage of those who, like the Kennedys, like the Roosevelts, like the Rockefellers, actually won elections by doing the dirty work of politics—courting obscure state party officials and shabby local politicians, speaking at their banquets, flattering their vanity, making them promises of patronage. In New York in 1960 prominent Stimsonians *opposed* Jack's candidacy; a number of important (non-Tammany) bosses, however, supported him (Peter Crotty, Charles Buckley, Eugene Keogh).[11] In the end it was the bosses who delivered the delegates.[12] The Kennedys didn't need the political support of the Stimsonians in 1960, but Jack Kennedy, perhaps because he was less proficient than Bobby in those bureaucratic arts at which the Stimsonians were supposed to excel, desperately wanted their approval. Kennedy, David Halberstam observed, believed in, was fascinated by, "the Establishment mystique."[13] His brother Bobby could not have cared less.

Halberstam was right: an establishment mystique *did* exist in America in 1960. But what of the establishment itself? Did it exist? And if it did, what part did the Stimsonians play in it? Certainly they constituted *an* established authority in the America of 1960. But they were hardly *the* establishment, and it would be misleading to describe the complex of institutions and individuals they represented as constituting something so solid and so supreme as to justify the use of the definite article. The very term "the establishment," and a half-dozen similar ones (the "Eastern" or "Northeastern" establishment, the "WASP ascendancy," the "Protestant establishment"), suggest that there existed in the United States in the first half of the twentieth century a single monolithic entity that somehow controlled American life, or was closely connected to the institutions that did—the "military-industrial complex," the "power elite," the "real" power structure that the "paper" one masked.[14] Such a supposition is misleading, for a nation as large as the United States will always contain not one, but a number of elites, a number of "establishments," and these elites will be not static and unchanging, but constantly evolving, growing, and, as it were, interbreeding in a complicated process of cross-fertilization and parasitical growth. There are today in the United States, as there were at mid-century, regional elites, business elites, the banking community, the capital markets, the military establishment, the great universities, the political parties, Hollywood, the legal profession, the medical profession, and a dozen others, and so interconnected are these various groups, and so fluid and mobile is the society in which they have their existence, that it would be impossible to assign them places in a neatly drawn schematic map of power in America. It is not wrong to speak of the existence of a "Stimsonian establishment," a nexus of men and institutions that during a large part of this century exercised a peculiarly extensive influence in American life, but it must always be borne in mind that this establishment was not the only one in the United States, that it was neither all-powerful nor all-controlling, and that in no sense was its jurisdiction in the various spheres in which it operated exclusive.

If absolute precision were required in the use of descriptive terms, the Stimsonians might with considerable justice be called a "court party," just as individual Stimsonians might with accuracy be described as aristocratic courtiers or mandarins, ones who were recruited from a variety of regional, hereditary, and scholastic elites. (The nation's founders used the term "court party" to describe factions that exercised an often hidden and usually sinister influence on the administration of government.) But the term "establishment" is not utterly out of place when applied to the Stimsonians, and can indeed more fittingly be applied to them than to the so-called Protestant ascendancy, the monolithic caste that supposedly dominated the life of the United States before World War II. The term "Protestant establishment" was never particularly helpful. Its weakness lay in its breadth: it encompassed too many people, too many regional elites, too many Protestant sects (Quaker, Puritan [or Congregationalist], Presbyterian, Episcopalian, Methodist, Lutheran, Baptist, etc.) to be analytically useful. It failed to take into account the fissures that divided what was all too often considered—in an age when the assumptions of Marx were all but inescapable—a single united class. But this class unity was largely specious; a prominent Middle Western family whose industrial fortune dated from the decades after the Civil War would have had, after all, next to nothing in common with a Brahmin family in Boston, one whose scions, supported by an older and smaller fortune, spent their lives toiling in the service of scholarship or one of the learned professions. Old money looked down upon new money; old cities looked down upon new cities; readers of old books looked down upon those who, they supposed, did not read books at all.* However subtle one's theory of an American Protestant "establishment"—of an American "upper class," a "WASP ascendancy," an "old school tie," a mythology of "old money," a "leisure class"—the reality was always more complicated.

At the same time, the term "Protestant establishment" exaggerated the religious tendencies of the people it purported to describe, as if religion were their most remarkable characteristic (and not simply one they happened to share with others), as if the Protestants themselves retained, in the twentieth century, the evangelical fervor or ascetic piety that had characterized their ancestors in the past. Nor can one escape the semantic difficulties of the term. In order to constitute an "establishment," as that word is defined by

---

*There will always be a difficulty in ascertaining just when a particular family entered the ranks of the so-called Protestant establishment, when it ceased to be nouveau, gauche, arriviste, non-U, and received the approbation of the arbiters of society. In his study *Philadelphia Gentlemen*, Digby Baltzell wrote that as late as 1940 families whose fortunes were made after the Civil War "were still considered 'new.'" But although men with freshly made fortunes are at first despised by the old guard, the snobs eventually relax their vigilance and are usually grateful to marry their daughters to the rich parvenu's sons. The processes by which one generation's plutocrats are transformed into the next generation's aristocrats are subtle and mysterious, and the careless historian is only too likely to overlook the intricate pattern of social fissures that separate the older elements of society from the new.

the Oxford philologists, the entity in question must either be maintained at the expense of the sovereign or in some way enjoy the patronage of the state (the military establishment, an established church).[15] Although this was not true of the Protestant establishment, it was eminently true of the Stimsonians. They were at home in the corridors of the federal government; they insinuated themselves into its affairs and made themselves indispensable to its rulers by developing expertise in programs and policies they themselves helped craft. Once in power, they tended to perpetuate themselves, to "establish" themselves, through a skillful practice of the arts of nepotism and favoritism (the "old boy network").

The "Stimsonian establishment," then, is not simply another name for the old Protestant elites, for those classes that Joseph Alsop labeled the "Who was shes?" (since the leading families in these classes were related to one another by marriage, it was particularly important to know a matron's maiden name. Hence the critical question "Now, let me see, who was she?").[16] But the Stimsonian establishment was to some extent descended from these declining elites; its members were largely recruited out of their ranks. The Stimsonians belonged to the same clubs (Century, Union, Links, Knickerbocker, Racquet, Somerset, the Brook, etc.) and took pride in the same hereditary organizations (Society of the Cincinnati, Mayflower Descendants, Daughters of the American Revolution) as their brothers and friends who made peace with the marketplace and devoted themselves more exclusively to the law, business, finance, or (more rarely as the century wore on) the Church (almost always the Episcopal one, although it was fashionable to have at least one member of the family enamored of the doctrines of Anglo-Catholicism or even of Rome itself). During the thirties tensions emerged between those patricians who worshipped capital and those who worshipped the state: while scions of some of the old-old and newly old families hated Roosevelt, others went to work for him. And yet even at the height of the New Deal FDR's patrician admirers were not as estranged from their brothers in finance and industry as might be supposed, and a surprising number of Stimsonians were able to lead double lives. In private life men like Harriman and Stimson were capitalists or the servants of capital; in public life they offered their services to a state increasingly eager to regulate and control capital. (Harriman, for example, served as an administrator of FDR's National Recovery Administration.[17]) The "Who was she?" classes were by no means united in their hatred of FDR, and indeed it was a rare patrician who would not have been happy to see his son benefit from the great man's patronage.

Not all Stimsonians, of course, were products of the "Who was she?" classes; as the century wore on, the Stimsonian club became an almost meritocratic one. A man who was considered "able"—a favorite Stimsonian term of praise—could expect preferment regardless of his background, provided, of course, that he was willing to embrace the fundamental tenets of the Stimsonian code. One of the more important achievements of the Stimsonians was to put an end to the gentle (and sometimes not so gentle) anti-Semitism that prevailed in the highest reaches of American public life in the first half of the century. Stimson himself recruited Felix Frankfurter for his staff in the United States Attorney's office; Dean Acheson considered Frankfurter his best friend.[18]

If religion was gradually ceasing to be a barrier to entry in the club, geography had never really been one. John W. Davis came from West Virginia, Bob Lovett from Texas, Clark Clifford from Missouri, George Kennan from Wisconsin, Adlai Stevenson from Illinois, Robert McNamara from California, Dean Rusk from Georgia, and William O. Douglas from Minnesota and Washington State. The very fact that they came from the South or the West made many of these men all the more ardent in their profession of the Stimsonian faith. Their first encounter with Eastern standards and institutions was often a decisive—sometimes a traumatic—chapter in their lives. George Kennan, who had suffered from an acute feeling of inferiority at Princeton in the twenties, wept over the pages in *Gatsby* in which Nick Carraway describes the cultural bewilderment experienced by those who come to the East from beyond the Alleghenies.[19] In time, however, even the most self-consciously Southern or Western of the Stimsonian statesmen established ties to the East and its aristocratic institutions. They spent summers in places like Fishers Island, Dark Harbor, the Vineyard, and Newport; packed their children off to schools like Groton, St. Paul's, and the Phillips academies; and sent updated information concerning new wives, children, houses, and yachts to the Social Register Association at New York.

Their anomalous position as an elite in a democracy helps to explain the curious isolation of the Stimsonians, their lack of engagement in the life of the great mass of the people, their lack of sensitivity to changes in public opinion. One is not surprised to discover that they were often out of touch with the deeper currents of popular feeling. When he was not in Washington administering an agency, or establishing a commission, or planning a clandestine operation, the Stimsonian could be found not actively engaged in the politics of his community, but in his law firm or investment house, at his country seat or on the Vineyard. Although the Stimsonians could plausibly claim to represent popular sentiment where the Cold War was concerned, even here they seem not to have chosen the most popular (or economical) way of fighting that war.[20] By the time Jack Kennedy became President, America had, Neil Sheehan wrote, "built the largest empire in history," and the most expensive one. The United States

had 850,000 military men and civilian officials serving overseas in 106 countries. From the combined-services headquarters of the Commander in Chief of the Pacific on the mountain above Pearl Harbor, to the naval base at Subic Bay in the Philippines, to the shellproof bunkers along the truce line in Korea, there were 410,000 men arrayed in the armies, the fleets, and the air forces of the Pacific. In Europe and the Middle East, from the nuclear bomber bases in the quiet of the English countryside, to the tank manoeuvre grounds at Grafenwöhr on the invasion route from Czechoslovakia, to the aircraft carriers of the Sixth Fleet waiting in the Mediterranean, to the electronic listening posts along the Soviet frontier in Turkey and Iran, there were another

410,000 soldiers, sailors, and airmen deployed. When the diplomats from the State Department, the agents from the CIA, and the officials of the sundry other civilian agencies were counted, the United States had approximately 1.4 million of its servants and their families representing it abroad in 1962.[21]

Some historians have found it convenient, by way of apology, to blame the excesses of the national security state on the pressures to which Joseph McCarthy and middlebrow Republicans subjected the Acheson regime in the early fifties. A tempting thesis, but not, finally, a convincing one. For after all, the first shot in the "Who lost China?" war was fired by Alsop himself, not McCarthy, in a series of articles that appeared in *The Saturday Evening Post* early in 1950. Three years before, in March 1947, Truman had ordered loyalty tests. The first State Department casualty of China, John Stewart Service, was a victim not of McCarthy's capricious whims, but of Acheson and Truman's blunt administrative fiat.[22] And this was at a time when Senator Robert Taft, "Mr. Republican," was *skeptical* of the need for an American empire, a Cold War waged on a dozen fronts. Taft, who voted against NATO legislation, worried that America, in the vainglorious pursuit of imperial power, would sacrifice her republican and democratic character on the altar of Empire, just as Athens and Rome had sacrificed theirs before her.[23] (Joseph Kennedy would call Taft's death in 1953 "the greatest tragedy to befall the American people in the loss of a statesman since the assassination of Abraham Lincoln.[24]") In the late fifties Ike believed that the national security state was secure enough, was perhaps *too* secure; in his farewell address he famously warned of the dangers of the "military-industrial complex." It was Acheson, Alsop, and Jack Kennedy who continued to insist on the precariousness of the nation's defenses; in 1960 Kennedy campaigned on a pledge to end a missile "gap" that didn't exist.[25] However much support Cold War policies may have had in the nation at large, the method of their execution bears the unmistakable impress of the Stimsonians.

If the Cold War policies of the Stimsonians had a solid basis of popular support, the same cannot be said of their domestic agenda. The Stimsonians' enthusiasm for the welfare and administrative state, an enthusiasm that lacked a foundation in what Bobby would later call "the shaping traditions of American life and politics," was increasingly at odds with the mood of the American people in the postwar period. A perceptive observer even in 1960 might have detected those undercurrents of dissatisfaction with bureaucratic bloat, regulatory overkill, and selective federal largesse that would later manifest themselves so signally in Ronald Reagan's rebellion against the welfare and administrative state. The Stimsonians, if they were adept at identifying the nation's problems, never sought to solve them in a way that was consistent with the nation's history and traditions. The crises were real enough, but the methods chosen to solve them, and the philosophy brought to bear upon them, tending, as they did, to exalt the grandeur of the state at the expense of the individual, were repugnant to the character and genius of the American people. It is not enough, Burke long ago observed, for a statesman to solve problems; he must make the additional effort of solving them in a way that furthers rather than undermines the first principles of his country.

Toward Camelot

JACK AND BOBBY might have chosen to question the prerogatives, the privileges, and the priorities of the Stimsonian establishment, but they did not. It was not in Jack's—or, at the time, in Bobby's—nature to be a heretic. Jack did not propose a radical overhaul of the Stimsonian system; he merely promised to get things "moving" again, whatever that meant. As a pledge of his good faith, he filled the executive establishment with Stimsonians of the highest caliber, men who had spent time in the best schools, the best colleges, and the best law firms in America. For his chief minister Jack wanted nothing less than a bona fide protégé of Stimson himself: among those he considered for Secretary of State were Bob Lovett, Jack McCloy, and McGeorge Bundy, each of whom had at one time worked for Stimson (as had Bundy's father). In the end Jack chose, in part on the basis of Lovett's recommendation, Dean Rusk.[26] Harriman, Bowles, and Stevenson were given diplomatic posts in the administration, Stevenson as Ambassador to the United Nations. Douglas Dillon went to the Treasury, David Bruce to London. Allen Dulles was kept on at the CIA, where Richard Bissell was a rising star and James Jesus Angleton performed with ponderous solemnity the role of high priest of the national security state. Kennedy made Robert McNamara, a Stimsonian by conviction and temperament rather than by blood, Secretary of Defense. McNamara's Defense Department could by itself have furnished an enviable Wall Street law practice; filling positions in the defense establishment were Roswell Gilpatric from Cravath, Cyrus Vance from Simpson, Thacher, Stan Resor from Debevoise & Plimpton, and Peter Solbert from Davis Polk. (Bill Bundy, Deputy Assistant Secretary of Defense for International Security Affairs, was an alumnus of Dean Acheson's law firm, Covington, Burling & Rublee; Bundy was also Acheson's son-in-law.) At the Department of Justice Bobby brought in a younger but no less respectable staff. The influence of Yale Law School was particularly strong, with Byron R. "Whizzer" White becoming Deputy Attorney General, Nicholas deB. Katzenbach heading the Office of Legal Counsel, Louis Oberdorfer the tax division, and John Douglas the civil division.[27] The Solicitor General's office went to Harvard's Archibald Cox.

Bobby's administration of the Justice Department remains a lasting example of Stimsonianism at its best; the department's work in securing the equal protection of the laws for blacks stands as one of the great achievements of the Stimsonian establishment. For once, the methods and tools the Stimsonians employed were equal to the crisis they confronted; for once, their lawyerly approach to human problems, their practice of hiring Ivy League lawyers and setting them to work to find legal and administrative answers to complex social and economic questions, resulted in accomplishments that withstood the test of time. Bobby himself became deeply involved in his department's civil rights work. He brought first-rate lawyers to the Civil Rights Division and put the admirable Burke

Marshall in charge of them. He traveled to Georgia to announce in person the administration's commitment to school desegregation. He battled segregationists in Mississippi when they refused to allow James Meredith to enroll at the State University at Oxford. He flew to Alabama, at a time when even brave men might have stayed away, to try to persuade Governor Wallace to permit the registration of black students at the University of Alabama. He helped to prepare the landmark civil rights legislation his brother sent to Congress in June 1963, and he served as the administration's lead witness before the Senate committees that initially reviewed the bill. He even found time to master the cases and issues involved in an important apportionment case, *Gray v. Sanders*, which established a "one man, one vote" standard in voting controversies. Bobby personally argued the *Gray* case at the bar of the Supreme Court; his wife, his mother, two sisters, his younger brother, a sister-in-law or two, and four of his children were present to hear him deliver his argument before the justices.[28] And yet if Bobby's civil rights work represented one of the great successes of his Stimsonian Justice Department, it at the same time revealed—to him no less than to his critics—the limits of the Stimsonian technique. Legal and administrative remedies might make it possible for oppressed minorities to enjoy the full complement of civil rights, but those remedies could do little to give them the self-confidence they needed to take advantage of their new opportunities.

The record of his brother's administration in other areas was less enviable. Most of Jack Kennedy's energy and imagination was consumed, during his presidency, by foreign crises, by the ongoing melodrama of Cold War confrontation, by the constant need to defend an empire whose far-flung frontiers the Romans themselves would have thought presumptuous. Jack Kennedy seems not to have foreseen, when he took office, the extent to which his achievements were destined to be the achievements of reaction—reaction to missiles in Cuba, to a wall in Berlin, to guerrilla activity in Indochina. His administration responded to history, responded, indeed, "flexibly" to it, to use the jargon of the time, but it did not shape history. History had been shaped for it—shaped by an earlier generation of

Stimsonians, by those who, in Dean Acheson's words, had been "present at the creation" of the postwar order.

But all of this lay in the future. The burdens of history were as yet unrevealed to Jack Kennedy when he took the oath of office on a cold sunny day in January 1961. David Halberstam has given, in *The Best and the Brightest,* the definitive account of the confidence and mutual admiration that prevailed during the first months of Camelot. The men who came to Washington to serve under the Kennedys, Halberstam wrote, believed that there "was no limit to what brilliant men, untrammeled by ideology and prejudice and partisanship, could do with their minds in solving the world's problems."[29] The administration was at once the culmination and the perfection of seventy-five years of Stimsonian aristocracy. Jack himself gracefully accepted the challenge of the moment, and articulated, more memorably than any other Stimsonian of his generation, the purposes and premises of their leadership, their vision of a group of Enlightened statesmen solving the problems of the nation and the world through a careful deployment of the resources of a powerful government. With its confident assertion that "man holds in his mortal hands the power to abolish . . . all forms of human poverty," with its famous pledge to "pay any price" and "bear any burden" to ensure the survival and the success of liberty and the American empire, Kennedy's inaugural address is a classic statement of the Stimsonian creed, an eloquent declaration of the principles on which the welfare state and the national security state rested.[30] Joseph Alsop could not have been more pleased, and when, a few months later, his dear friend the President came to dine at his house on Dumbarton Avenue, and complimented him upon his selection of wines (a stomach complaint prevented Kennedy from actually drinking them), we may fairly suppose that Alsop's ecstasy was complete.[31]

It is, perhaps, more than a coincidence that the Kennedys were not simply the last, but in some ways the most brilliant representatives of a dying aristocracy. As is so often the case with aristocratic castes, the rich and fermenting processes of decay brought forth the most splendid growths. The repeal of the Corn Laws in England meant the end of the Tory Party as it had been constituted in that country for two centuries, but its leadership was never more memorable than at the time when its fortunes began to decline and its principles came to be discredited, when it brought forth Disraeli (who like Jack and Bobby had not been born into the aristocracy he was later to lead) and Randolph Churchill. It was during the last years of its ascendancy that the ancient republican aristocracy of Rome produced its most memorable men: Cato the Younger, Brutus, and Caesar himself. The extinction of the Roman aristocracy coincided with the collapse of the Republic, and afterward the emperors filled the Senate with mediocrities and nobodies, with scribes and centurions and the sons of former slaves.[32] In America half a century of Stimsonian aristocracy culminated in the rise of Jack and Bobby Kennedy—outsiders to begin with, but men whose names came in time to be synonymous with the idea of aristocracy in the United States.

PART II

The Portrait of a Rebel

8

⟨⟨⟨⟨⟨⟨⟨⟨⟩⟩⟩⟩⟩⟩⟩⟩

ON THE MORNING OF FRIDAY, NOVEMBER 22, 1963, THE
Attorney General presided, in his office in the Department of Justice, over a discussion of the problem of organized crime in the
United States. Among the federal prosecutors in attendance were
Robert Morgenthau, scion of a prominent New Deal family and
now in Henry Stimson's old job as United States Attorney for the
Southern District of New York, and his assistant, Silvio Mollo, the
chief of the criminal division in the Southern District. When, about
noon, the meeting adjourned, Bobby invited the two lawyers to
luncheon at Hickory Hill. The day was warm, and the three men
sat out of doors, on a patio beside the swimming pool, where a meal
of tuna fish sandwiches and New England clam chowder was served.
Later Ethel joined them, and Bobby swam in the pool.[1]

The Kennedys had recently added a new wing to the house, and
in the distance a group of workmen were painting it. Some time
after one-thirty one of the workmen, a radio in his hand, came
running toward the luncheon party in a state of agitation. At the
same time, a maid, or possibly a butler—Morgenthau's memory was
uncertain—approached the little group and announced that the director had telephoned and wished to speak to the Attorney General.
The director, of course, was J. Edgar Hoover, and he was not in
the habit of telephoning the Attorney General at home. Bobby went
to the telephone, and all at once Morgenthau began to comprehend

the agitated workman's words. A moment later Bobby put his hand to his mouth; Ethel went to his side. When he put the telephone down, Bobby was at first silent. At last he spoke, and told the group that his brother had been shot.[2]

The four of them returned to the house. Morgenthau and Mollo were shown to a television set in the drawing room; Bobby and Ethel went upstairs, where Bobby attempted to telephone Kenny O'Donnell in Dallas. Failing to reach O'Donnell, he spoke instead to Clint Hill, the Secret Service agent who a short time before had leapt aboard the presidential limousine in a Dallas street. The President, Hill said, was gravely wounded. Bobby asked whether they had summoned a priest, and Hill replied that they had. Half an hour later the Attorney General spoke again by telephone to Dallas; this time he was informed that the President was dead. Bobby went downstairs. "He's dead," he announced, in an oddly casual way, to Morgenthau and Mollo, and then he went outside.[3]

In the gathering dusk he paced the great lawn of his estate. Friends and lieutenants joined him for brief periods of time, as did his own children, whom Ethel had fetched from school.[4] "He had the most wonderful life," he told them as he embraced them. He shed no tears, but Ethel gave him a pair of dark glasses, lest his red-rimmed eyes betray him. In the early evening he changed clothes, put on a black suit, and was driven to Secretary McNamara's offices at the Pentagon; from there he traveled by helicopter to Andrews Air Force Base. When, about six o'clock, the Boeing 707 bearing the new President, the dead President, and the dead President's widow taxied to a halt on the Andrews field, Bobby, avoiding the television lights that illuminated one side of the great airplane, slipped through the shadows to the darkened side of the jet and climbed aboard unnoticed. He hurried past President Johnson and his party, who were gathered at the front of the plane, and went at once to the private apartments in the rear of the aircraft, where his sister-in-law, in her bloodied clothes, had kept a vigil beside her husband's coffin. Bobby held her hand as they stepped out into the brilliant glare of the television lights, and escorted her to the ambulance that was to bear the coffin, first to the Naval

Hospital at Bethesda, and then to the White House itself.[5] Bobby slept in the Lincoln Bedroom that night; his friend Chuck Spalding brought him a sleeping pill. After Spalding closed the door, he heard an anguished cry from within: "Why, God?"[6]

Death and the Attorney General

ISAIAH BERLIN HAD been distressed to find, during a visit to Washington in the early sixties, that the relationship between Jack Kennedy and his aides-de-camp resembled that between Bonaparte and his marshals; some of Kennedy's courtiers were "physically in love with him."[7] They had loved him in life, and now that he was dead, even the strongest among them were broken in spirit. "For a time after Jack Kennedy's death," Joseph Alsop recalled, "the sense of emotional loss was so staggering among those who had known and worked with him that the Washington landscape" seemed "littered with male widows."[8] "I suddenly realized," the tough old Cravath lawyer Roswell Gilpatric said, "that I felt about [the President] as I've never felt about another man in my life."[9] McGeorge Bundy confessed that the President's death struck him more deeply than the loss of his own father.[10]

If the effect of the President's death on Alsop and Bundy and Gilpatric was great, how much greater must its effect have been on Bobby himself. He appeared to Ben Bradlee to be the "strongest of the stricken," but this apparent strength was deceptive, for he, too, was at heart a broken man.[11] In the months that followed the assassination he would sit for hours at a time at his desk in the Justice Department, staring out the window.[12] Or he would wander aimlessly through the streets of Georgetown, dressed in an old tweed overcoat that had belonged to his brother.[13] He lost so much weight that his clothes ceased to fit him.[14] There was a "hollow" look in his eyes.[15] In a quiet voice he talked of leaving politics altogether, and of devoting himself to other pursuits. He would teach, or write, or travel. His humor, always dark, became morbid. "Been to any good funerals lately?" he asked a friend. "I don't like to let too many days go by without a funeral."[16] For a time he escaped, to Douglas Dillon's house at Hobe Sound, Florida, and found release, in that enclave of tastefully displayed wealth, in games of touch football. They were, Pierre Salinger recalled, "really vicious" games. "It seemed to me," Salinger said, that Bobby "was getting his feelings out . . . knocking people down."[17] But still the pain remained.

At length his spirits began to revive. A regimen of athletic competition at Hobe Sound might have been good for the body, but the insipid rhythms of life at a *Social Register* watering hole could not have been good for the soul. For spiritual nourishment Bobby was forced to wait until the spring of 1964, when he traveled to the house of Mrs. Paul Mellon in Antigua. There his sister-in-law Jacqueline gave him a book called *The Greek Way* by Edith Hamilton. Miss Hamilton, a classical scholar and former headmistress of Bryn Mawr, had first published her meditation on the salient characteristics of the Hellenic mind in 1930. Bobby found himself unable to put the book down. "I remember he'd disappear," Jacqueline Kennedy recalled. "He'd be in his room an awful lot of the time . . . reading and underlining things."[18]

Not merely the period of life in which we first read a book, but the place and the circumstances in which we begin to turn its pages, has everything to do with the nature and potency of its effect upon us.[19] Under the tropical sky Miss Hamilton's pages revealed to Bobby a far larger universe than he had previously had any conception of. The Stimsonian creed in which he had been bred up was an intensely *practical* creed; Miss Hamilton, however, taught that practicality alone was not enough, that greatness lay in the union of practical and spiritual excellence, in the "fusion of rational and spiritual power" which she believed the ancient Greeks and the Renaissance Italians had achieved.[20] Although the Greeks possessed the raw strength and tenacious willpower that wins battles and prostrates enemies, they were at the same time devoted to poetry and to what Miss Hamilton called the "imponderables" of high civilization.[21] The Greeks succeeded in escaping the fate of so many peoples who have excelled in works of practical genius; their closeness to the mysteries of human existence, their intimacy with the world of the imagination, the world of dreams—the dark ecstasies of Dionysus, the sunlit excellence of Apollo—saved them from spiritual superficiality. Miss Hamilton's fifth-century Athenians were as "hard-headed" as the Stimsonians, and won as many famous battles and wars, but they took, as the Stimsonians did not, "a delight in the things of the mind"; they possessed a "love of beauty" and "delicate feeling" that was quite foreign to the protégés of Colonel Stimson.[22] Bobby's own debt to Miss Hamilton's brilliant Hellenes was evident when he said that the two virtues he most admired were "courage and sensitivity."[23]

Although a faint odor of the Middle Age hung about their seigneurial pretensions, the Stimsonians were curiously oblivious of the life of the spirit, and this blindness helps to explain certain shortcomings in their approach to man's problems. So unconscious were they of the mechanics of human pain, so blind were they to its power, that they believed it could be done away with through a more Enlightened deployment of society's resources. Stepchildren of the Enlightenment, the Stimsonians possessed a complacent faith in a painless future, a future bred to splendor by science and rational planning, the same faith that had characterized the eighteenth-century *philosophes* before them. Bobby was at the beginning of his life sympathetic to the Stimsonian point of view; but Miss Hamilton's pages forced him for the first time to question it. He discovered in her book the mysterious processes by which tragedy and suffering defy so many of man's rational and Enlightened efforts in the world (the relevant word, of course, is "hubris"). At the same time, he came to understand that pain is a necessary precondition for any great or worthwhile achievement. Oedipus himself, after all, had once been a Stimsonian, a technocrat, a solver of riddles, the Enlightened deliverer of his city.[24] But he, too, had eventually grown up.

Carrying the Torch

THE DIRECTION IN which his private thoughts tended did not initially influence his public politics. He became, if anything, even more zealous in his advocacy of the principles of Stimsonian governance in the months that followed his brother's death. This was so in part because of the duty he believed he owed his brother's memory. Jack Kennedy had pledged himself to upholding the ideals of the welfare state at home and the Pax Americana abroad: he had declared that Americans would pay any price to ensure the survival and the success of liberty and the American empire around the world; at home he had been troubled by the pain and poverty depicted in Michael Harrington's book *The Other America* and had vowed to do something about it. Inevitably history would judge him by how well he had served the causes to which he had dedicated his presidency. The truth, of course, was that his administration had been characterized by a remarkable degree of reticence. The rhetoric was dazzling; the actions were cautious, cool, and pragmatic. Kennedy had rejected Arthur Schlesinger's advice that he adopt an ambitious domestic program along the lines of FDR's New Deal; Schlesinger, the President said, "couldn't get it through his head" that this was "1963, not 1933."[25] In foreign policy Jack Kennedy had been no less circumspect; he had been more interested in reducing the scope of America's commitments abroad by means of carefully negotiated settlements (as in Laos) than in extending America's influence by concluding fresh alliances around the world. Kennedy privately criticized Eisenhower's promiscuous promises of American support to all and sundry; he seemed, at times, reluctant to defend even those governments, like the regime in South Vietnam, to which the United States—and his own Vice President—had given unconditional assurances of support. But it is boldness, not prudence, that turns the heads of historians, and so cautious a record as President Kennedy's was unlikely to win him an enviable place in the history books. Bobby knew how cruelly posterity treated those leaders who, in his words, failed to "press"; he was therefore determined to foster the notion that his brother had been a consummately progressive President, one whose last wish had been to launch a great federal war to "end" poverty.[26]

The fact that Jack Kennedy had been, in Bobby's view, so distinctly progressive a President made it all the more necessary for Bobby himself to embrace the progressive cause with a becoming zeal. Somebody, after all, needed to carry on Jack Kennedy's legacy. Bobby decided, not unnaturally, that he was the best man to do it. He had been closest to his brother in life; why should he not carry on his brother's legacy after his death? Certainly Lyndon Johnson, he believed, could not be trusted with so important a task; for Johnson, Bobby argued, was at heart a conservative. "People just don't realize," Bobby said as he rode in the elevator to Robert McNamara's office a few hours after his brother's murder, "how conservative Lyndon really is."[27]

Bobby's problem lay in the fact that he himself didn't *seem* like a progressive politician. Jack may not have been a truly progressive statesman, but his eloquence, his grace, his generous and open nature, had combined to make him seem the very model of progressive liberality. Bobby, by contrast, with his crew-cut head and hard Irish face, seemed too ruthless, too bellicose, too unapologetically vindictive, too apparently petty, to be a really liberal statesman, a happy warrior in the tradition of Charles James Fox and Franklin Roosevelt. Nor was Bobby's style alone a problem; his record was just as troubling. The liberals in his party had not forgotten his apprenticeship under Senator McCarthy. They had not forgiven him for threatening to "get" Hubert Humphrey in 1960, or for humiliating Chester Bowles at the time of the Bay of Pigs crisis.[28] They remembered his work to expose the malversation of their allies in the labor movement. Only the most substantial atonement would cause the liberals to forgive; if Bobby was to make up for the deficiencies of his past conduct, he would have to redouble the zealousness of his exercises in liberal virtue. Even as he turned the pages of the Greek tragedians, even as he began to question the fundamental assumptions of the Stimsonian state, Bobby was forced, by the political realities of the moment, to be an enthusiastic, even aggressive, promoter of the idea of grand government.

The personalities he found himself opposing in the pursuit of power and the defense of his brother's legacy only intensified the pressures upon him. On a hot day in July 1964 Lyndon Johnson summoned Bobby to the Oval Office to inform him, during the course of an unpleasant forty-five-minute interview, that he had decided against asking him to be his vice-presidential running mate in 1964. The following weekend Bobby flew up to Hyannis Port to ponder his future. Arthur Schlesinger was there, and so were Averell Harriman and Dave Hackett. Together the four men reviewed Bobby's options. Though the possibility of a State Department post initially intrigued Bobby, Schlesinger and Harriman persuaded him that a man of his restless temperament would never be content in Dean Rusk's foreign policy shop. That left one other possibility: moving to New York and running for the Senate. Though Bobby had ruled out a Senate bid in June, he was now prepared to reconsider his earlier decision. Within days Kennedy loyalists were canvassing New York politicians in search of support.

In order to secure the nomination, Bobby needed to do more than find a house and establish residency in New York (a house was quickly obtained for him in Glen Cove, Long Island). He was forced to turn to the bosses. Men like Charles Buckley of the Bronx, Peter Crotty of Buffalo, and John English of Nassau County were, in style and stature, the antithesis of the Kennedys; they were unimaginative machine politicians of the type that good Stimsonians had been struggling against ever since the days when Stimson himself and Paul Drennan Cravath had worked together to draft legislation designed to curb the power of the Tammany bosses.[29] The Kennedys had, however, given abundant proof, in 1960, of their ability to do business with Daley-style machine politicians, and Bobby found himself unable to reject their support now.[30] The bosses were willing to put their power and influence at his disposal at a time when respectable Stimsonians—Adlai Stevenson, Mayor Wagner, Mrs. Herbert Lehman—were skeptical of his candidacy.[31] Stevenson, who was serving as Ambassador to the United Nations and was frequently mentioned as a candidate for the Senate himself, angrily turned away Steve Smith when the smooth-talking brother-in-law showed up at Stevenson's apartment in the Waldorf Towers looking for a kind word and an endorsement.[32] The presence of the bosses in Bobby's camp, however necessary it might have been, made it all the easier for the Stimsonians to discredit Bobby, to revive unpleasant memories of a man whose sole concern was power, a man who had grabbed poor old Chester Bowles by the shirt collar and poked a finger in his portly belly, a man who had told New York's liberals that he "didn't give a damn" about their reform committees and that his only concern was to get his brother elected President.[33] Only the most dramatic of mea culpas, only the most persuasive of demonstrations of fidelity to the Stimsonian faith, would overcome the animosity of the liberal Stimsonians in New York.

Bobby the mean kid brother, Bobby the McCarthy sympathizer, Bobby the bane of the Eleanor Roosevelt wing of the Democratic Party—this picture of Bobby as a "little Torquemada" (Gore Vidal's characterization) had a plausibility in 1964 that is difficult to comprehend today. He won the nomination easily enough. But no sooner had he done so than a number of distressingly respectable people—artists, scholars, grand old liberals—broke party ranks and threw their support behind his Republican opponent, Kenneth B. Keating of Buffalo. Although Keating was neither a memorable nor an inspiring political figure, his record in the Senate was progressive enough to make him a credible opponent. He was an amiable, pink-faced granddaddy, and many felt sympathy for him as he prepared to fight for his political life in an unequal contest against an arrogant rich kid, Joe McCarthy's brat, the Catholic Roy Cohn.[34] Even so passionate a Kennedy supporter as Arthur Schlesinger conceded that Keating's "vaguely liberal reputation" was justified by the "passable record" he had compiled in Washington.[35] Gore Vidal helped form a Democrats for Keating Committee. Vidal's antipathy toward Bobby might perhaps be ascribed to spite or envy; Schlesinger has suggested that Vidal, whose own quest for public office ended in failure, resented Bobby's political successes and was piqued by Bobby's failure to recognize him when the two met in 1960.[36]

More troubling, no doubt, were the defections of such respected scholars and honorary Stimsonians as Archibald MacLeish, Richard Hofstadter, Barbara Tuchman, and (this was really embarrassing) Schlesinger's own father, Arthur M. Schlesinger, Sr.[37] John Roosevelt, the youngest son of Franklin and Eleanor, condemned Bobby for implying that his mother would have supported his candidacy.[38] Stevenson himself noted the "widespread disaffection" that he detected among liberals, reformers, and organized labor.[39] Even the NAACP climbed aboard the Keating bandwagon.[40]

As the election approached, Keating, who had been shrewd enough to repudiate Barry Goldwater, his party's standard-bearer in 1964, could plausibly claim that he was a truer liberal, a truer progressive, than his ambitious young opponent. Bobby's campaign, which had begun with great promise and a commanding lead in the polls, lost momentum. In the opening days the campaign had been fueled by the fire of his celebrity and the memory of his brother's martyrdom. But these things could not sustain it indefinitely. Bobby's odd and unpredictable humor, his evident struggle to reconcile his customary reserve with his love of the large crowds that gathered to cheer him—and the crowds *were* large in the beginning—made him a curiously appealing candidate. When, not long after Labor Day, Bobby arrived, five hours late, in the town of Glens Falls, he was "astonished" to find—for it was well after midnight—a thousand people waiting for him at the airport and thousands more in the town square.[41] By October, however, the novelty was gone, and the flame of celebrity had expired; Bobby himself seemed at times to forget where he was, and acted less like a man who wished to triumph at the polls than one who wished to pay a perpetual homage to the memory of his brother.[42] When the Warren Commission report was made public, Bobby spent the day in seclusion, unable to campaign.[43]

His attitude toward the Warren Commission's work reveals much about the state of his mind during the Senate campaign. The period of mourning and melancholia was not yet over. Not only did Bobby not read the Warren report, he was reluctant even to talk about it, and once asked Arthur Schlesinger "how long he could continue to avoid comment" on its conclusions.[44] Although there was, of course, much to criticize in the Warren Commission's work, Bobby was unwilling to speak out and thereby "reopen the whole tragic business."[45] Some thought this out of character: surely the question of who murdered Jack Kennedy ought to have perplexed a man as passionately devoted to his brother as he was more than it apparently did. And yet it's not clear that Bobby bothered even to learn Oswald's name; several years after the assassination he was still referring to "that fellow Harvey Lee Oswald."[46] Was he afraid that a more thorough investigation of the assassination would reveal facts that were better off left in obscurity? Did he fear revelations of Mafia ties and plots to kill Castro? Or did his indifference to the circumstances of his brother's death stem rather from his conviction that to dwell upon an act so horrible, so blasphemous, so profane—a stain upon the honor of the world—was itself a kind of sacrilege, a form of disrespect? Jack Newfield, sitting next to him on an airplane, observed how Bobby's eyes would avoid any reference to the assassination in a newspaper.[47] He could "only speak around the event," Newfield said, "or in euphemisms."[48] When Newfield asked him "when he began to read poetry," Bobby replied, "Oh, at the very end of 1963, I think."[49]

"Get out of this mysticism," Paul Corbin told him. "Get out of your daze. . . . Goddamn, Bob, be yourself. You're real. Your brother's dead."[50] With his poll numbers dropping and his campaign adrift, Bobby launched a massive advertising offensive in the middle of October and harshly criticized Keating for his failure to support a host of welfare state legislation: laws authorizing the construction of new housing projects, the creation of a larger federal education bureaucracy, the extension of the minimum-wage law.[51] Bobby's efforts to tie his candidacy to the future of the welfare state were in the end successful, and he won the election by some 720,000 votes.[52]

The Predicament

HE NEEDED DESPERATELY to discard prior selves, to reinvent himself, to re-create himself; only then could he hope to win over critical constituencies in his own party. If in order to do this he had to betray his own deepest self, no matter: the act of betrayal could itself be turned to political advantage. His different selves—the "good" Bobby and the "bad" Bobby of the famous Jules Feiffer cartoon—became evidence of his complexity and depth, of everything that separated him from the packaged politicians of the era, of everything that made him "authentic" in a way that Johnson and Nixon and Humphrey were not and could never be. Was he struggling with his own dark passions? So much the better; the higher journalists loved it. "God!" Murray Kempton exclaimed after interviewing him. "He's not a politician! He's a character in a novel!"[53] It hardly matters that much of what made Bobby interesting to intellectuals in the middle sixties hasn't worn well, that the quotations from McLuhan, the allusions to Camus, seem curiously trite. Posterity may sniff; the brightest journalists of the day did not.

The pressures that forced him to embrace the Stimsonian ideals of federal noblesse oblige in the 1964 campaign did not diminish with his elevation to the Senate in January 1965. On the contrary, Bobby's difficulties increased when Lyndon Johnson, whom he had expected to be a cautious and conservative president, rapidly emerged as the most progressive occupant of the White House since Franklin Roosevelt. The sentimental Johnson had hung, in a conspicuous place in the White House, an old photograph of himself with President Roosevelt; beneath the picture he had written, "I listen." Listen he did. Sometime in 1964 (speechwriter Richard Goodwin said that the decision was made during the course of a swim in the White House swimming pool) Lyndon Johnson determined to build a Great Society.[54] What conceptions of policy, what considerations of interest, what intimations of glory, caused Johnson to embark upon so fantastic a project cannot now be deduced with a precise or scrupulous accuracy. The genesis of so vast, so lavish, and so impossible a scheme cannot be reduced to discrete causes or simple motives. A hundred circumstances influenced Johnson's decision. He was influenced by the spirit of the age, and by the promptings of his advisers; by an urge to direct the destiny of a nation, and by a desire to secure a just historical fame for himself; by the wish to emulate his heroes, and by the hope of disgracing his enemies. Not least among his motives was his desire to prove to the Stimsonians, who had always regarded him as a coarse and primitive man and who had "laughed at him behind his back," that he was no less worthy than they, and that he could play the part of federal philanthropist-in-chief just as effectively as the best of them.[55]

In order to maintain his image as a progressive, Bobby was forced to assert, improbably, that Johnson was not doing enough to expand the welfare state. In his attempts to outdo Johnson in feats of liberal virtue, Bobby criticized the President for failing to fund federal poverty programs adequately.[56] He blamed him for failing to allocate sufficient monies for the creation of public housing.[57] Johnson's Great Society was, Bobby said at one point, a mere "drop in the bucket."[58] In his eagerness to out-Johnson Johnson, in his eagerness to tell the Arthur Schlesingers of the world what they wanted to hear, Bobby reached for easy, facile solutions—increased government spending, higher taxes, more federal programs. He hadn't yet begun to do the hard work—and the hard *thinking*— that produce persuasive answers to complicated problems.

When he entered the Senate in 1965, Bobby could not be called an original statesman; he was still a conformist. The qualities that seemed so original and refreshing in the 1964 campaign—the shy humor, the tousled appeal that was even then being compared to that of a rock star—were qualities of style, not substance. Nothing better illustrates Bobby's lack of originality than the way he conformed his politics to the precepts of Stimsonian liberalism. Politics and circumstance may have played a part in his decision to conform; but so, too, did his inability to see any alternative body of political principles on which to base a political career. The Stimsonian creed was the only respectable creed available to him, and in 1965 Bobby was still a man who cared deeply about respectability. Lionel Trilling's claim that liberalism was not only the dominant but even the "sole" political tradition in the United States was no less true in 1965 than it had been when Trilling's book *The Liberal Imagination* first appeared in 1950. The liberalism Trilling had in mind—a liberalism grounded in a faith in an "educated class" committed to "progress, science, social legislation, planning, and international cooperation" and possessed of a "mild suspiciousness of the profit motive"—was an unmistakably Stimsonian liberalism.[59] The old nineteenth-century tradition of liberal individualism, the tradition of Lincoln and Emerson, was in the New Deal and postwar periods known as "conservatism," and it was distinctly unfashionable. However privately skeptical Bobby might have been of certain facets of Stimsonian liberalism, he must have believed, at the time he entered the Senate, that he had very little choice but to embrace it. His mind was afire with striking thoughts and startling conceptions, with Aeschylus and Plutarch, but in his public politics he remained, at the beginning of 1965, a most conventional statesman.

9

━━◁๐/๑/๑▷━━

IN APRIL 1965 BOBBY VISITED TENEMENTS IN HARLEM, where, he said, "the smell of rats was so strong that it was difficult to stay there for five minutes."[1] They came out of holes in the wall and mauled little children, who, Bobby said, "slept with lights turned on their feet to discourage attacks."[2] In a Brooklyn slum he encountered a young Puerto Rican girl with a mangled face; her mother "explained that the rats had bitten her face off when she was a little baby."[3] In a ghetto school he watched a young boy identify a picture of a teddy bear as a rat.[4] To complacent middle-class audiences Bobby liked to cite a startling statistic: there were more rats in New York City than people.[5]

He had been in the Senate for only a few months. He had not really wanted the job. "I remember and regret," he said shortly after he took his seat, "the situation that gave rise to my being here."[6] Unlike his older brother, he derived no imaginative stimulus from the Senate itself, from its history, its ceremony, its ritual pomp. He thought it "too archaic," Pierre Salinger said, "too slow and inactive."[7] Jack Kennedy had felt the charm of the place, had reveled in its very archaisms; to him they were relics of the Republic's Silver Age, the age of Calhoun and Webster, a time when Senators had filled the chamber with a neoclassical rhetoric so carefully wrought as to have possessed an almost voluptuous quality. Jack had, indeed, been something of an unofficial historian of the Senate: his *Profiles in Courage* was a study of the careers of eight illustrious Senators; in May 1957 he delivered a speech on the floor of the Senate entitled "The Senate's Distinguished Traditions."[8] But the historic grandeur of the Senate made little impression upon Bobby; for intellectual and imaginative sustenance he would have to look elsewhere.

When he found the stimulation he craved, he found it not in Washington, but in New York. During his years in the Senate Bobby flew up from Washington at least twice a week, sometimes more often. In New York there would be a school to visit, a speech to deliver, a banquet to attend. He took an apartment high above the little park beside the United Nations, in a fashionable building at 870 United Nations Plaza—Truman Capote was a neighbor—and had an office at Lexington and 45th Street in the old Post Office building. (The Kennedy house at Glen Cove, Long Island, a twenty-five-room mansion in the Dutch colonial style, was less frequently used.[9]) He had his favorite hangouts in the city: after a day of hand-shaking and speech-making he would meet a small group of friends for a drink at the 21 Club, a hamburger at P. J. Clarke's, or a chocolate sundae at Elaine's. But all that was best in the city—the museums, the theaters, the opulent dinners at restaurants like La Côte Basque and La Caravelle, where Bobby frequently dined—could not disguise that which was worst. On the long drive from the airport, on the tours of the slums, on visits to his constituents, Bobby became aware, in a way that he had not been before, of the city's evils, of its "blackened tunnels," its dilapidated schools, its terrible housing projects, its dirt, its stink, its careless "brutalities," its "grotesque" violence, its "congestion," its "filth," its "danger and purposelessness."[10] His very appreciation of the sun-washed brightness of the old Hellenic poetry—ever since Antigua he had devoted his leisure hours to the literature of ancient Greece—worked rather to increase his sensitivity of the terrible urban poetry that now confronted him, a dark poetry that haunted his mind and troubled his dreams. The world of the Greek poets had, of course, also been filled with pain and suffering and horror. But it had at least been free of rat shit.

The January Speeches

AS A CANDIDATE for the Senate, Bobby had portrayed himself as a devoted champion of the welfare state, and it was only natural that, after he had taken his seat in that body in January 1965, he should have immediately set out to obtain for his state as large a slice of the federal welfare pie as possible. The tables had hardly been cleared following the luncheon Ethel and Bobby gave at Hickory Hill on the afternoon of Bobby's induction into the Senate before the new Senator went to work trying to find ways to bring more federal dollars to his state. He sought to make thirteen New York counties eligible for aid-to-Appalachia funds.[11] He announced a federal grant of half a million dollars to fight poverty in Syracuse.[12] And yet in even the earliest speeches of his senatorial career an element of heresy is detectable. In April 1965, a month after he climbed a fourteen-thousand-foot mountain in Canada's Northwest Territory (the peak had recently been renamed in honor of President Kennedy), Bobby declared that "we have gone as far as goodwill and even good legislation will take us."[13] He continued to chant the standard liberal mantras of the times: more government money, more government programs. But he had begun to waver in his faith.

In the late summer of 1965 rioting erupted in the Los Angeles district of Watts. There was bloodshed, and there was death: thirty-four people died and more than a thousand were injured. In a speech delivered at Spring Valley, New York, a few days afterward, Bobby did more than elucidate the underlying causes of urban violence—the dearth of jobs, the absence of the "purpose, the satisfaction, [and the] dignity" that steady work provides.[14] He explicitly questioned the reasonableness of the welfare state. "A way must be found," he declared, to stop the "waste of human resources and the resulting financial drain on the rest of the community" that the existing welfare regime encouraged.[15] He insisted the country could not "afford to continue, year after year, the increases in welfare costs which result when a substantial segment of the population becomes permanently unemployable."[16] These were bold words, but they were overshadowed by another passage in the speech in which Bobby asserted that in the United States the law was the "friend" of the white man and the "enemy" and "oppressor" of the black. This last assertion was much gazetted in the press, and as a result Bobby's more controversial remarks about the deleterious effects of the welfare state went largely unnoticed.[17]

He sensed the inadequacy of the existing welfare regime, but he had as yet no conception of an alternative. His speeches of the period are to be faulted for their vagueness and their tendency toward dreaminess; for all the grandeur of the aspirations expressed, they say little about how the speaker's dreams of felicity were to be realized in the life of the nation. Bobby sensed their shortcomings, and shortly after his appearance in Spring Valley he asked the brightest of his bright young aides, Peter Edelman and Adam Walinsky, to translate his felt but as yet inarticulate dissatisfaction with the methods of the welfare state into a comprehensive critique of the assumptions upon which it rested. Edelman and Walinsky's work in the autumn of 1965 formed the basis of a series of speeches that Bobby delivered in New York City that winter.

The speeches—they were given on three successive days in January 1966—were not delivered in a famous university; they did not bear the imprimatur of a splendid endowment, like the Godkin Lectures or the Bollingen Foundation; they were never collected into a book and separately published.[18] But the delivery of the January speeches was as momentous an event in the history of the welfare state as any; Bobby was at last prepared to nail his theses to the cathedral door. At the heart of the speeches was a simple proposition: no genuine and lasting improvement in the conditions of life in the ghetto would occur unless such improvement resulted primarily from the efforts of the individuals who inhabited it. The welfare state failed because it was premised on the idea that governments, bureaucracies, programs, laws can by themselves, or with a very minimum of cooperation, lift people out of poverty and pain. But of course they cannot. Bobby himself knew as much about the strengths and weaknesses of bureaucracy as anyone of his generation. He knew how intransigent and inflexible even the most efficient bureaus could be. They were often unable to solve the smallest problems. Could they really be expected to lift large numbers of people out of poverty and pain? The massive postwar federal establishment, Bobby would later declare, had "foundered" as new agencies had "proliferated, splitting tasks and energies among dozens of distant and unconnected bureaus."[19]

He had developed a horror of bureaucracy. Bureaucracy, he would write in his book *To Seek a Newer World*, amounted to a "denial of individualism," a denial that "human beings matter," a "suppression of individuality," a trivialization of human action.[20] There is not, he declared,

> a problem for which there is not a program. There is not a problem for which money is not being spent. There is not a problem or a program on which dozens or hundreds or thousands of bureaucrats are not earnestly at work. But does this represent a solution to our problems? Manifestly it does not. We have spent ever-increasing amounts on our schools. Yet far too many children still graduate totally unequipped to contribute to themselves, their families, or the communities in which they live. . . . We have spent unprecedented sums on buildings of all kinds. Yet our communities seem less beautiful and sensible every year.[21]

Bobby, among the greatest managers of his time, had developed a horror of the very bureaucracy he himself was so adept at managing. His revulsion was partly the product of his own experience; his career as an administrator had made him conscious of the limits of such vast administrative wastelands as the Justice Department, the State Department, the Defense Department, and the Central Intelligence Agency. But his revulsion was a product, too, of the preoccupations of the age, of the criticisms of the modern bureaucratic mentality that men like C. Wright Mills, David Riesman, Paul Goodman, Sloan Wilson, and W. H. Whyte had put forward in the fifties, criticisms of managerial (as opposed to entrepreneurial) capitalism, organization men, and a bureaucratic approach to human life that stifled the imagination and poisoned the soul.[22]

Bobby's reservations about the nature and direction of the bureaucratic state found expression in a series of explicit criticisms of the welfare regime that had grown up under its aegis. The last thing the nation needed, he asserted in the second of his January speeches, was "a massive extension of welfare services."[23] The welfare state had "largely failed as an anti-poverty weapon."[24] It had "destroyed family life."[25] The welfare state had not only failed to make things better, it had in a number of instances actually made things worse:

> Opponents of welfare have always said that welfare is degrading, both to the giver and the recipient. They have said that it destroys self-respect, that it lowers incentive, that it is contrary to American ideals. Most of us deprecated and disregarded these criticisms. . . . [But] the criticisms of welfare *do* have a center of truth, and they are confirmed by the evidence. Recent studies have shown, for example, that higher welfare payments often encourage students to drop out of school, that they often encourage families to disintegrate, and that they often lead to lifelong dependency. [It has been] said that welfare was the worst thing that could have happened to the Negro. Even for such an extreme position, there is factual support. [But because] most of us were committed to doing something we *thought* was good, we ignored the criticisms.[26]

If they were to prosper, the inhabitants of the ghetto would have to dig themselves out of despair; they would have to rebuild, with their own hands, the fallen cities in which they lived.[27] Every instance of genuine individual success was, Bobby believed, the result of individual effort. Only through their own hard work—"work which is dignified," work "which is hard and exacting"—could people make a better place for themselves in the world.[28] Change would not come about "by fiat from Washington," or by order of the President, or as the result of a law passed in Congress; it could come about only through "the work and effort" of individuals.[29] In "the last analysis," Adam Walinsky said, Bobby believed that "people had to do whatever they did for themselves. . . . He did not believe in the government just taking large sums of money and handing it out to people."[30] The "rebuilding" efforts that Bobby proposed in the January speeches were to be the work of individuals and communities, not of government bureaus; Bobby called upon individual citizens themselves to "take the first steps" toward a restoration of their blighted neighborhoods.[31] "Concessions wrung from an unwilling bureaucrat or absentee owner," he later declared, would "never equal, in quality or permanence," the achievements "of a self-reliant community."[32] One of the things he found most inspiring about Cesar Chavez's effort to organize migrant farmworkers was the fact that Chavez and his followers were doing it themselves: with little assistance from the government they had seized the initiative and with their own hands were working to improve the quality of their lives. "You are winning a special kind of citizenship," Bobby told Chavez's people in Delano, California "no one is doing it for you—you are winning it yourselves—and therefore no one can ever take it away."[33]

But could Chavez's success be replicated in the ghetto? Chavez, after all, confronted, in the valleys of California, conditions just as terrible as those in the slums of the cities, but he had nevertheless succeeded, against every expectation, in inspiring his people to act, in giving them a sense that there was more to life than the misery their broken bodies had long since learned to accept. Could one apply the lessons of Delano to the human problem at the heart of the ghetto? Like the migrant workers before Chavez, the children of the cities exhibited all the signs of people who had never been given any sense of their value, their potential, their unique human worth. "A lot of those looters are just kids in trouble," Bobby said at the time of the riots in Watts. "*I* got in trouble when I was that age."[34] The apathy, the dejection, the sullenness that characterized so many of these men and women resulted in an atrophy of nerve, a paralysis of will, a listlessness that the unsympathetic outsider was likely to confuse with laziness or stupidity. A bureaucratized system of handouts could only perpetuate the problem, could only humiliate those whom it was intended to help:

> In our generosity [Bobby declared] we have created a system of hand-outs, a second-rate set of social services which damages and demeans its recipients, and destroys any semblance of human dignity that they have managed to retain through their adversity. . . . In the long run, welfare payments solve nothing, for the giver or the recipients; free Americans deserve the chance to be fully self-supporting.[35]

So far from improving the self-esteem of the individual, the welfare state undermined it even more. Impersonal, sterile, and gray, the welfare bureaus reinforced in those who had become dependent upon them their already marked sense of powerlessness and hopelessness, and contributed to the "sense of helplessness and futility" that overwhelmed so many of those who were in the grip of its power.[36] The welfare bureaucracy did nothing to instill in its beneficiaries those feelings of self-confidence and self-respect that might have made it possible for them to seize the initiative and take control of their lives.[37] The welfare state "destroy[ed] self-respect," it "lower[ed] incentive," and it led to "lifelong dependency."[38] The time had come to reform it.

IO

THE PROBLEM OF THE UNDERCONFIDENT SOUL IS A REL-
atively new one in human history. It seems not to have existed, on
a large scale, before the eighteenth century. Men and women who,
had they lived a few centuries earlier, would have occupied a definite
place in life—however dismal that place might have been—found
themselves, in the modern age, forced to make their own way in
the world, a world that was bigger, more complicated, and more
impersonal than it had been in the past. To succeed in finding places
for themselves in the modern world, men and women needed to
possess far greater reserves of self-confidence than was the case in
the past.

In the past self-confidence had been a problem of the few and
not the many; it was a problem only for those who were supposed
to make something of themselves in the world. Machiavelli's prince,
for example, *needed* self-confidence, for only a highly self-confident
man could succeed in conquering Fortune.[1] Princes needed to possess self-confidence; much of the rest of the world did not. And yet
Machiavelli's slender handbook for princes is itself an indication of
how rapidly the world was changing; the very fact that a commoner
like Machiavelli should have been so intrigued by the connection
between self-confidence and success, the very fact that he should
have been so fascinated by the impact the self-confident man (Ces-
are Borgia, for example) can have on history, is an indication that

the problem of self-confidence had come, by the beginning of the sixteenth century, to have a wider significance than ever before. Self-confidence was no longer a problem for princes and generals alone, a problem for those who by tradition were supposed to possess what Machiavelli calls *virtù* (strength, self-confidence, audacity); self-confidence was—or was becoming—a problem for everyone, from civil servants like Machiavelli to strongmen like Borgia himself. Sainte-Beuve informs us that, in seventeenth-century France, it was thought exceedingly "strange" that La Rochefoucauld should have been "so embarrassed in public that if he had to speak on official matters before six or seven persons his courage failed him."[2] That a French nobleman should have been as unself-confident as La Rochefoucauld was thought unpleasantly queer; at the same time, none of his contemporaries would have been in the least surprised to learn that La Rochefoucauld's valet de chambre was equally incapable of expressing himself confidently in a crowd. "Why ever should a valet need to express himself confidently in a crowd?" they would have wondered. Today, however, everyone is expected to be able to act confidently in a crowd, to make something of himself in the world, and thus the problem of self-confidence has become, for the first time in history, a mass problem.

Some natures, of course, adjusted quite readily to the changed conditions of the modern world; others did not. The intellectual-priest type was one victim of the new age; there was less need of such a type in the demystified world that the Renaissance and the Enlightenment brought into being. The decline of the intellectual-priest was not, perhaps, a great loss: intellectual-priests never accounted for more than a small percentage of society, and those few who are still to be found today have by and large found a decent refuge, not indeed in the Church, but in the university. Other groups, however, present a more serious problem. There are in every American city young men and women who lack the resources, intellectual or material, to carve out satisfactory places for themselves in the world. One sees them hanging out on streetcorners and in shopping malls, idle, bored, cynical, a refutation in themselves of the faith of the *philosophes*, a testament to the naïveté of the Enlightened belief that progress in the arts and sciences would inevitably work a fundamental change in human character. We know less about their fears and anxieties than we do about those of the priestly intellectuals and the neurasthenic "sick" souls of the upper and upper-middle classes, whose depressions and eating disorders are the object of so much scrupulous study. But this much we do know: the neurasthenic "sick" soul of the upper and upper-middle classes and the "depraved" or "fallen" soul of the lower and lower-middle classes are alike in being unself-confident souls.

That underconfident souls should constitute so large a proportion of our population is troubling. But are those who occupy the other end of the confidence spectrum any less a matter for concern? Are our society's supremely self-confident men and women any less disturbing? Do we care—should we care—whether they are admirable figures? Have they anything at all to do with the humane and liberal traditions of the West? Or are they merely the possessors of certain narrow technical competence, magicians with money, possessed of an uncanny ability to manipulate capital or technological know-how? For there can be little doubt that, if the Machiavellian prince was the archetypically self-confident figure of four or five centuries ago, today it is the modern entrepreneurial hero who, more than any one else, embodies the idea of self-confident action in the world. But should our underconfident youth really *want* to be like the entrepreneurial hero? Should they really want to be like Rockefeller, or Gates, or Gatsby, or Reginald Lewis, or Joseph Kennedy? The great-souled men of the past, the supermen whom Machiavelli and Nietzsche and Stendhal celebrated in their writings, the godlike beings whom Aristotle described in the *Politics*, had their shortcomings, to be sure. But does the modern entrepreneurial hero—the hero whom we are taught today to admire and envy— really represent an *improvement* on the heroic idea? Did Morgan, Rockefeller, and Ford advance beyond the point that Alexander, Borgia, and Bonaparte reached? Caesar might have been a bad man, as Cato said, but still he was undeniably a great man; he set the standard against which we continue to judge great men. When admirers of Jack Kennedy celebrated their hero's coolness under pressure, his heroism in battle, his literary achievements, his attractiveness to women, they invoked an ideal that is recognizably Caesarian in its derivation: Caesar, the brilliant warrior, the master of literary form, the seducer of women, the charmer of Catullus. In *The Making of the President 1960*, Teddy White very explicitly compared Jack Kennedy with Julius Caesar.[3] When, however, we come to the modern entrepreneurial hero—when we come to Gatsby— we are disappointed to find him a duller creature than either Caesar or Kennedy. Here is Gatsby on his (make-believe) youthful adventures:

> After that I lived like a young rajah in all the capitals of Europe—Paris, Venice, Rome—collecting jewels, chiefly rubies, hunting big game, painting a little, things for myself only, and trying to forget something very sad that had happened to me long ago. . . . Then came the war, old sport. It was a great relief, and I tried very hard to die, but I seemed to bear an enchanted life.[4]

Gatsby is unlikely to have charmed Catullus. Caesar's tale of the youthful adventure in which he was captured by Mediterranean pirates is not only far more winning than Gatsby's (Caesar's story reads like a chapter of *Candide*), it has the additional merit of being true. The very phrases Gatsby uses are "so worn and threadbare," Nick Carraway says, that they evoke "no image except that of a turbaned 'character' leaking sawdust out of every pore as he pursued a tiger through the Bois de Boulogne."[5] Gatsby is not a great-souled man of the type beloved of Stendhal and Nietzsche and Machiavelli; he is a curious mixture of disciplined Puritan (he drinks little and boasts that it took him only three years of disciplined work to "earn" the money he used to buy his house) and eighteenth-century rogue charmer, a cross between Benjamin Franklin and Lovelace, the anti-hero of Richardson's *Clarissa*, a man with a winning smile who is handy with accounts, a seducer of women who can read an income statement. His dreams of glory are sadly, oppressively, overwhelmingly pedestrian. His heart, we are told, was in a constant, turbulent riot. The most grotesque and fantastic conceits haunted him in his bed at night. A universe of ineffable gaudiness spun itself out in his brain while the clock ticked on the washstand and the moon soaked with wet light his tangled clothes upon the floor.[6]

It is possible, of course, that Fitzgerald's narrator, Nick Carraway, the Middle Western patrician whose family claims to be descended from the Dukes of Buccleuch, has distorted the qualities of Gatsby's plebeian imagination; Carraway admits that Gatsby is the embodiment of everything for which he has an "unaffected scorn." And yet the fact remains that the modern entrepreneurial hero is *not* a particularly interesting character; by the standards of Old World greatness he is not a great man at all. The East Egg patricians who, like Theodore Roosevelt, attempted to revive those standards in the late nineteenth and early twentieth centuries could not help but despise the new breed of entrepreneurial West Egg heroes who, like Gatsby and Joseph Kennedy himself, fell so far short of their lofty, great-souled ideal.

If the entrepreneurial hero is not an intellectually or spiritually compelling figure, he nonetheless tells us a good deal more about the requirements for success in the modern world than Caesar and Alexander or even Teddy Roosevelt do. Ordinary men and women might not need the superabundant self-confidence of a Jay Gatsby or a Joseph Kennedy to get by in the world that the Renaissance and the Enlightenment brought into being, but even modest success in our complicated system of political economy requires a degree of the confidence that the tycoons possessed. The Stimsonians, however, turned away from the problem of self-confidence. Their programs did nothing to strengthen self-confidence in those who were without it. Their public policies, like those of the kings and emperors of the Old World, were conceived in almost exclusively heroic and monumental terms; one finds in those policies little sympathy for the aspirations of the individual men and women they were supposed to benefit. Robert Moses's public architecture, a public architecture conceived with little understanding of the soil

...ich it was planted, is a perfect example of the Stimsonians' attraction to the grandiose and the monumental, a perfect example of their indifference to the individual. Moses, the prodigy of Yale and Oxford, succeeded in creating a public architecture that Haussmann and Napoleon III might have envied. Like Caesar Augustus, who said that he found Rome a city of brick and left it a city of marble, Moses, too, fundamentally altered the character of his city. He found New York a city of neighborhoods and elevated trains and left it a city of reinforced concrete and elevated highways.

The vast bureaucratic structure of the welfare state is a no less telling monument to the Stimsonians' love of the grandiose at the expense of the individual. Emblematic of the Stimsonian approach were the great housing projects the bureaucrats built, monuments to Enlightened intentions gone awry, behemoths conceived without any conception of human proportion or scale. Looming hideously over the nation's decaying ghettos, the projects had been built, Bobby said, without "relevance" to the "underlying problems" of "alienation" that had caused many people to "need assistance in the first place."[7] They had become places of "despair and danger."[8] In conceiving these and other bureaucratic programs, the architects of the welfare state had "ignore[d] the shaping traditions of American life and politics."[9] Having no relation at all to the individuals they were intended to serve, the welfare bureaucracies did nothing to endow those individuals with a feeling of confidence in themselves.

Emerson, Lincoln, and the Idea of "Self-Trust"

IN QUESTIONING THE ability of government agencies and government programs to solve the human problem at the heart of the ghetto, Bobby did more than rebel against his own Stimsonian heritage, he drew inspiration from a much older liberal tradition, the liberal individualism of Emerson and Lincoln.

Emerson and Lincoln were perhaps his two greatest American heroes.[10] Emerson was his favorite American poet; Jack Newfield remembered him reading Emerson's poem "Fame" aloud one evening in his New York apartment.[11] And Bobby was a careful student of Emerson's *Essays*.[12] His admiration for Lincoln was, if anything, even greater. Bobby purchased, at considerable expense, a rare copy of Lincoln's Emancipation Proclamation; an acquaintance who toured Lincoln's house in Springfield, Illinois, with him in 1956 remembered how "deeply moved" Bobby had been by the experience.[13] After the burial of his brother in the cemetery at Arlington on November 25, 1963, Bobby, riding back to the White House with his widowed sister-in-law, ordered the driver to take them to the Lincoln Memorial, where they paused in silence to gaze up at the Daniel Chester French statue of the sixteenth President.[14]

Bobby's devotion to the greatest of America's propounders of the power of the free unfettered individual was not merely fortuitous, he believed as passionately as they in the promise of the individual. Bobby derived from his study of Emerson's philosophy and Lincoln's life not only an admiration for the ideal of the self-reliant individual, but also an insight into the central obstacle to the creation of a nation of self-reliant individuals: the absence in large numbers of men and women of self-confidence, or what Emerson in his *Essays* calls "self-trust."[15]

The Emersonian influence on Bobby's evolving thought is important enough to make a closer examination of the *Essays* themselves desirable. A great part of the first series of essays is devoted to the problem of self-trust. In self-trust, Emerson says, all the other virtues are comprehended.[16] Emerson attempted, in such essays as "Self-Reliance," "Heroism," and "History," both to understand the ways in which ordinary men and women—the "cowed" and the "trustless"—develop self-confidence and at the same time to instill a degree of this confidence in the ordinary men and women who were his readers.[17] The *Essays* have some claim to being the first, as they have certainly a claim to being the greatest, of American self-help books. (The term "self-help" was itself first used by Emerson's friend Thomas Carlyle in his book *Sartor Resartus*). A man "takes up Emerson tired and apathetic," John Jay Chapman wrote, and "presently finds himself growing heady and truculent, strengthened in his most inward vitality, surprised to find himself again master in his own house."¹⁸ The *Essays* are the literary equivalent of Prozac; they admonish the reader to put aside his timidity and his reticence, his fear and his embarrassment, his tendency to bow down before great names and august personages; they urge him to "believe" his own thoughts, to "trust" himself, and to be unashamed of the "divine idea" that he represents.¹⁹ If we develop a faith in ourselves, Emerson tells us, we will succeed in banishing "discontent," which he said is only another name for "the want of self-reliance" and self-confidence.²⁰ Bobby himself was moved by such Emersonian celebrations of self-confidence as this one, which he underscored in his copy of the *Essays:* "When you have chosen your part, abide by it, and do not weakly try to reconcile yourself to the world."²¹ Bobby praised Allard Lowenstein, the liberal activist whose confidence in himself and his principles helped ignite the Bust Johnson movement in 1968, in similarly Emersonian terms:

> For Al, who knew the lessons of Emerson and taught it [*sic*] to the rest of us: "They do not yet see and thousands of young men as hopeful, now crowding to the barriers of their careers, do not yet see that if a single man plant himself on his convictions and then abide, the huge world will come round to him." From his friend Bob Kennedy.²²

Drawing both on Romantic theories of creative genius and radical Protestant conceptions of a divine "inner light" that revealed itself in certain men and women, Emerson developed a novel democratic theory of self-reliant individualism. Lincoln's life was in many ways a perfect illustration of that theory; Emerson prophesied that America's democratic civilization would produce men fully as great as the great-souled men of the past, fully as great as Plato and Caesar and Shakespeare. Lincoln, who emerged, unschooled and unpolished, from the frontier towns of Kentucky and Illinois to become one of the great world-historical figures of the nineteenth century, appeared to be a striking vindication of Emerson's philosophy of self-confident, self-reliant individualism. The vision of Emerson and

Lincoln powerfully influenced Bobby; one can trace the intellectual origins of his own antipathy to handouts to Emerson's and Lincoln's contempt for them. Bobby did not, like Emerson, go so far as to condemn as a "wicked dollar" every dollar that men doled out to charity.[23] But he shared with Lincoln the conviction that a dole tended to undermine an individual's capacity for exertion and achievement.[24]

The Neuroses of the Unconfident Self

THE DIFFICULTY WITH Emerson's project lay in the fact that so many Americans—in Bobby's time no less than in Emerson's—lacked the self-confidence that Emerson celebrated in his writings. How much talent, how much energy, Bobby wondered, did his nation forfeit merely because the possessors of that talent and energy had grown up under conditions that destroyed their self-confidence and prevented them from developing their gifts to the fullest degree? This absence of self-confidence was especially evident in the inner city. But it was not limited to the inner city. The "pathological fear and anxiety" that Robert Coles detected in ghetto children could be found in many other Americans as well.[25] That overwhelming and almost obnoxious self-confidence that European visitors like the Duc de Liancourt and Alexis de Tocqueville believed to be a universal American trait in the late eighteenth and early nineteenth centuries was not encountered nearly as frequently in 1965.[26] In some ways this was good: Americans had matured as a people; they were less complacent than they had been in the past; they were more conscious of the difficulties of existence, and had perceived the terror of life. But even the stereotypical shallow and self-satisfied American of the period before the Civil War might be preferable to the people Bobby saw too frequently in his own time, and we ourselves encounter so often today—men and women who, crippled by pain and neurosis, shrink from life, become dependent on drugs (tranquilizers thirty years ago, antidepressants today), and are so acutely conscious of their own deficiencies that they find relief from the burdens of self only by engaging in a variety of self-destructive behaviors. These behaviors are the intellectual strategies by which men and women prevent themselves from doing that which they could do were they not so morbidly afraid of failure and humiliation. They are the neuroses of the unconfident self, neuroses that have transformed America from a vale of soul-making into a vale of soul-breaking.

Had America failed? Had it lost its way? Or had the country and its philosophical system been doomed from the beginning? Critics of the American democracy believed that it was bound to fail precisely *because* it was so hopelessly premised on the ideal of the self-reliant individual. These skeptics believed that individual Americans, cut off from the sustaining nourishment of ancient cultural traditions, would inevitably become either shallow, self-confident successes (entrepreneurial heroes) or neurotic, self-doubting failures (almost everyone else). Commerce might flourish, but not art, or manners, or learning. Henry James maintained that the American atmosphere was too culturally thin to sustain a very high or happy level of civilization. In a famous passage in his book on Hawthorne, James drew up a list of reasons why an artist—and by implication a civilized man—must find American society insupportable:

> No State, in the European sense of the word, and indeed barely a specific national name. No sovereign, no court, no personal loyalty, no aristocracy, no church, no clergy, no army, no diplomatic service, no country gentlemen, no palaces, no castles, nor manors, nor old country-houses, nor parsonages, nor thatched cottages, nor ivied ruins; no cathedrals, nor abbeys, nor little Norman churches; no great universities, nor public schools—no Oxford, nor Eton, nor Harrow; no literature, no novels, no museums, no pictures, no political society, no sporting class—no Epsom or Ascot![27]

Edmund Wilson made a similar point in his diary:

Good abilities degenerate, go to waste—I think of all the friends of my school and college years who showed such promise and didn't pan out. . . . The vulgarity of life in the United States shows up in one of its very bad aspects in the inability of professional men to persist beyond their youthful years in living up to any standard of civic conscience or science or art. Since standards are not there in clear sight, since they are not supported by a hierarchy, the individual has to make more of a moral effort, which, combined with the effort involved in mastering any field with its skills, is likely to prove too much for him.[28]

The point of James's catalog of American deficiencies, the point of Wilson's longing for "standards" and a "hierarchy," the point of T. S. Eliot's essay "Tradition and the Individual Talent," is that the individual, by himself, is *not* enough.[29] Such an individual may be self-confident (although in most cases he will not be), he may be self-reliant (but only in the most elementary economic sense), and still he will never be as fully developed a being as he might have been in a more civilized climate, in a world where he was not so relentlessly thrown back upon himself and his own (meager) resources. Eliot and James—and before them Edmund Burke—believed that traditions, and the institutions that perpetuate them, are essential to the health and vitality not only of civilizations, but also of the individual men and women who compose them. "We are afraid," Burke said, "to put men to live and trade each on his own private stock of reason, because we suspect that this stock in each man is small, and that the individuals would do better to avail themselves of the general bank and capital of nations and ages."[30] It is the very antithesis of Emerson's idea of "self-reliance."[31]

Unlike Henry James and T. S. Eliot, Bobby did not reject the American, the Emersonian, theory of a civilization of self-confident, self-reliant individuals in favor of the system that had produced what James called the "denser, richer, warmer European spectacle." Nor did Bobby believe, as so many patricians of Eliot's own generation believed, that Americans must forsake the severe individualism of their democratic creed and learn to rely instead on the Enlightened wisdom of aristocratic mandarins. Bobby continued to believe, as Emerson had believed, that self-reliant individualism could be made the basis, not merely of a system, a vast commercial empire, but of a civilization. It was true, Emerson conceded, that America lacked the institutions—the monarchy, the aristocracy, the clergy—on which the Old World had relied to foster the kind of creativity that makes civilization possible. In his book *English Traits* he uncannily anticipated the arguments of James and Eliot and analyzed the ways in which English institutions fostered a high degree of civilization in that country. In his *Essays*, however, as well as in lectures like "The American Scholar," Emerson set out to demonstrate that the absence of ancient cultural traditions in America was a good thing, not a bad thing, that a race of self-confident individuals, relying on nothing but their own genius, could create a civilization no less splendid and no less satisfying than the civilization of the Old World. Over and over again he throws down the challenge. It was only right, he maintained, that men should be thankful to the civilization of the Old World, to "history, to the pyramids, and the authors." "But now," he continued,

> our day is come; we have been born out of the eternal silence; and now we live,—live for ourselves,—not as the pallbearers of a funeral, but as the upholders and creators of our age; and neither Greece nor Rome, nor the three Unities of Aristotle, nor the three Kings of Cologne, nor the College of the Sorbonne, nor the Edinburgh *Review*, is to command any longer. . . . A false humility, a complaisance to reigning schools, or to the wisdom of antiquity, must not defraud me of the supreme possession of this hour.[32]

This is all very well, but how exactly were Americans to develop the kind of confidence in themselves that would enable them to take "supreme possession" of their time? By taking Dale Carnegie's course? By learning how to win friends and influence people? Emerson does not give a satisfactory answer to this question, and when we look to the *Essays* for a method and a program, we are disappointed to find that the inspiring prose dissolves into the sugary vagueness of the author's own inexorable optimism.

Unself-Confident Ghetto, Unself-Confident Nation

THE QUESTION OF whether America's system of self-reliant individualism could produce not merely a commercial empire, but a true civilization, was one that Americans who lived in the ghetto did not have the luxury of being able to ask. The more immediate problem of the ghetto was the problem of pain. Physical pain, of course, but even more the kind of psychological pain, the mental anguish, that lack of faith in oneself causes. The cycle is a vicious one. One feels bad about oneself because one lacks the confidence to believe in oneself, and the worse one feels about oneself, the more difficult it becomes to act confidently in the world. It is hard enough even for a member of the more prosperous middle class to muster the kind of confidence that makes progress possible in an indifferent, even hostile world. For the citizen of the ghetto, with fewer resources at his disposal, the struggle to attain self-confidence—and the good grades, job offers, mortgage loans, and credit ratings it brings—is all but impossible. Self-confidence is the fragile foundation upon which much of middle-class life is built; its relative scarcity in the ghetto helps to explain the absence there of a middle-class culture and a middle-class economy. It is true, of course, that racism has had a great deal to do with the failure of a middle-class institutions to develop in the ghetto; no person, however industrious, can achieve economic success if he is barred from competing in the marketplace on equal terms with his fellows. And yet the most insidious effect of racism is not the barrier it throws up between the individual and the marketplace, but its tendency to undermine the self-confidence a person needs to make his way in the world, to break down the barriers.

America ignores this crisis of confidence at its peril. In the ghetto Bobby saw, in an exaggerated form, the same problems that, he was certain, would one day haunt the prosperous middle class itself. Time would prove him right; thirty years after Bobby's death, crime, violence, and drugs, those unmistakable indicia of underconfident selves, have begun to disturb the complacent dreams of Middle America as well. Although Americans of all races and classes continue to aspire to the old Emersonian ideal of self-reliance, when I look around me today, I am more often conscious of how sadly lacking in many even of the relatively successful men and women among us is the self-confidence that makes self-reliance possible. How much crippling pain has the want of self-trust caused? How often has it caused a person to forbear to say a word, or perform an act, or undertake an enterprise that might have improved the quality of his own life, or that of others? How often has it caused a person to watch his more confident neighbor, in the classroom or the boardroom, receive credit for an idea he was too timid to profess himself?

> To believe your own thought [Emerson wrote], to believe that what is true for you in your private heart is true for all men,—that is genius. Speak your latent conviction, and it shall be the universal sense. . . . A man should learn to detect and watch that gleam of light which flashes across his mind from within. . . . Yet he dismisses his own thought, because it is his. In every work of genius we recognize our own rejected thoughts: they come back to us with a certain alienated majesty. . . . [T]omorrow a stranger will say with masterly good sense precisely what we have thought and felt all the time, and we shall be forced to take with shame our own opinion from another.[33]

A person may be inferior to another in intelligence, or beauty, or wit, but such inferiority is not half so terrible as possessing an inferior degree of self-confidence.[34]

Few American politicians could have been better prepared to take on the problem of self-confidence than Bobby Kennedy. His own battle to achieve self-confidence had been a difficult one.

Looks, E.M. Forster says, have their influence on character, and Bobby was painfully conscious, during much of his life, of following in the footsteps of bigger, taller, handsomer brothers.[35] As a boy he had been extremely shy and something of a loner, "whimsical and a little bit solitary."[36] His mother had worried about his apathy. While Jack "has had the most astounding success," Rose Kennedy reported to her husband,

> Bobby is in a different mold. He does not seem to be interested particularly in reading or sailing or his stamps. He does a little work in all three but no special enthusiasm. . . . I am trying to get Bob to do some reading. He doesn't seem to care for sailing as much as the other boys. Of course he doesn't want to go to any of the dances.[37]

He was a poor student; his teachers made fun of him. A Milton instructor once began a class by declaring that two "great things" had recently occurred: "One was that Rommel was surrounded in Egypt," the other that Bobby Kennedy "had passed a math test."[38] Dave Hackett remembered that "everything he did was very difficult for him. Athletics for him—which he loved—were always difficult. Studies, the same thing. And also, I think, with his social life. . . . I don't think he ever had anything easy."[39] When, in adolescence, Bobby began to be interested in girls, he discovered that he was deeply bashful in their presence, and though in his fourth-form year at Milton he fell in love with a girl named Ann Appleton, he never dared to say even a word to her. For many years he lacked the confidence to speak effectively in public; friends remembered him stammering painfully through a toast delivered at Jack's wedding to Jacqueline Bouvier in Newport in 1953.

Slowly, of course, he overcame his fears and began to develop faith in himself and his abilities. But he remained, to the end of his life, a shy man. Diana Trilling, though she thought him "infinitely better-looking than" Jack, noted that he "didn't exude anything like his brother's power."[40] Unlike Bobby's face, Jack's exuded self-confidence: it "radiated strength," Trilling remembered, a "power so compressed that you felt it was about to explode."[41] Bobby lacked this "absolute confidence in himself and his charm."[42] When he spoke, Jack Newfield said, he "stammered and his hands trembled."[43] He "walked in a slouch like a man who did not want to be noticed." His handwriting "was small and squiggly."[44] He differed, Robert Coles observed, from those "glib, articulate, well-psychoanalyzed, well-intellectualized people who always know what to say, who always know where and how to get it across through either the printed or spoken word."[45] Jack Newfield concluded that Bobby was "basically introverted and nonverbal," and noted how frequently his confidence deserted him: "If a reporter asked him why some people hated him, or thought he was ruthless, he would freeze, and mumble like a little boy."[46] One supposes that what often appeared to the world to be arrogance or insolence was really a form of concealed shyness. Much has been made of Bobby's brusqueness and rudeness, but, of course, it is precisely with this kind of aloof behavior that shy people so often seek to disguise their want of confidence in themselves. If in the end Bobby surmounted these difficulties and became a brilliantly successful statesman, he himself would have been the first to concede that he had been specially blessed by Fortune. Had he not been born a Kennedy, he once told Jack Newfield, he would probably have become a juvenile delinquent.[47]

Bobby's own struggle to achieve self-confidence cannot, however, explain why he embraced the notions of entrepreneurial self-confidence that he did, the kind of self-confidence that enables men and women to go out into the world and hold down jobs in a competitive economy. Bobby's father, after all, had not *wanted* his sons to empathize with the entrepreneurial virtues; Joseph Kennedy had wanted his sons to emulate patrician standards of greatness, to become great-souled men in the tradition of Teddy Roosevelt, a man who despised shopkeepers' arts, denounced entrepreneurial success as a manifestation of greed, and celebrated Old World ideals like military glory and conquistadorial prowess. Bobby's embrace of free-market and entrepreneurial virtues, his belief that a private-sector job could do more for a man's soul than a government-sponsored handout, startled both his liberal Stimsonian and his radical left-wing friends. "I guess you don't like all the things I say about free enterprise," Bobby told the socialist Michael Harrington when the two met in 1968.[48] Neither Stimsonian liberals nor the socialist left could accept Bobby's belief that if only people could develop the self-confidence to take advantage of its opportunities, the free market would do more to improve the quality of their lives than a government bureaucracy could. They stared blankly at him, and were astonished at his doctrine. They had ceased to understand him. He had broken with their faith.

Beyond the Welfare State

HE HAD ONCE uncritically accepted the Stimsonian idea that an Enlightened government could sweep down, deus ex machina, and improve the conditions of peoples and nations. By the spring of 1966, however, Bobby was ready to challenge the conventional Stimsonian wisdom. "The inheritance of the New Deal," he declared, had been "fulfilled."[49] He did not talk, in the esoteric language of the Stimsonians, of the ability of bureaucracies and programs to transform the "structural" conditions that "caused" poverty in America; he instead worked strenuously to recover the older and more compelling language of Emersonian self-reliance, a peculiarly American moral code that emphasized the importance of liberating the talents and energies of ordinary men and women by giving them the self-confidence to realize the "divine idea" that each of them represented. Bobby had at last reconciled himself to the Emersonian idea that our streets, our houses, our communities are not a reflection of "structural" economic conditions, they are the mirror of our souls. If we would heal the melancholia of the ghetto—if we would transform dreary streets and decaying neighborhoods into something more and something better—we must first transform the melancholy souls, the stagnant intellects, the sagging spirits, the underconfident selves of the people who inhabit them. We knowing moderns can't quite believe *that*; schooled in Freud and the horrors that are present in even the most innocent minds, we cannot put our faith in a world that mirrors the confident soul. Emerson no doubt exaggerated the beneficial effects of self-confidence. But he did not exaggerate the terrible effects of its absence.

What distinguished Bobby from the typical Stimsonian of his day was his desire to solve the problem of urban poverty in a manner consistent with "the shaping traditions" of American life and thought, in a manner consistent with the character and genius of the American people. The welfare state, with its emphasis on centralized planning, centralized control, and a vast centralized bureaucracy, was not a characteristically American institution; its intellectual origins are to be found not in American traditions of self-reliant individualism, but in eighteenth-century French theories of rational planning and nineteenth-century socialist theories of economic oppression. Those theories had been conceived with the political and social conditions of highly centralized, highly stratified European states in mind, and they were bound to have a pernicious effect in the very different moral climate of America. Bobby did not call for the wholesale dismantling of this alien welfare regime; however unfortunate it in many ways was, it could not be done away with in an instant without causing great hardship. But he didn't *like* it; he hoped that over time its importance would diminish, as individuals began to work themselves out of poverty and despair. He was certain that if the peculiarly American solutions he proposed to the problems of the ghetto were adopted, if the Emersonian rebuilding projects he envisioned were conscientiously carried out, self-confidence would grow, dependency would diminish, crime would decrease, and urban neighborhoods would become once again aesthetically pleasing places in which to live.[50] The welfare state would, in time, wither away.

It is one thing, of course, to make Emersonian speeches about the importance of self-reliance and self-confidence. It is quite another to give people that confidence, to help them find the will to begin rebuilding their lives and their neighborhoods. By the spring of 1966 Bobby realized that any genuine solution to the problems of the inner city must involve giving its inhabitants confidence in themselves and their abilities. But how was this to be accomplished? Could it indeed be accomplished in a manner consistent with American traditions of individual liberty? He understood the problem, but in the spring of 1966 he was still groping for a solution.

I I

━━◦∕◦∕◦━━

O N   A   C O L D ,   C L O U D Y   F E B R U A R Y   A F T E R N O O N   I N   1966
Bobby came to Bedford-Stuyvesant.[1] Because Bed-Stuy would be-
come the site of one of his bolder attempts to reverse urban decay, it
is tempting to think that his experience that day, as he toured the dismal streets, was a somehow critical one, a transformative experience,
a dark afternoon of the soul from which illumination and insight proceeded. The more prosaic reality is that Bobby had for some time
been casting about for a suitable venue in which to launch an urban
renewal program, and he and his advisers had discussed a number of
possible sites. Political and tactical considerations were as important
as any in the final selection of Bedford-Stuyvesant; there was no miraculous epiphany that day, no blinding revelation.[2] The visit, in fact,
wasn't even a particularly successful one. At the YMCA Bobby was
chewed out by residents demanding to know where the hell the
swimming pool they'd been promised was. By the time he drove back
to Manhattan, he was in a foul mood. "I could be smoking a cigar
down in Palm Beach," he said. "I don't really have to take that."[3] He
would, however, get them the swimming pool.

His initial efforts in Bedford-Stuyvesant appeared to signal a
retreat from the revolutionary ideas of the January speeches, a re-
version to old dogmas and discredited ideas. The months that followed his visit to Bedford-Stuyvesant saw him on Wall Street,
knocking on patrician doors. It was almost a parody of the Stim-

sonian technique: summon the Wise Men. Half a decade earlier, his brother Jack, in forming an administration, had scoured the Street for recruits: Lovett, McCloy, Gilpatric, Dillon, etc., had all been approached and offered jobs. Now Bobby turned to the same people in order to create a council to revive Bedford-Stuyvesant. He asked old friends and sailing companions like Thomas J. Watson, Jr., of IBM for help. He called on William Paley, the chairman of CBS, and asked for his assistance (Paley was the stepfather-in-law of one of Bobby's own bright young men, Carter Burden). He talked to Douglas Dillon, who had left the Treasury and was back at Dillon Read. He sought out Benno Schmidt, Sr., the legendary J. H. Whitney banker and father of a future president of Yale. André Meyer of Lazard Frères was approached (at the time Meyer was Jacqueline Kennedy's investment adviser), as were George Moore of the National City Bank, J. M. Kaplan of Welch's Grape Juice, and Ros Gilpatric, who had recently returned to Cravath. McGeorge Bundy received a long letter from Bobby: could the Ford Foundation see a way to advancing funds?[4] It was a perfectly Stimsonian method of operation: gather the best and the brightest; together they would solve the problems of the slums.[5]

The Stimsonian architecture of the Bedford-Stuyvesant project was, however, deceptive, was in many ways a mere facade. In contrast to Stimsonian ventures in places like Vietnam and the Tennessee Valley, the role of the Wise Men in Bedford-Stuyvesant was sharply limited. The voice of the community's own citizens, under the leadership of Judge Thomas R. Jones, was to be the decisive one in the project; the patrician advisers were to defer to the citizens of Bedford-Stuyvesant in all matters of significance.[6] Government was to play a much smaller part than was typically the case in New Deal and Great Society programs.[7] The success of the project would turn primarily on the ability of the community to attract private enterprise and private capital. The capitalist system, Bobby asserted in the January speeches, was not the enemy of the ghetto, the oppressor of the underclass; on the contrary, the businessman was a potential friend.[8] Bobby called for the "active participation" of the business community in every facet of the revitalization efforts.[9]

Later he would propose a variety of tax incentives designed to stimulate private investment in the inner city, a proposal that anticipated the various "empowerment" and "enterprise" schemes more recently championed by Jack Kemp and Al Gore.[10] For the time being, the best he could do was ask the Wise Men to lend their names and their Rolodexes to the cause.[11]

Restraining the Wise Men

IT IS A wonder—and a testament to the tenacity with which Bobby and his aides insisted on the principle of community control—that the Stimsonians did not take over the project entirely. The Wise Men whom Bobby summoned to Bedford-Stuyvesant were accustomed to giving orders and being obeyed; how would they suffer the leadership of a plebeian board? The Stimsonians' protégés in academic and legal circles had names to make and careers to build; they were always looking for an opening, a break, a chance to make a simple idea more complicated, a chance to get a crack at federal funds, a chance to build a bureaucracy. Bobby and his aides received dozens of letters from such academic and legal hustlers. The letters do not make for edifying reading: there can be few things so unctuous as the tone of a professor on the make, pimping his pet theories and ideas. "Just a note," one Yale Law School professor wrote Walinsky in January 1967, "to let you know that I am presently working with an embryonic inter-disciplinary group involving architects and planners who are thinking of putting together a proposal relating to the Bedford-Stuyvesant project." The mind recoils; what sort of baroque bureaucratic scheme was such an "interdisciplinary group" of "planners" likely to evolve? The professor observed that Walinsky's "influence" was "pervasive indeed" in the little academic orbit in which he moved; he said that he himself was particularly "intrigue[d]" by Walinsky's "sale and lease-back" ideas.[12] After more demeaning flattery of this kind—the professor claimed to be "awed" by Walinsky's "familiarity with the tax laws" and wondered how he had ever been able to "learn it all"—he pleaded for "any further tidbits" Walinsky might be able to give him; Washington's table scraps were never enough to fill the insatiable academic maw.[13] Walinsky kept his distance.

There was no shortage of expertise available to Bobby and his aides; the difficulty lay rather in preventing the experts from ruining the project by introducing needless complexity. It is true that Bobby could, when necessary, play the Stimsonian card as well as anyone; he knew how to massage Stimsonian egos with blather about their extraordinary qualities of prescience and vision. His proposal to McGeorge Bundy's Ford Foundation is a textbook example of how to get a Stimsonian to open his checkbook. In most of his statements about Bedford-Stuyvesant Bobby took pains to emphasize the importance of community leadership; in his Bundy proposal, however, Bobby made it seem as though the *Stimsonians* would be the dominant force in the neighborhood. Bobby's staff described the Bedford-Stuyvesant project to Bundy as "the first time the leaders of the American business community" had "assumed the *primary responsibility* for dealing with the problems of the ghetto."[14] The proposal compared the project to the TVA, the Marshall Plan, and the Manhattan Project.[15] This, of course, was nonsense. The community board, headed by Judge Jones, possessed primary responsibility for solving the community's problems; it was, so to speak, the sovereign entity in the project, a mechanism that provided for "the full and dominant participation" of the residents of Bedford-Stuyvesant.[16] The Stimsonian board, the board on which Paley, Dillon, Watson, and Schmidt sat, would have to content itself with a secondary role. The project as a whole was conceived not as a variation on a New Deal theme, but as an alternative to government-sponsored programs like the TVA. The point of Bedford-Stuyvesant was to ensure that solutions were "not imposed from the top" on an indifferent community.[17] Bobby, however, knew his man; he realized that nothing was more likely to appeal to the biographer of Colonel Stimson than the prospect of brilliant philosopher-kings "educating the community" and solving "in new ways" problems that had heretofore "defied solution by all other effort."[18] The "potentially catalytic combinations" of genius and talent that such men could generate, Bobby assured Bundy, would inevitably "suggest new techniques and new approaches" to the problem of urban poverty.[19] Nor was the "deeper value" inherent in the project to be overlooked, the value of "exposing" the elite "to frontier social problems."[20] As Mr. and Mrs. Leonard Bernstein introduced high society to the Black Panthers, so Bedford-Stuyvesant would introduce Mac Bundy to the ghetto. This was, after all, the age of radical chic; there was no better way of drawing attention to oneself than to be seen in a Park Avenue drawing room with the Panthers, or in a Wall Street boardroom with Judge Jones and the good citizens of Bedford-Stuyvesant.[21] The social and intellectual nobility was only too happy to respond to Bobby's summons. I. M. Pei, who among other things was busy designing the Temple of Kennedy that now graces Boston Harbor, took charge of creating so-called "super blocks" for the neighborhood; Cravath, Swaine & Moore agreed to provide legal counsel; Mrs. Astor and the Astor Foundation supplied valuable funds; and Bundy's Ford Foundation underwrote a generous grant of capital.[22]

Beyond Radical Chic

THERE WAS A radical chicness to it, and at times Bobby seemed almost like a Robin Leach in reverse, a rich and famous person trying desperately to learn about the lifestyles of the miserable and obscure. But Bobby carried his concern beyond radical chicness. He left Mrs. Leonard Bernstein, nibbling at hors d'oeuvres with Eldridge Cleaver, in the dust; his own pilgrimages, to Bedford-Stuyvesant, to the Mississippi Delta, to the slums of South America and the shanties of South Africa, amounted almost to a new medievalism. Even if it were impossible to change the world, one nevertheless had an obligation, Bobby believed, to expose oneself to its sufferings, to don an intellectual hair shirt, as penance for its pains. In the Mississippi Delta he came upon "the dirtiest, filthiest, poorest" houses imaginable, houses that stank of "mildew, sickness, and urine."[23] Charles Evers, who in addition to being Medgar Evers's brother was himself active in the civil rights movement, remembered that the "odor was so bad" that visitors "could hardly keep the nausea down."[24] And yet Bobby went into these hovels; in one of them he sat upon a foul bed and cradled a little black boy in his arms. The child was covered with "open sores" and his "belly was bloated from malnutrition." Bobby rubbed the boy's grotesquely distended stomach.[25] "I wouldn't do that!" Marian Wright Edelman later said. "I *didn't* do that."[26] But Bobby did. It was a ritual he acted out, with slight variations, over and over again. In Brazil, in the slums of Salvador, he crouched to speak to barefoot children in a street "where the open sewers and humid heat combined to create a stench so foul" that the Brazilian security police deserted their senatorial charge in order to "find sanctuary in their closed cars."[27] In rural New York he found migrant workers living in abandoned buses that reeked of filth, and to his horror found the workers' children covered with unhealed scabs and putrefying sores.[28]

This Bobby, the passionate pilgrim, the earnest seeker, the Bobby whom we so easily picture walking along a desolate Western airport tarmac, against a background of great mountains, with his little dog, or kneeling, in the midst of a remote orange grove, with Mr. Chavez and a group of migrant farmworkers, or bending to grasp the hand of one of those little children with whom, like the Lord, he felt such instinctive sympathy: this Bobby is familiar enough to us.[29] It is the Bobby whose purity, whose compassion, and whose peculiar sweetness of nature made him seem like a secular saint. But we are suspicious; we do not trust secular saints. We wonder what he was *really* about. A sentimental fool? A cynical manipulator? An expert purveyor of modern melodrama? And what about Marilyn Monroe? We wonder whether his sense of charity was not misplaced. Brother Ted is beginning to drink his life away; the kids are getting into drugs; sister-in-law Joan is freaking out. Shouldn't we be tending to the home fires?

Of course, there was always more to it than medievalism and Mrs. Jellyby. Bedford-Stuyvesant was as much about politics as it was about compassion; the documents in the Kennedy archives make the political purpose of the project abundantly clear. In a confidential 1966 memorandum to Bobby, Adam Walinsky argued that Bedford-Stuyvesant, not Vietnam, was the issue that would enable him to usurp the heights, would propel him to the highest places in the republic. Bed-Stuy, Walinsky said, was a "job which only you can pull off," a "job which will pay dividends to you" in the future. "If you can make this work," he told Bobby, "it will be the 'Kennedy Plan' everywhere." The word would get out; it could "be spread, among other things, by the subcommittee of which you are a member," a subcommittee that, under the leadership of Senator Ribicoff, was about to begin landmark hearings on the question of urban poverty. Bed-Stuy, Walinsky predicted, would dramatically boost Bobby's popularity in New York, where he found himself in competition with the energetic Rockefeller and the handsome and proverbially charismatic Lindsay. Success in Bed-Stuy, Walinsky said, would emphasize the "contrast between what [Lindsay] has done in a year and what you [can] do in a month." And it would raise Bobby's national stature. Johnson, Walinsky said, had dropped the ball on urban poverty; there was now "a complete vacuum of poverty leadership" in the United States. "You can seize the lead," Walinsky told his boss.[30]

No surprise there. Like every other United States Senator who pledges to do something about a problem, Bobby pledged to do something about Bedford-Stuyvesant only after he and his aides had carefully weighed the political implications of such a promise. Politics played a part—a large part—in the decision to take on Bedford-Stuyvesant. But it was politics of the highest and boldest sort, politics characterized by an audacity rarely found in the Senate. Here was a Senator who, in a year in which he attained new and extraordinary heights of popularity, was willing to wade into the morass of the ghetto and gamble his career and his future on the chance that he could do something about it. Senators are not in the habit of doing things like this. Daniel Patrick Moynihan, who today occupies the Senate seat that Bobby then held, privately warned his friend not to make the attempt.[31] Doubtless many other Senators would have taken Moynihan's advice.

Practical politics, the fashion of radical chic, even a kind of false charity all played a part in Bobby's pilgrimages in pain, and all contributed to his decision to come to Bedford-Stuyvesant. But more than anything else Bobby's pilgrimages were exercises in an ongoing attempt to explore the relationship between compassion and self-confidence. They were Bobby's way not merely of immersing himself in the facts and metaphysics of human suffering, but of understanding the way in which the compassionate act nurtures a person's confidence in himself.

12

IN NOVEMBER 1962, JAMES BALDWIN PUBLISHED "LETter from a Region in My Mind" in *The New Yorker*. In it he told of ghettos where

> the wages of sin were visible everywhere, in the wine-stained and urine-splashed hallway, in every clanging ambulance bell, in every scar on the faces of the pimps and their whores, in every helpless, newborn baby being brought into this danger, in every knife and pistol fight on the Avenue, and in every disastrous bulletin: a cousin, mother of six, suddenly gone mad, the children parceled out here and there; an indestructible aunt rewarded for years of hard labor by a slow, agonizing death in a terrible small room; someone's bright son blown into eternity by his own hand; another turned robber and carried off to jail.[1]

Baldwin told of watching old friends degenerate, of finding them, "in twos and threes and fours, in a hallway, sharing a jug of wine or a bottle of whiskey, talking, cursing, fighting, sometimes weeping."[2] He told of a past, "the Negro's past, of rope, fire, torture, castration, infanticide, rape; death and humiliation; fear by day and night, fear as deep as the marrow of the bone; doubt that he was worthy of life, since everyone around him denied it."[3] Tame stuff, perhaps, compared with the sentiments expressed by groups like the Black Panthers a few years later. But in 1962 Baldwin's was as powerful a statement of black rage as most *New Yorker* readers had ever encountered. It shocked genteel liberals out of their paternalistic complacency; something, they said, had to be done.

The article moved Bobby to seek Baldwin out. The two had met before, briefly, at a White House dinner; now Bobby invited him to breakfast with him at Hickory Hill.[4] Though he had in the past ridiculed Baldwin's homosexuality—he and Jack used to quarrel over who had first thought to call Baldwin "Martin Luther Queen"—Bobby now developed a respect for the man, and asked him to arrange a meeting with a group of blacks to talk about the problems of the ghetto.[5] The meeting took place on a late spring afternoon in 1963 at the Kennedy family apartment on Central Park South in New York. Burke Marshall accompanied Bobby. Several black artists and entertainers were present, among them Lena Horne, Harry Belafonte, and Lorraine Hansberry. So, too, were two experts on urban problems: Kenneth B. Clark, the social psychologist, and Edwin C. Berry of the Chicago Urban League.[6]

Also present was a young man named Jerome Smith, a civil rights worker who had spent time in Southern jails and who had on several occasions been beaten to a pulp by white supremacists.[7] He was less prominent than the artists and scholars who had gathered to meet the Attorney General, but he quickly established himself as the dominant presence in the room. He was not famous, Baldwin observed; he "didn't sing or act or dance."[8] But he nevertheless became "the focal point" of the debate.[9] Smith began by saying, in an angry, stammering voice—for he stammered when he was angry—that it "nauseated" him to be in the same room with a man who as Attorney General had been as negligent in the performance of his duties as Bobby.[10] Unprepared for this hostility, Bobby politely ignored Smith and turned to the others in the room, to those whom he took to be the "reasonable, responsible, mature representatives of the black community" present. This was a mistake; the others insisted that he listen to Smith. And Smith was merciless. Kenneth Clark remembered his harangue as "one of the most violent, emotional verbal assaults" he had ever witnessed.[11] The atmosphere in the room became, Baldwin said, "very tense, and finally very ugly."[12] Bobby himself, who appeared to Clark to be "extraordinarily insensitive" to the plight of black people in the United States, became, as the meeting proceeded, "more silent and tense, and he sat immobile in the chair. He no longer continued to defend himself. He just sat, and you could see the tension and the pressure building in him."[13] And yet Smith refused to relent, and the verbal pummeling continued. Smith said he did not know how much longer he could remain nonviolent. He said he did not know how much longer he could endure, with patience, with meekness, with humility, the indignity of being spat upon by whites, and of being beaten by them to within an inch of his life. Smith's parting words were blunt: "When I pull the trigger," he told the Attorney General, you can "kiss it good-bye."[14]

The encounter in New York left Bobby not only shaken, but also profoundly angry. "I think he was always a little mad at me," Baldwin said afterward.[15] And yet however wounded Bobby might have been by the tongue-lashing he received on that late spring afternoon in 1963, in subsequent years he ritualistically subjected himself to similar abuse; he seemed almost to enjoy the degree of humiliation involved. And these encounters *were* exercises in humiliation, exercises in which Bobby very deliberately abased himself, made himself "low and humble in position," and bore with meekness and humility the taunts and insults of others.[16] After the funeral of Dr. King in April 1968 prominent black leaders, among them Ralph Abernathy, James Bevel, and Hosea Williams, gathered at Bobby's suite at the Regency Hotel in Atlanta.[17] There was, Andrew Young recalled, "a whole lot of undirected hostility present." People were "just angry and bitter and grieving."[18] A quantity of profane language was used, and when "preachers get to cuss," Young observed, they "cuss good."[19] But Young hesitated to silence his colleagues; he was "impressed" by the way Bobby accepted their calumnies. Bobby "listened," Young said, "while we blew off steam . . . he wasn't upset."[20]

A short time later Bobby addressed an angry black audience in

Oakland. It was, John Seigenthaler remembered, a "rough, gut-cutting" affair. Members of the audience variously denounced white people, the Kennedy family, obsequious blacks, and "technicolor niggers"; Bobby himself they derided as a talker, a hypocrite, "just another politician."[21] "Look, man," one participant said to him when he attempted to speak, "I don't want to hear none of your shit."[22] Unperturbed, Bobby "sat there and listened and took it."[23] Afterward, driving back to San Francisco, he said that he was "glad" that he had gone to the meeting. "They need to know," he said, that "somebody [will] listen." After "all the abuse the blacks have taken through the centuries," he continued, "whites are just going to have to let them get some of these feelings out."[24] He had come a long way from the man who had once said he could have been smoking a cigar in Palm Beach.[25]

The Ritual Discipline of Humiliation

THE EMERGING THEME is one of ritual humiliation: it explains much in Bobby's career that is otherwise inexplicable; his very campaigns for public office partook of it. There *was* a medieval quality to Bobby, a part of him that was in love with the idea of the mortified flesh. The body, in the idiosyncratic philosophy he evolved, had been created for punishment as well as pleasure. Hence his predilection not only for the most dangerous rapids of rivers and the sheer faces of mountains, but also for the frenzied crowds that reached out to touch him.[26] In his own campaigns, and when he campaigned for others, he was literally bloodied by his supporters, and yet he continued to submit to them. "They tore at his buttons and his hair . . . they tried to pull him out of his convertible." His bodyguard Bill Barry, a big man who had played football at Kent State, was forced "to hang on to him with all his strength."[27] "People were coming up to him," Dolores Huerta recalled, "and they would grab him and hug him and kiss him on the mouth!"[28] They would shout, "Un gran hombre . . . un gran hombre"—"a great man"—and "his hands were all bloodied where people had pulled him."[29] Teddy White, who traveled with Bobby during the '68 campaign, remembered the "near-sexual orgy of exultation" of the crowd, the "frenzy of their love."[30] The "hands would reach for him, grabbing for a thread, a shoelace, a shoe; in the near-hysteria, anyone in the car with Bobby would become a bodyguard, protecting him."[31] At one point, White said, the "clutchers seized him and pulled so hard that in tumbling over the edge of the car he had instinct enough only to throw his elbow over his eyes to protect them; and slammed his jaw on the door of the car, breaking a front tooth and cutting open his lip."[32] His tie, his cuff links, even his shoes were taken from him, and still the "touching . . . and the pulling and the pushing and the screaming" continued.[33]

> A lot of people [the television reporter Charles Quinn remembered] were crushed and fainted and got hurt, and we had some close calls in the motorcade when little kids fell under cars. It was hairy. . . . I have a vivid picture of a lady grabbing him by the tie and pulling him down by the neck; his little head bobbing up and down.[34]

It was more than a modern form of self-flagellation, it was a kind of fatal dance, as Bobby himself acknowledged when he said that each time he stepped into the mass of tangled, moving, pressing flesh he was playing a game of Russian roulette.[35] The crowd, for its part, sensed his willingness to be a sacrifice, and attributed to the garlanded hero extraordinary and undefinable qualities, qualities that made it all the more eager to reach him, to grab him, to make some sort of tactile contact with him, as if the touch of his hands, swollen and scratched—as if his very skin and hair—were a cure for all our modern scrofulas.[36]

History teaches us to be cautious about labeling particular phenomena unique. Bobby grew up, Jack Newfield observed, "with cardinals, movie stars, diplomats, and financiers, but he was killed reaching for the hand of a $75 a week Mexican dishwasher."[37] Newfield implies that there is something singular in this, but of course, the phenomenon of aristocratic statesmen sympathizing with the cause of the downtrodden is at least as old as the Gracchi. Bobby, however, went further than any other major American statesman in trying not simply, like the Stimsonians, to mitigate the pain of the poor and the powerless, but to feel it himself.[38] The Stimsonians, with their great-souled, Alexander-spared-the-daughters-of-Darius notions of charity, saw pain from a distance: Bobby looked it in the face. He told Newfield that he envied the fact that Newfield had grown up in a slum. "I wish I had that experience," Bobby said.[39] Much as Franklin Roosevelt sympathized with the Forgotten Man, and pitied the terrible privations that must have marked his growth to manhood, one may doubt whether he himself even for a moment wished that he had grown up anyplace other than on his Hudson River estate.

In "the greater part of the Benefactors to Humanity," Keats wrote, "some meretricious motive has sullied their greatness—some melodramatic scenery has fascinated them."[40] It cannot be denied that Bobby himself craved the kind of "melodramatic scenery" of which Keats spoke. For years his imagination had been circumscribed by the narrow limits of the Stimsonian creed in which he had been bred up; he had at length gained his freedom, and in this newly liberated state found himself impelled by an impetuous desire to plumb the depths of experience, to probe the limits of the universe. With a ferocious appetite he delved into books, shot the rapids of rivers, climbed mountains, recited Shakespeare, provoked the frenzy of crowds, explored poverty, toured the world and found out countries, and dreamed of being a revolutionary hero. His pilgrimages to the most abysmal places of human suffering threatened to become simply another facet of a romantic effort at universality, a vain and Faust-like quest for impossible experience. Jacqueline Kennedy said of her husband that he "lived at such a pace because he wished to know it all."[41] The statement was truer of Bobby than it was of Jack. Like so many apparently stoical men, Bobby was at heart a sensualist.[42] Just as he had become addicted to the narcotic of the campaign, to the windswept airport tarmacs, the sun-soaked crowds, the roar of the jet airplane engines, to that constant sensual stimulation that, Pascal said, is the primary reason men seek public office, so had he also become addicted to other rare and curious forms of existence.[43] He was now, more than ever, Schlesinger said, "a collector" of personalities: one "never knew whom to expect at Hickory Hill novelists, entertainers, columnists, decathlon champions, astronauts, football stars, diplomats, politicians, mountain climbers, international beauties, appearing in every age, sex, size, color."[44] The more exquisite forms of human suffering threatened to become simply another exotic delicacy in his extensive menagerie, another means of stimulating an already overindulged palate, one more Lucullan delight in the epicure's feast of experience.

And so the worst that can be said of his emerging philosophy of ritual humiliation, his evolving theology of compassion, has been said; that it was marred by vanity, and egotism, and romantic desire, and mere sensuality; that it was tinged with ambition. The good in it was not therefore wholly lost. His journey into the darker territories of human suffering—his desire to expose himself to the pain of others, even when it meant humiliation for himself—had a value that transcended his own egotism. The effect of Bobby's compassion may have been limited, but the insight he gained into the role of compassion in society was an important one. He did not really believe, when he was in the *barriada* in Brazil and begged the barefoot children to stay in school as a favor to President Kennedy, that this gesture, the impulse of a moment, would have any lasting effect on the lives of the children who swarmed around him. That is precisely why he is said to have been so dejected afterward: "On the plane north he sat by himself, his head buried in his arms."[45] The people he encountered in the slums, the ghettos, and the barrios were, he believed, uttering a "cry for love."[46] But the love he bore them was of necessity too brief, too remote, too impersonal, to transform their lives in the way that a more durable love sometimes can. He recognized the problem: In the slum, the ghetto, the barrio, as well as in other parts of American society, self-confidence had diminished as the traditional bearers of durable love, the institutional vessels of compassion—the families, the schools, the churches—cracked and broke. This circumstance, more than any of the "structural" economic conditions described in the bureaucrats' reports, was at the root of the apathy and underconfidence that characterized so many of the inhabitants of the inner city. The children of the ghettos were not born with dead souls. In a conversation with Robert Coles, Bobby observed that slum children had, at the age of three or four, "a certain vitality and beauty in their faces that well-fixed middle-class children being pushed around in their baby carriages on Fifth Avenue did not have." But by the age of eight or ten or twelve the faces of these children began to change as the children themselves sensed the "oppressiveness" of the world in which they were fated to grow up.[47] Bobby went among them, and tried, as he said, to "bind up [their] wounds." But there was only so much he could do.

Confidence Games

HOWEVER LIMITED WAS the efficacy of the compassion he was able to convey through his own ritual exercises in humiliation, he had identified the importance of compassion—as cultivated in families, schools, churches, and neighborhoods—in nurturing the self-confidence that makes self-reliant citizenship possible. It is difficult for us today to put any great degree of faith in a concept like "compassion"; so frequently has the word been invoked in empty sermons and vacuous editorial writing that it has altogether lost its intellectual edge, its moral point. Bobby's own contribution lay in his attempts to restore its edge. He helped to recover the older meaning of the word—and to endow it with new importance. Emerson, in the severe individualism of his creed, had supposed that a man was complete in himself, and that he had only to look inside himself to discover the strength that makes the good life possible. There is in Emerson's thought a suggestion of the radical Protestant idea that an individual must find his own way to salvation; that he must find God in himself, or not at all; that he must save his soul through his own efforts, and not through the mediation of institutions like the family, the church, the school, the community. Though "I prize my friends," Emerson wrote, "I cannot afford to talk with them and study their visions, lest I lose my own."[48] "I chide society," he said, "I embrace solitude."[49] Emerson was suspicious of churches, schools, friendship, even marriage; for Emerson, the greatest man was never less lonely than when completely alone. One sees this radical aloneness in Lincoln, the Emersonian hero who, growing up among people greatly inferior to him in genius and ambition, never learned to rely on anyone other than himself. Lincoln did not depend on his family and friends the way other men do. Judge David Davis, who rode the Illinois circuit with Lincoln in the 1840s and 1850s (Lincoln later elevated him to the Supreme Court), recalled that "when all the lawyers of a Saturday evening would go home to see their families and friends, Lincoln would find some excuse and refuse to go."[50] Lincoln could, it is true, open himself up, as private men are sometimes able to do, in a crowd.[51] In his public performances—in his storytelling and his speech-making—he exuded a warmth he was incapable of displaying in his private life.[52] But if he was a man capable of touching, to the depths of their beings, men and women whom he did not know, he was separated from his friends and his family by an impenetrable barrier. He was, his law partner William Herndon concluded, not merely a private but a cold man.[53]

Most people are not like Lincoln; their fruits will ripen only where love and compassion have stimulated and nourished them. So bewitched was Emerson by the spectacle of individual genius that he failed to recognize the processes by which such genius is (in most cases) uncovered, the social processes by which an individual's imagination and talents are unlocked and revealed to the world in their fullest splendor. "Everyone," Nietzsche said, "possesses inborn talent, but few possess the degree of inborn and acquired toughness, endurance, and energy actually to become a talent, that is to say to *become* what he *is:* which means to discharge [one's talent] in works and actions."[54] The development of individual genius is not always or even usually a matter of spontaneous combustion; it occurs, rather, as a result of the love and compassion of others: Most people are not *born* self-reliant; they are instead persuaded, by a compassionate parent, teacher, or priest, to *become* self-reliant; they are persuaded, in other words, that in spite of their doubts and fears and worries, they have a self that is strong enough to be relied upon. It is a lesson of Shakespeare's: if you treat Christopher Sly like a lord, he will soon enough act with the confidence of one.[55]

It is not surprising that Bobby should have been more sympathetic than Emerson to the idea of compassion. Emerson inherited, even as he struggled to escape, the old Puritan problems and preoccupations; Bobby was a product of a less austere Roman Catholic tradition that emphasized the important role institutions (such as the apostolic succession) and other human beings (such as priests) play in transmitting to individuals the divine compassion that Christians perceive in the figure of Christ. Bobby had seen this principle of compassion at work in his own life and in the lives of his brothers and sisters. It was in part because his father had instilled in his children the belief that they *could* be successful that they actually became so. "Aren't you foolish," Joseph Kennedy wrote to the young Jack Kennedy, "not to get all there is out of what God has given you?" "You have the goods," Kennedy told his son, "why not try to show it?"[56] By making his sons believe that they could do great things, Joseph Kennedy enabled them to do great things. Bobby said that his father "called on the best that was in us." "We might not be the best, and none of us were, but we were to make the effort to be the best."[57] "If it hadn't been for that," Jack said, Teddy would "be just a playboy today."[58] Some might question whether Teddy ever became anything more than that. But the fact remains that at the age of thirty this otherwise unremarkable young man was elected to the United States Senate.[59] It is of course true that Teddy had money, connections, and a presidential brother on his side, but he also possessed—it is impossible to deny it—an unusually high degree of self-confidence. In *The Fruitful Bough*, a privately printed book edited by Teddy, Bobby declared: "What it really adds up to is love—not love as it is described with such facility in popular magazines, but the kind of love that is affection and respect, order, encouragement, and support."[60] Joseph Kennedy constantly sought to reinforce his children's confidence in themselves with loving support—even when they made mistakes, even when they were under great pressure.[61] Of course, all parents—or most parents, at any rate—*try* to do this, but few can have done it as persistently, as successfully, as religiously, as Joseph Kennedy. One may call him a Sinister Capitalist if one likes, but one cannot deny that he was a wonderful parent. "I still don't know how I did," Jack Kennedy joked after talking to his father by telephone at the time of the second debate with Nixon. "If I had slipped and fallen flat on the floor, he would have said, 'The graceful way you picked yourself up was terrific.' "[62] Joseph Kennedy's letters and telegrams to his children are among the best things he ever wrote. When Kick Kennedy was struggling with the question of whether to accept Billy Hartington's proposal of marriage and marry outside of the Roman church, her father cabled her:

I FEEL TERRIBLY UNHAPPY YOU HAVE TO FACE YOUR BIGGEST CRISIS WITHOUT MOTHER OR ME. YOUR CONFIDENTIAL MEMORANDUM WORTHY OF CHESTERTON MAGNIFICENT. WITH YOUR FAITH IN GOD YOU CAN'T MAKE A MISTAKE. REMEMBER YOU ARE STILL AND ALWAYS WILL BE TOPS WITH ME. LOVE DAD.

When at a later time Kick contemplated marriage to Peter Fitz-william, a British aristocrat whom Joseph Alsop described as "astonishingly good-looking, wonderfully easy and jolly, and with that curious aura of glamour sometimes conferred by great possessions long held and a great place in the world long maintained," Rose Kennedy took the position "that if Kick married outside the Church a second time," she would never speak to her daughter again and would "cut off relations with any members of the Kennedy family" who did.[63] Years later, long after Kick and Fitzwilliam had died in a plane crash en route from Paris to the Riviera, Alsop asked Jack Kennedy, who was by then President, whether he would have sided with his sister or his mother (and the Church) in the event Kick had lived to marry Fitzwilliam. "With Kick, of course," the President responded at once.[64] His father had taught the son the supreme importance of devotion to family—and continued to remind him of its importance even after the son had reached the White House. In the spring of 1961, Arthur Schlesinger wrote, Jack Kennedy was in Hyannis Port

> walking to his father's house for dinner when Caroline, his daughter, came off the porch crying to him. As he started to comfort her, the kitchen door opened, and someone said, "Mr. President, they want you on the White House phone— they said it's important." Kennedy said, "Caroline, I'll be back in just a moment. Let me go take this call." When dinner began, there was an edgy silence. Finally Mr. Kennedy said, "Jack, I saw what happened outside. Caroline was in tears and came out. You had a call from the White House. I know there are a lot of things on your mind about your meeting with Khrushchev. . . . But let me tell you something: nothing that happens during your Presidency will be as important as how Caroline turns out. And don't forget it."[65]

Self-confidence is at the heart of the Kennedy phenomenon. Not the self-confidence of the New World entrepreneur or the Old World great-souled man: the Kennedys invented their own system of confidence-building, created their own inventory of tools and techniques. The father carefully nurtured the myth of Kennedy exceptionalism; the children grew up with the myth, believed it, drew strength from it. They *were* exceptional; theirs was, the father assured them, the grandest, the most exclusive club of all, a far more splendid affair than Porcellian or A.D. Joseph Kennedy taught the children to love one another even as he loved them, and love one another they did, as any number of witnesses have attested.[66] The younger siblings worshiped the older ones with a cultlike devotion. Eunice worshipped Jack, Teddy worshipped Jack, they all worshipped Jack, and Bobby never spoke of his brother other than as a person apart, a sacred being. Jack himself had the self-confidence of one accustomed to commanding the love and even the idolatry of others: when he chose to project, nakedly and unapologetically, his high confidence in himself, the effect was striking. Opponents were quite literally undone. Ted Reardon, a Kennedy aide, remembered the first time Richard Nixon saw the young Jack Kennedy in action at a congressional hearing in the late forties. When "Jack started to talk," Reardon said, "Dicky Boy sort of looked at him . . . with a look between awe and fear and respect."[67] Years later, when Kennedy, looking, television news producer Don Hewitt said, "like a young Adonis," arrived in a Chicago television studio for the first of their presidential debates, Nixon was "physically overwhelmed" by his rival's self-confident presence.[68] From "the moment Kennedy strode in," Nixon was "not the same man."[69] "Visibly deflated by his rival's matinee-idol aura and seeming nervelessness," the Vice President "slouched in his chair, his head turned away, a man in retreat."[70]

The Kennedy cult of self-confidence had its rituals and its rites. Whenever he greeted his father, Jack Kennedy would make a fist, and the old man would wrap his hands around it, as if to affirm the son's strength.[71] The Kennedys learned to draw strength from the most elemental things: the sun, the wind, and the sea "elated" Bobby and Jack; clouds and rain "depressed" them.[72] Bright sunshine, Jack Newfield observed, "quickly lifted Bobby's spirits."[73] Their aides took to calling the brilliant sunny weather in which they so obviously delighted "Kennedy weather." A friend recalled how Bobby, closeted one morning in a hotel suite, was unable to concentrate on his work: so entranced was he by the perfection of the cloudless blue sky he saw through the window that he could not apply himself to the business at hand.[74] Jack Kennedy rehearsed for his first debate with Nixon in dazzling sunshine on the rooftop of his Chicago hotel; there he burnished the tan he had nurtured during a swing through California the week before. In an age when no one worried about melanoma, the Kennedys were astonishingly vain of the fact that their faces reflected the dazzling power of the sun. The sun, Jack Kennedy said, "gives me confidence. . . . It makes me feel strong, healthy, attractive."[75] When he was unable to escape the northern winter by flying to the tropics, he used a sun lamp instead.[76] The sea and the sky similarly elated the Kennedys. They loved to sail and to fly, loved boats and airplanes, the exhilaration of motion. Emerson once said that he "never was on a coach that went fast enough for" him.[77] The Kennedys knew what he meant. They, too, loved the *feel* of motion, loved the heightened sense of consciousness it produced, loved the way it stimulated the soul, the hundred thousand nerve endings that make human beings capable of ecstasy. The Kennedys' capacity for exhilaration was directly related to their capacity for self-confident action; the joy they took in the world corresponded to the joy they took in themselves, as if they as much as the sun, the sky, and the sea were a manifestation of God's plan, an extension of His divinity, an expression of His glory. There is a degree of narcissism at the heart of all the higher forms of self-confidence.

So pronounced was Jack Kennedy's self-confidence that his rare stumbles seem inexplicable, out of character, the actions of another man. Why did the man who had taken down Cabot Lodge, Hubert Humphrey, Lyndon Johnson, and Richard Nixon lose it in Vienna, where his self-confidence deserted him and where he allowed Khrushchev to bully and intimidate him? The Bay of Pigs, too, shook Jack's confidence in himself, and the experience was so novel to him that he is said to have done something that Kennedys do not do—he is said to have been on the verge of weeping, to have been "practically . . . in tears."[78] He soon enough recovered his customary equanimity, however, and he remained, to the end of his life, a supremely self-confident man.

Though Bobby studied the tools and techniques Jack Kennedy used to bolster his confidence in himself, he never achieved the same degree of self-assurance. Friends and family, Arthur Schlesinger said, sensed Bobby's vulnerability and tended to be protective of him; they never thought that his self-confident brother needed protecting.[79] When in March 1968 Bobby finally made up his mind to run for President, Teddy Kennedy warned Schlesinger not to try to dissuade him. If you "discuss it any longer," Teddy told him, "it will shake his confidence" and undermine the magical self-possession a Kennedy needed in order to do those things that ordinary mortals could not.[80] The less than supremely confident Bobby shrank from face-to-face encounters with opponents like Eugene McCarthy and Kenneth Keating, and he never became as confident a debater as Jack had been.[81] When Bobby debated the question of Vietnam in a televised debate with Ronald Reagan, "the general consensus," David Halberstam wrote, "was that Reagan . . . destroyed" him.[82]

If he never became as self-confident as his older brother, Bobby had by the early sixties come a long way from the underconfident young man who in 1953 had stammered through a toast at Jack's wedding. The teenager who had been painfully shy around girls was capable, in 1962, of captivating Marilyn Monroe.[83] The man whom Lyndon Johnson called the "runt" of the Kennedy litter "came to inhabit the fantasies" of a screen goddess's last summer.[84] Bobby's relationship with Monroe foreshadowed, indeed, the *over*confident behavior that has characterized the Kennedys in the years since his death, years in which the family's confidence in itself has at times been so excessive as to constitute a kind of hubris. In Bobby and Jack self-confidence was generally commensurate with talent and ability; it's not clear, however, that these corresponded as closely in Teddy's case or in the case of the third generation. David Horowitz, who with Peter Collier wrote a book about the Kennedys in the 1980s, described how self-confidence became a form of arrogance in Robert F. Kennedy, Jr., Bobby's second son. In his memoirs Horowitz recounted the "surreal experience" of listening to a Harvard roommate of Bobby Junior's—a person who knew of the young Kennedy's heroin addiction—talk as though his friend's intention to run for Congress in the next election was "perfectly natural."[85] Like so many other cults, Joseph Kennedy's cult of self-confidence had entered an irrational phase, had become what Horowitz called a psychosis. At the "center of the psychosis," Horowitz wrote, was the idea that a self-confident Kennedy "could get away with *anything*."[86]

The decadence in which Joseph Kennedy's cult of self-confidence culminated must not be permitted to obscure the achievements of its prime. Joseph Kennedy, it is often said, believed that it matters less what you are than what you seem to be.[87] Like Sallust's Caesar, he is said to have cared less about being virtuous than seeming to be so.[88] This is usually taken to be yet another evidence of Joseph Kennedy's dishonesty, and of the essential hollowness of the Kennedy phenomenon as a whole.[89] In retrospect, however, it's clear that the "confidence" games the elder Kennedy played were more than sleights-of-hand designed to fool a gullible public; in a more important sense they were tricks he wanted his boys to play on themselves. Joseph Kennedy seems instinctively to have realized that a self-confident person inevitably involves himself in an infinite number of acts of deception, of self-deception; the self-confident person, he knew, must think himself better than the facts at any given time would seem to admit. If one is to have any hope of becoming that which one wishes to become, one has to believe, in spite of the evidence, that one *can* become it. Only by believing—perhaps wrongly—that you are good enough to win will you have any chance of actually winning. Was he deceiving his boys—and inviting them to deceive themselves—when he told them that they were the best, that they "had the goods," that with such talents and abilities as they possessed they need never settle for second place? Perhaps. Joseph Kennedy was a cunning man. But in his cunning it is possible to discern the methods not merely of a cunning man, but of a compassionate one as well.

The Anatomy of Self-Confidence

WHEN SOME FUTURE Burton comes to write his anatomy of self-confidence, he will have the unenviable task of explaining a quality that is at once difficult to define, difficult to obtain, and difficult to retain. Self-confidence is, along with love, hatred, and genius, among the most mysterious and elusive of human qualities. One need not be an absurd mystic to see that a highly self-confident person can, if he chooses, quite literally *undo* the self-confidence of another, can drain a less self-confident person of whatever self-esteem he possesses. Thus a supremely self-confident Jack Kennedy rapidly drained Richard Nixon of his self-confidence at their first debate in Chicago in 1960; thus the supremely self-confident Kennedy tribe slowly drained Joan Bennett Kennedy of her self-confidence during the years of her association with the family.[90] On the other hand, the self-confident person can, if he wishes, choose to share his confidence with others, and through his compassionate acts can raise others to his own exalted level.

In formulating his ideas about the role of compassion in stimulating self-confidence, Bobby could look not only to his family's example, but also to a wealth of Christian teaching on the subject. Compassion, in the traditional Christian view, involves an act of humiliation, of lowering oneself to the level of the object of one's compassion: the person who occupies what is, in the eyes of the world, a higher and more responsible station in life—the priest, the parent, the teacher—lowers himself to the level of the student, the child, the parishioner, and by so doing assures the less exalted being that, in spite of the differences of their worldly positions, they possess a common humanity. In the ancient rituals of Christian humiliation, the well-born, the prosperous, the successful man was required to lower himself to the level of the least favored of men through a symbolic act, such as washing the feet of the poor on Maunday Thursday.* In so abasing himself, the prosperous man declared to the world that, notwithstanding the accidents of fate and fortune, he and the least favored of men were equals in the sight of God. Created in His image, the poor man and the rich man, the great man and the little man, were both of them brothers in Christ. For centuries this ritual of compassionate humility was repeated by the great ones of the earth; we read in Gibbon of Theodosius, "stripped of the ensigns of royalty," appearing "in the midst of the Church of Milan" in a "suppliant posture" and humbling "in the dust the pride of the diadem."[91] The message was clear, and the poor man was supposed to be inspired by it: the humblest of human beings had within themselves the same divinely

---

*The ritual of the washing of the feet on the Thursday before Easter is still carried on in the Roman Catholic Church.

inspired potential of the great ones of the earth. Bobby's own desire to walk among the least favored of men, to see and to touch the untouchables of our society, was nothing so much as a revival of this ancient Christian conception of compassion: he did then much of what Diana was later to do. In Harlem, in Watts, in Bedford-Stuyvesant, Bobby's very presence proclaimed the revolutionary truth of the Gospels, that all human beings—Senators and street-walkers alike—have been endowed by God with an unalienable dignity and value. It is, of course, the message of Christ himself, who in spite of His divinity, kept company with publicans and sinners, and "with sick people that were taken with divers diseases and torments, and those which were possessed with devils, and those which were lunatick, and those that had the palsy."[92]

In time this Christian conception of compassion was corrupted by snobbery and indifference; it was transformed into a merely donative charity, a matter of gold coins and silver ducats. The Maundy ceremony itself ceased to involve the poignant act of royal and other eminent persons washing the feet of the poor; all that remains today of the ritual is the distribution of Maundy Money by the sovereign. The old belief that an act of compassion—an act of love—might cleanse the heart of the cleanser and inspire the imagination of the cleansed was for the most part lost, to be kept alive only by organizations like the Salvation Army.[93] And while, of course, practical—as opposed to ritual—acts of compassion continue to occur every day, they seemed to Bobby to occur less frequently now than in the past. This was particularly true, he believed, in the inner city. Bobby liked to tell the story of a priest who worked with a young gang leader whose gang had acquired "a reputation for violence that struck fear in the hearts of adults and children alike."[94] The priest "spent a great deal of time getting to know" the young man and his cohorts.[95] He "counseled him in all sorts of troubles," persuaded him of the value of learning, and eventually obtained for him a scholarship at university, where the young man flourished as a student.[96] Bobby knew, however, that such Monseigneur Myriels are not so commonly met with in this world, and it was the very rarity of their compassion that made it seem to him notable.

When Bobby and a handful of other important men came to Bedford-Stuyvesant in 1966, they came as agents of a truer compassion than is embodied in the faceless, bureaucratized charity of the welfare state. The welfare state, so far from slowing the deterioration of the traditional institutional bearers of compassion—the schools, the families, the churches—undermined those institutions even more. For all the Enlightened thought that went into its construction, the welfare state was, like the Maundy Money itself, a feudal corruption of an older and better conception of compassion—a means of buying off the poor with gold coins, a means of making people content with their mediocre place in the hierarchy of society. This was not, Adam Walinsky observed, compassion: it was a kind of bribery, a way of perpetuating poverty, a method of keeping people in their place.[97]

13

⟨⟨⟨≈⟩⟩⟩

THE AMERICAN REPUBLIC, 1966. ON TELEVISION AMER-
icans watched *Gomer Pyle, U.S.M.C.*, *Petticoat Junction*, *My Favorite
Martian*, and *Batman*. The Beatles released *Revolver*, Jacqueline Su-
sann's *Valley of the Dolls* was a best-seller, and *Mame*, with Miss
Lansbury in the title role, was the toast of Broadway. Truman Capote, fresh from the success of *In Cold Blood*, gave his famous black-
and-white masked ball at the Plaza, and Susan Sontag published
Against Interpretation. The Methodist Church merged with the
United Brethren Church to become the United Methodist Church,
the largest Protestant denomination in the country, and three Gem-
ini series rockets were launched at Cape Kennedy. The Supreme
Court handed down its decision in *Miranda v. Arizona* in June, and
in September the first episode of *Star Trek* was broadcast on NBC.
In July Richard Speck murdered eight student nurses in a house on
the South Side of Chicago, and in August Charles Whitman killed
sixteen people and wounded thirty others with a high-powered rifle
fired from the tower of the University of Texas at Austin. It was a
year in which *Gilligan's Island* and *Flipper* coexisted uneasily in the
national consciousness with campus protest and alienated youth, in
which pictures of dropouts and hippies in San Francisco contrasted
oddly with the airbrushed glamour of the models depicted in ad-
vertisements in magazines and on television. It was the era of the
Dean Martin Show and the *Jack Benny Hour*; of Barbara Garson's

MacBird and Megan Terry's *Viet Rock*; of Danny Kaye, Stokely Carmichael, and Gary Player.

An American Senator in 1966

AT THE END of January 1966 President Johnson ordered a resumption of the bombing of targets in North Vietnam. In February the Senate Foreign Relations Committee, under the chairmanship of Senator Fulbright, held hearings on the progress of the war. Bobby, about to leave Washington to go skiing in Vermont, urged the administration to negotiate an end to the conflict, and asserted that no lasting settlement would be possible unless the Americans invited "discontented" elements in South Vietnam (like the Communist National Liberation Front) to the bargaining table and admitted them to "a share of power and responsibility" in the government at Saigon.[1] President Johnson, who was still convinced that the United States could win a military victory in Indochina, was furious. Although Bobby would in the ensuing weeks soften his remarks about the necessity of admitting Communists to a share of "power and responsibility" in the south, he continued to believe that the war was unwinnable. His doubts were reinforced when, in March, he lunched in New York with the French statesman Pierre Mendès-France, who told him that Hanoi and Peking could afford to pursue the war indefinitely, and that in the end they would exhaust America's patience.

But there was more to Bobby's life in 1966 than Vietnam. In June, the same month in which he dedicated a new swimming pool in Bedford-Stuyvesant, he made a triumphal tour of South Africa and several other African nations.[2] The trip was extensively covered in the newspapers and on television, and Bobby's own popularity soared. "Senator Kennedy," Joseph Alsop wrote, "has now reached the status of an unprecedented political phenomenon." Alsop likened him to "the young Theodore Roosevelt returning from Cuba" with all eyes upon him.[3] By the end of the summer Bobby had moved "dramatically ahead" of Lyndon Johnson in public opinion polls, and people began to talk of the inevitability of another Kennedy administration.[4]

During the second half of 1966, however, Bobby found himself on the defensive, forced to devote much of his time to the sordid and unfashionable pursuits of conventional politics—hand-shaking, speech-making, king-making. In July he helped elect Sam Silverman, a former Paul, Weiss partner, to the New York City Surrogate's Court. After the Silverman victory he turned his attention to the November elections. Nelson Rockefeller, who had taken the Governor's Mansion from Averell Harriman in 1958, was standing for reelection as Governor of New York. Bobby weighed the merits of a number of potential opponents: Sol Linowitz, the Rochester lawyer and Xerox executive; Franklin D. Roosevelt, Jr., to whom Bobby was under a personal obligation (Roosevelt had helped Jack Kennedy win the West Virginia primary in 1960); Eugene Nickerson, a Long Island politician who, though he was more obscure than his competitors, would in Bobby's view make as good a Governor as anyone. But Bobby hesitated to spend his political capital in the expensive effort of making a king, and in the fall his party, meeting at Buffalo, nominated Frank O'Connor, a machine politician from Queens. Bobby endorsed his party's nominee without enthusiasm.

In September there was a brief respite; Bobby put aside the burdens of politics and went sailing off the coast of Maine. Word reached him there that General de Gaulle, on a visit to Cambodia, had offered to broker a peace between Washington and Hanoi. Bobby thought the offer worth exploring, and was disappointed to learn that Johnson had summarily rejected it. He spent much of the rest of the fall campaigning for fellow Democrats—O'Connor in New York, G. Mennen "Soapy" Williams in Michigan, Pat Brown in California, Paul Douglas in Illinois. It was not a good year for liberals. Ronald Reagan was elected Governor of California, and many of the candidates for whom Bobby campaigned lost their races.[5] In New York the Rockefeller machine spent some $11 million to defeat O'Connor, making it one of the most expensive gubernatorial contests in American history.

Exhausted from the rigors of campaigning, Bobby flew to the Bahamas to recuperate in the sun. When he returned to Washington, he faced still more bad news, allegations that as Attorney General he had authorized illegal wiretaps on telephones and other impermissible forms of electronic surveillance. Nor was this his only problem. William Manchester had recently completed his manuscript on the assassination of President Kennedy; *Look* had secured prepublication serialization rights; the book itself was scheduled to appear in bookstores in 1967. Jacqueline Kennedy did not want the book published. Indeed, she did not want *any* history of the assassination published.[6] Bobby reluctantly agreed to press her cause. In November, the same month in which he feted Averell Harriman at Hickory Hill, Bobby showed up at the Berkshire Hotel in New York, where Manchester was staying in a suite maintained by *Look*, and demanded a meeting. Manchester refused to open the door to the suite, leaving Bobby to pound on it in impotent fury.[7] Rebuffed by Manchester, the Kennedys went to court. Jacqueline Kennedy authorized Simon Rifkind, another Paul, Weiss lawyer, to seek an injunction preventing publication of *The Death of a President* on the ground that Manchester had breached his contract with the Kennedys. (The Kennedys' ties to Paul, Weiss, among the most liberal of New York's preeminent law firms, had been strengthened when Theodore Sorensen became a partner there in January 1966; Adam Walinsky's father-in-law was the firm's real-estate partner.[8]) Bobby, on the slopes at Sun Valley, condemned what he called Manchester's greed (*Look* had agreed to pay him $665,000 for the serialization rights) even as he privately acknowledged that the affair was damaging his own reputation.[9] (The accusation of greed was unfounded; Manchester would eventually donate more than a million dollars in royalties from *The Death of a President* to the Kennedy Library.)[10]

As 1966 drew to a close Bobby talked about getting out of the United States for a time; the struggles of the past few months had left him tired and dispirited.[11] "I gotta get out of the country," he told friends.[12] A European itinerary was soon put together. The trip, a combination of business and pleasure, would give him a chance to see old friends like the Radziwills, Rudolf Nureyev, and Margot Fonteyn.[13] There was a lunch at Blenheim with the Duke of Marlborough; a dinner party in Paris given by Hervé Alphand, the former French Ambassador to the United States, and his wife, Nicole (Pierre Cardin, Shirley MacLaine, and Catherine Deneuve were among the guests); dinner with Candice Bergen at a cozy little place on the Left Bank; drinks with Elizabeth Taylor and Richard Burton in Rome; and a shopping tour with Contessa Crespi.[14] There was, too, a series of obligatory calls on heads of state and other movers and shakers in the highest political and diplomatic circles. During the course of the trip Bobby met Prime Minister Wilson, President de Gaulle, Ambassador Bohlen, Chancellor Kiesinger, Mayor Brandt, Premier Moro, Cardinal Cicognani, and the Pope.[15]

The Idea of Community

THUS THE PUBLIC life of a powerful American Senator thirty years ago. What of the intellectual life, the life of the mind? Bobby has consistently been celebrated by his admirers as one of the most creative political personalities of his day, a man whose capacity for intellectual growth distinguished him from the other politicians of the period. "Most people," Tony Lewis said, "acquire certainties as they grow older; he *lost* his."[16] Bobby "grew" more than anyone Lewis had ever known. Arthur Schlesinger said that Bobby possessed to an "exceptional degree" what T. S. Eliot called an "experiencing nature," one that permitted him to respond to the turbulence of his times "more directly and sensitively than any other political leader of the era."[17] Jack Newfield was awed by Bobby's "capacity to grow and change"; he contrasted it with the less credible transformations undergone by Nixon, Reagan, and Dole: "Below the surface of these packaged politicians," Newfield said, "there was no authentic growth."[18] We have, in a previous chapter, seen how Bobby believed that a crisis of confidence lay at the heart of the tragedy of the ghetto (as well as of many other places in American society), and we have seen that he further believed that this deficit in self-confidence could be made good only through the compassion of others. But quite obviously he himself could not visit every slum; he could not touch the life of every person who had been scarred by pain or seared by terrible experience. He could not personally persuade each drug addict, each delinquent, each hardened criminal, each teenage mother, that he or she had been created in God's image, and had a life that was worth living. He needed to find some more comprehensive dispensary of hope and affirmation, needed to find a broader means of effecting the "cure through love" that he envisioned.

During much of 1966 he was still groping toward a solution. His notes in committee show him struggling with the question of how to formulate a comprehensive response to what he called the "pathology of the ghetto." It was not simply a matter of creating self-confident and self-reliant citizens in the inner city. It was, in a more important sense, a matter of demonstrating that the nineteenth-century tradition of liberal individualism, the tradition of Emerson and Lincoln, was not an anachronistic one. According to critics of liberal individualism, the cult of the individual had no place in twentieth-century American life.[19] The nineteenth century's faith in the powers of an archetypical "American Adam," with his limitless horizons, his extensive opportunities, his relative freedom from restraint and coercion, had ceased to be compelling in the more complicated world of the twentieth century.[20] The early-nineteenth-century American, it was argued, was far freer to shape his destiny than his twentieth-century counterpart; he was not beholden, as his twentieth-century descendant was, to institutions over which he had no control; he was not at the mercy of vast corporations, a larger and more intrusive government bureaucracy, an educational establishment for whose credentials he must pay dearly if he was to have any hope of success. In this larger, more impersonal, more bureaucratic world, the typical American had far less opportunity than the free and unshackled "American Adam" of Tocqueville's time; hence the need for a neo-feudal welfare state presided over by benevolent technocrats.

Were its critics right? Was the nineteenth-century tradition of liberal individualism an archaic throwback to an America that no longer existed? Only sentimentality could make us think so. The railroad-building, factory-creating nation that gave the world Emerson and Lincoln was not an overgrown village. Americans in the early nineteenth century were oppressed by many of the same confidence-killing things that weigh upon them so heavily today. They, too, felt the pressure of mortgages, bills, employers, and tax collectors. In *Walden* (1854) Thoreau wrote that on applying to the assessors at Concord he was

> surprised to learn that they cannot at once name a dozen in the town who own their farms free and clear. If you would know the history of these homesteads, inquire at the bank where they are mortgaged. The man who has actually paid for his farm with labor on it is so rare that every neighbor can point to him. . . . What has been said of the merchants, that a very large majority, even ninety-seven in a hundred, are sure to fail, is equally true of farmers. With regard to the merchants, however, one of them says pertinently that a great part of their failures are not genuine pecuniary failures, but merely failures to fulfill their engagements, because it is inconvenient; that is, the moral character breaks down. But this puts an infinitely worse face on the matter, and suggests, beside, that probably not even the other three succeed in saving their souls, but are perchance bankrupt in a worse sense than those who fail honestly. Bankruptcy and repudiation are the spring-boards from which much of our civilization vaults and turns its somersaults.[21]

America was always a nation of desperate men. The very things that do so much to undermine our spirits and sap our confidence today existed, in only a slightly different form, a hundred and fifty years ago. Mortgages, debt, bankruptcy, the interest rate, the necessity of making a living, the necessity of paying taxes did as much to limit freedom of action and inhibit the development of a self-confident attitude toward the world in the nineteenth century as they do today. Social class, ancestry, and religious affiliation were often a far heavier burden then. If the world is more complex today, it is no more antipathetic to the individual's desire to express himself freely and self confidently in it. And yet there was, Bobby knew, an important difference between Emerson's world—the world of the early and middle nineteenth century—and our own. A hundred and fifty years ago the confidence-crippling effects of bills, mortgages, debts, tuition, and taxes were mitigated by an institution that we in the twentieth century have allowed to fall into disrepair and desuetude—or so Bobby argued. He argued that our contemporary civilization, in destroying the small communities and neighborhoods that once flourished in the land, robbed us of the very things that had once made Americans such a spectacularly self-confident people. In destroying the close-knit civic units, the little platoons to which Americans had once belonged, and which had once given them comfort in the midst of their desperation, our modern civilization had destroyed the very things that had once sustained and nurtured self-reliant citizens.[22] Bobby concluded that if Americans were, in the middle of the twentieth century, suffering more acutely from feelings of anxiety and worthlessness than they had in the past, it was in part because they no longer lived in the kind of communities that had once given them a sense of stability, a sense of order, a sense of belonging, a sense that there existed around them a network of friends, neighbors, churches, clubs, and associations to which they could turn for help and guidance, and that could in turn lift up their spirits and stimulate in them a feeling of confidence in their powers.

The individual and the community were closely connected in Bobby's mind: a compassionate community could liberate an individual from his crippling pain, and so give him a degree of control over his destiny; liberated individuals, in turn, could contribute to the vitality of the community that had nurtured them. Bobby believed that participation in the life of the community worked to awaken the soul, stimulate the moral sense, and strengthen self-confidence. The question he asked in 1966 was how a sense of community could be restored in America's neighborhoods, how people could be made to feel again a sense of "larger common purpose."[23] How, Bobby wondered, was it possible to tap the "nucleus of leadership and community concern" that existed in even such a place as Bedford-Stuyvesant, a "decaying, dying city," the "worst slum" in America, a place where thirty percent of the housing was classified as deteriorating or dilapidated, a place where the rates of crime, venereal disease, alcoholism, and infant mortality were far above national and even New York City averages?[24]

The mechanism upon which he eventually settled was the community development corporation.[25] The prototypical community development corporation was the Bedford-Stuyvesant restoration project itself. Bobby outlined the basic theory of these corporations during the Ribicoff hearings in August 1966, when he took the "unusual step" of testifying before a subcommittee of which he himself was a member.[26] In testimony in which he quoted Aristotle and Lewis Mumford, Bobby lamented the destruction of the "thousand invisible strands of common experience and respect which tie men to their fellows."[27] He lamented the decline of the "civic pride" and "human dialogue" that enabled each citizen to feel his "own human significance in the accepted association and companionship of others."[28] "The whole history of the human race, until today," Bobby declared, had "been the history of community." But community was now "disappearing," disappearing "at a time when its sustaining strength" was "badly needed."[29] An older America, an America in which "the values of nature and community and local diversity" found "their nurture in the smaller towns and rural areas," had vanished; it had been replaced by a bigger and more impersonal world, one in which Americans were condemned to live their lives "among stone and concrete, neon lights and an endless flow of automobiles." Detached from the vital warmth of community, men became "more and more both perpetrators and victims of coldness, cruelty, and violence."[30]

> Bigness, loss of community, organizations grown far past the human scale—these [Bobby declared] are the besetting sins of the twentieth century, which threaten to paralyze our very

capacity to act . . . our ability to preserve the traditions and values of our past.[31]

All Americans, he declared, had "suffered somewhat the loss of personal identity" brought about by "the disintegration of the neighborhood as the basic unit of local democracy."[32] Even the affluent "child of the suburbs" had "suffered from the loss of community":

> He lives, after all, in a vast bedroom, removed by ribbons of concrete from the city, where his father's work and the cultural and social amenities that are the heart of community life are located. He, too, suffers as he grows up from a sense of being unable to be an active, determining force in his own life.[33]

And yet if suicide, drugs, and delinquency had come to the suburbs, still it was the "child of the ghetto" who "suffered most" from the loss of community.[34] The ghetto child was "the prisoner" of a "vast, gray, undifferentiated slum, isolated physically and in every other way from the rest of the city and its resources."[35] Only by restoring a sense of community in the ghettos could Americans hope to create the self-confidence that would lead to economic self-sufficiency there; only by creating a sense of civic pride in the inner city could Bobby's entrepreneurial vision of bringing "the people of the ghetto into full participation in the economy" be realized.[36]

Under Bobby's plan members of the community would themselves control the community development corporation; the corporation, in turn, was charged with attracting employers to the area, putting unemployed citizens to work rebuilding neighborhoods, and doing what it could to engender a sense of civic pride in the community as a whole. Unlike many advocates of community (e.g., Rousseau), Bobby did not believe that civic spirit was incompatible with private enterprise. On the contrary, he hoped that a strong community would attract private investment, and that this investment would in turn lead to the creation of jobs that would give purpose and meaning to the lives of the community's citizens. "We must," he said, "combine the best of community action with the best of the private enterprise system."[37] Government funds in the form of an "initial grant of capital" would be necessary to jump-start the project. But "for their ongoing activities [the community development corporations] should need and receive no significantly greater subsidy than is ordinarily available to nonprofit housing corporations under present law."[38] Community development corporations could not "and should not be owned or managed by Government, by the rules and regulations of bureaucracy, hundreds of miles away."[39] Bobby was hopeful that, once the essential viability of the program was demonstrated, private capital would play the most important part in the project.[40] (The number of overlapping agencies to which the Bedford-Stuyvesant community development corporation was forced to apply for initial funds and approvals was itself an indication of just how bloated the bureaucratic state had become; the Department of Labor, HEW, HUD, the Office of Economic Opportunity, the Small Business Administration, the Economic Development Administration, the Model Cities Program, the Lease Guarantee Program, the Federal Housing Administration, and the City of New York each had some measure of jurisdiction over the project).[41]

To cover start-up costs, the Bedford-Stuyvesant community development corporation sought, and eventually obtained, $7 million in "special impact" funds for a construction and training program. ("Special impact" funds could be obtained only where there was a likelihood that such funds would lead to "private investment" and the creation of "for-profit enterprises" in a particular area; Bobby and Jacob Javits had themselves sponsored the legislation creating the "special impact" program in 1966.[42]) Special impact funds were to be used to teach unemployed, underconfident residents of Bedford-Stuyvesant how to restore old houses and build new ones; the process of construction would itself function, Walinsky observed, as a "social change lever."[43] The act of building houses would provide Bedford-Stuyvesant's citizens with the best as well as the most productive kind of therapy. Bobby hoped that the Bedford-Stuyvesant community development corporation would serve as a model of how to enlist "the energies and labor of the ghetto" in a "massive program of physical reconstruction," a program of reconstruction "consciously directed at the creation of communities—the building of neighborhoods in which residents can take pride, in which they have a stake."[44] It was a good idea; the problem lay in unsympathetic labor unions that did not like to see their monopoly on construction in New York challenged.[45] By May 1967 the goal of putting people to work building their own houses was in danger of being lost.[46]

During the fall of 1966 Bobby, his staff, and members of the Bedford-Stuyvesant community worked out the details of the Bed-Stuy community development corporation (the organization is now known as "Restoration"). It was necessary to "be vague" about the precise details of the undertaking; it was essential that its inherent drama not be undercut by premature disclosures.[47] The launch of the Bedford-Stuyvesant project was to be what Walinsky called a Kennedy-style blitz in which the element of surprise would be crucial; all the procedures that had brought the Kennedys victory in the past—secrecy, organization, careful preparation, and, as the decisive moment drew nearer, a massive investment of time and energy—were to be scrupulously followed.[48] The planning and preparation would culminate in what Walinsky called "a month of intensive effort" in anticipation of the launch date. To students of Kennedy tactics this "intensive-concentration" method was familiar enough; Bobby and Jack had pioneered it during the 1960 campaign and perfected it during the crises of Jack's presidency—the Bay of Pigs, the Berlin Wall, the missile crisis, Oxford, Mississippi. The Kennedys, Walinsky said in a memorandum to Bobby, were masters at developing "the urgent sense of concentration that great enterprises require." The tactics that had worked against Khrushchev and Ross Barnett would work against urban poverty; these tactics could pay off, Walinsky said, "where lesser efforts go piddling."[49] Walinsky urged Bobby not to go abroad in November or December 1966; Bedford-Stuyvesant would need his undivided attention during those months. The point, the young staffer said, "was to build an organization" that, in a single month in 1966, could "begin to make demonstrable progress towards rebuilding" a community.[50]

Walinsky advised Bobby to "maintain contact with Lindsay" in the weeks preceding the "crash effort" but to withhold the key dates from him; by surprising Lindsay and other officials, the Kennedy team would throw its rivals off balance.[51] The urban crisis had become a hot political topic; each politician had his own preferred solution, and none was above stealing the best features of a competitor's program. Javits was busy pushing his own ideas; after Bobby completed his August testimony, Javits hectored him about the inferiority of the community development corporation concept to proposals he had put forward.[52] When the Ribicoff hearings resumed at the end of November 1966, Edelman urged Bobby to "hit as many witnesses as possible" with the community development corporation idea and contrast it with the "monolithic" federal approaches favored by Javits and Ribicoff.[53]

In October the Senator made a final decision to go ahead with the project.[54] On December 10, 1966, the mighty and the humble gathered together in the auditorium of Public School 305 on Monroe Street in Bedford-Stuyvesant.[55] Lindsay was there, and so was (an undoubtedly envious) Javits.[56] Bobby began his speech with a quotation and a question: " 'If men do not build,' asks the poet, 'how shall they live?' "[57] It is difficult today to comprehend the optimism that prevailed during the early days of the Bedford-Stuyvesant project; there was a sense among all involved that they were participants in a "pioneering effort" to remake the ghetto, that they could transform an impoverished slum into what Bobby called a "self-reliant community."[58]

The optimism soon faded. It was not that the program failed; indeed, it can today boast of important achievements. But neither was its success as great as its promoters hoped; Bedford-Stuyvesant did not solve the problem of the ghetto. Would it have been more successful if Bobby had lived? Perhaps. Kennedy aides William vanden Heuvel and Milton Gwirtzman said that the "most important element in Bedford-Stuyvesant's survival was Kennedy's own involvement."[59] But, of course, the whole point of the project was to demonstrate that the ghetto did *not* need the help of a Kennedy in order to flourish; it was supposed to be able to make progress on its own. It was not Bobby's death that created problems for Bedford-Stuyvesant, it was the project's reliance on the efficacy of a single fundamental idea. The Bedford-Stuyvesant restoration project was premised on the idea of community, and that idea has had a troubled history.

14

$\equiv\!\infty\!\equiv$

THE BELIEF THAT MEN MUST REVIVE A SENSE OF COM-
munity is among the oldest in the intellectual's repertoire of ideas,
and has over the centuries been the cause of uncounted elegiac
laments and prophetic exhortations. Bobby was not the first statesman to call for the restoration of community; if we are to evaluate
his program, we must see it in the context of the larger intellectual
tradition to which it belonged.

The roots of the communitarian creed are ultimately Hellenic;
the prototypical ideal of its communicants is the Greek polis. Aristotle described the essential philosophy that underlay the cult in
a few pregnant passages in the *Politics*. Man, he declared in that
treatise, was a *zoon politikon;* he was, that is, a political animal, a
creature of a polis. Aristotle was a dispassionate philosopher, an
objective student of natural phenomena; in describing man as a political animal, he believed that he was stating a scientific fact. But
the attitude of the typical Hellene toward the polis in which he
lived was, if the ancient commentators are to be believed, anything
but dispassionate. The polis, in Aristotle's words, made possible life
on a "plane" that was neither too high nor too low for "the divine
element of human nature." Man was neither a beast nor a god; but
he yet possessed an element of divinity within him, and only by
participating in the life of the polis—only by offering up "liturgies"
in its name, sacrificing to its gods, attending to its public business,

and participating in the purifying spectacles of the comic and the tragic drama—only by doing these things could he fully realize the divinity lodged within him. The typical Hellene was, we are told, devoted to his city, and the special quality of his devotion made a lasting impression upon the imagination of the West.

Intellectuals have never succeeded in reconciling themselves to the decline of Athens; and ever since the demise of that splendid city they have never ceased to lament the death of public virtue. Sophisticated Romans living in the age of empire, enamored of the old Hellenic ideal of community, lamented the corruption of their own once-virtuous city, and looked back wistfully to a golden age when citizens supposedly possessed a high purpose in life, lived on friendly terms with their neighbors, and spent their days contributing to the welfare of the res publica. A thousand years after the fall of the Western Empire, European intellectuals rediscovered the city-states of antiquity; they contrasted the virtue of Rome and Sparta with the mean and selfish spirit of their own times. Machiavelli lived in what we all know to have been one of the most brilliant ages man has ever known, and yet he cursed Fortuna for having been born in the midst of the Renaissance. He cursed the "malignity of the time": in it one came across nothing "but extreme misery, infamy, and contempt"; all was "besmirched by filth of every kind."[1] It was, of course, an age of genius: Machiavelli himself knew Leonardo. Leonardo's plan to divert the Arno, and deprive Pisa of it, seized Machiavelli's imagination, and he used all of his influence at Florence to get the plan accepted.[2] But if Machiavelli admired the scientific genius of Leonardo, he admired it not as a thing worthy in itself, nor even as a thing instrumental in the discovery of truth. He admired it as a means of realizing those communitarian ideals that he cherished—those ideals of public virtue, civic glory, and republican heroism, which were the central passions of his life.

The same communitarian ideal that inspired the Renaissance sages inspired their counterparts in the seventeenth and eighteenth centuries. Men as different as Milton, Bolingbroke, Rousseau, and Jefferson were each seduced by the idea of community. Jefferson's ideas about community were of particular importance to Bobby. In his book *To Seek a Newer World* Bobby noted Jefferson's belief that "the salvation of the Republic" lay in "the regeneration and spread of the principles of the New England townships," communal structures that were in Jefferson's time already beginning to be "overshadowed by growing state governments."[3] To meet the problem, Bobby observed, Jefferson "urged the division of the nation" into a " 'republic of wards'—areas perhaps a fourth the size of a (nineteenth century) county—that would provide for their own elementary schools, a company of militia, their own lower courts, police, and welfare services." Bobby noted with approval Jefferson's assertion that each "ward would thus be a small republic within itself and every man in the State would thus become an acting member of the common government, transacting in person a great portion of its rights and duties, subordinate indeed, yet important, and entirely within his competence."[4]

In recent decades the idea of community has continued to provoke enthusiasm. Critics like Edmund Wilson studied the influence of old-fashioned civic ideas on Robert E. Lee, Justice Holmes, John Jay Chapman, and Woodrow Wilson.[5] Scholars like Lewis Mumford and Edith Hamilton drew from their study of the Greek polis conclusions about the importance of community in modern life. (Mumford testified at the Ribicoff hearings; following Aristotle, he declared that "democracy, in any active sense, begins and ends in communities small enough for their members to meet face to face").[6] During the 1960s a younger generation of scholars that included J. G. A. Pocock, Bernard Bailyn, and Gordon Wood demonstrated the extent to which classical notions of citizenship and community influenced the founders of the American republic. Their researches inspired a number of contemporary theorists of community, among them Amitai Etzioni, Michael Sandel, and Bruce Ackerman. In his second inaugural address President Clinton himself paid homage to the communitarian tradition, declaring that Americans' "greatest responsibility" was to "embrace a new spirit of community."[7] Hillary Clinton's book, the title of which derives from the saying "It takes a village to raise a child," would have made perfect sense to an Athenian, who would have understood it to mean "It takes a polis to make a citizen."

The idea of community is for intellectuals what snake oil used to be for traveling salesmen; there has scarcely been a time, since the dawn of the Renaissance, when a skillful academic or literary charlatan could not earn his bread by peddling the notion of public-spiritedness and palming it off on naive takers. The very complexity of our modern Enlightened world has made men peculiarly suscep-tible to the appeal of a golden age of small villages and pristine republican virtue. But the attractiveness of the communitarian ideal does not make it an intellectually compelling one, and at a distance of thirty years even his most devoted admirers may wonder whether Bobby, in making the communitarian ideal central to his attempts to reinvigorate the ghetto, did not stumble into a blind alley.

It's easy to understand why Bobby should have been attracted to the communitarian tradition. When Aristotle said that men fully become men—that they become indeed partly divine—when they participate actively in the life of their city, when Pericles said that those men who did not participate in the public affairs of Athens were idiots, ciphers, savages, both men were saying, in the idiom of old Greece, that citizenship gives men self-confidence; that it makes them vital, capable, fully developed human beings; that it permits them to realize their highest potential. And this, of course, is pre-cisely what Bobby hoped the restoration of the communitarian idea would accomplish in places like Bedford-Stuyvesant—that it would transform underconfident, underperforming, underdeveloped men and women into self-reliant citizens. But if it was ingenious of Bobby to have made the connection between the communitarian tradition of old Hellas and America's own late-twentieth-century problems, he failed to perceive the extent to which the tradition in which he placed such great faith was a chimerical one.

If community is the snake oil of the intellectuals, it is the opium of disgraced politicians and idealistic dreamers. At no time in history does the ideal res publica of which the communitarian philosophers dreamed seem ever actually to have existed; the extant literature is almost exclusively nostalgic, it is almost exclusively elegiac.[8] The great civic philosophers never celebrate the *existence* of community; they always lament the lack of it. We are shown not virtue, but the memory of it. Neither Sallust, nor Machiavelli, nor Rousseau ever saw, with his own eyes, the ideal communities each of them celebrated in his writings; they could do no more than claim to have discovered, in the uncertain and fragmentary record of the past, dim evidences of a civic felicity that had long since vanished from the earth. Rousseau's description of classical Sparta and Machiavelli's description of early republican Rome belong to the realm of myth and fiction, not of history and fact; they are civic mirages, fantasies that comforted their troubled creators in the midst of difficult lives. Rousseau dwelt, throughout his life, in a world of solipsistic dreams, and after the return of the Medicis to Florence, so, too, did Machiavelli. They escaped a sordid reality and lost themselves in the pages of Livy and Plutarch.[9] Their writings on the idea of community are best regarded as a form of personal therapy, and as such must be treated with the utmost wariness by statesmen who, like Bobby, would resurrect their ideas and put them to a practical use. The community that is at once wholly loved and wholly loving: it doesn't exist and never has existed. (Friedrich von Hayek went so far as to say that it *shouldn't* exist; classical republican politics, he argued, is bad policy.[10]) Bobby, in emphasizing the importance of human dialogue and political participation in the ghetto, accepted the communitarian fiction that these activities necessarily improve and elevate the soul. They don't. Jack Newfield tells us that Bobby admired Tacitus more than any other Roman writer. But he seems to have overlooked the great lesson of Tacitus—that the virtuous republic is a beautiful but impossible thing.[11]

He was concerned with the problem of the unself-confident man and the pain a lack of self-confidence causes. The Enlightenment, so adept at mitigating physical pain, could not alleviate this crippling spiritual or psychological pain. And so Bobby looked beyond the Enlightenment, looked to the creed of the city, the cult of the polis: in the City of Man the unself-confident man lost sight of his own inferiority in the dazzling brightness of his city's reflected glory; he gained a confidence in his public self that he could never have enjoyed in a merely private station. But the transformation of private loser into public winner, however wonderful it might seem, is not always a happy one; we have only to remember the example of Adolf Eichmann to know that this is so. And even if we discount the sinister civic impulses that produced men like Eichmann, the colorless loser who, casting about for a cause or a creed, was on the point of joining a Freemasons' lodge when he decided to join the Nazi Party instead—even if we disregard the darker side of the civic tradition, and forget about Robespierre and Saint-Just—it's not clear that the self-confidence of the wholly civic man, the wholly public man, is a desirable thing.[12] Machiavelli and Rousseau were themselves fascinating, somewhat introverted, highly imaginative men; but the ideal public citizen whom they sketched in their works, a citizen who committed his body and soul to the republic, is an unappealing and curiously rigid figure, a block of marble, a sort of Coriolanus without the psychological scars and aristocratic pride that make Coriolanus interesting. Civic boosterism doesn't give people the kind of self-confidence that's worth having; it gives them instead the banal self-confidence of the bureaucrat and the martinet.

Of Bolingbroke, Alcibiades, and the Jefferson Airplane

FOR THE EPIGRAPH of his book *The Kennedy Imprisonment*, Garry Wills selected Walter Bagehot's précis of the character of Henry St. John, Viscount Bolingbroke, the great eighteenth-century celebrator of community and civic virtue. Bagehot reveals how that notorious statesman combined an acute but superficial brilliance with an inner moral hollowness. Bolingbroke, in Bagehot's view, was a splendid fraud, a dazzling impostor—just like the Kennedys themselves, or so Wills implied. Was Wills right? *Was* Bobby a fraud, an impostor? Did he flirt with the rhetoric of community in the same flippant way he flirted with the radical left, sipped cocktails with Staughton Lynd and Tom Hayden, praised Che Guevara to gullible journalists, and affected to enjoy the music of the Jefferson

Airplane? Perhaps. Perhaps his rhetoric of community was simply one more attempt to demonstrate that he was an "authentic" man, that he was capable of "growth," that he had read McLuhan and mastered the philosophy of Camus. Perhaps his motives *were* bad—as bad as Bolingbroke's, whom Wills thinks the Kennedys so greatly resembled; as bad as Alcibiades', whom Bagehot thought Bolingbroke so greatly resembled.

Whatever the motive that underlay it, the insight that led Bobby to the idea of community was itself a valuable one. Without repudiating the Enlightened world of markets and modernity, Bobby sensed that something was missing. He was sympathetic to the individualist creed of Emerson and Lincoln, but he was also conscious of the shortcomings of that creed. The individualist creed was in some ways a very modern creed, but its strength diminished in direct proportion as it grew apart from the premodern sources of faith that originally sustained it. The individualist creed was in some ways a highly Enlightened creed, but it required something more than reason to make it work. The Enlightened mind tried to understand the soul, as if it were a machine; in doing so, it lost sight of those pre-Enlightened creeds that, without pretending to understand the soul, had nevertheless given it strength, confidence, and the ability to endure pain. In looking to the cult of the polis for a solution to the problem of modern pain—the pain of Bedford-Stuyvesant, the pain of the nation itself—Bobby looked to the wrong pre-Enlightened cult. But the instinct that prompted him was a sound one, and honest.

15

⟨⟨⟨⟨⟩⟩⟩⟩

THREE DECADES LATER THE PICTURES STILL MOVE US: pictures of Bobby roughhousing with his children at Hickory Hill before putting them to bed, or teaching them how to throw a football on the lawn at Hyannis Port, or splashing about with them in the swimming pool at Palm Beach. To call him a family man is to understate the case considerably; so devoted was he to the cause of family, so completely did he identify himself with the interests of his own family, that his father, himself an expert on the making of families, bestowed upon the third son the highest of compliments: "Bobby's a tough one," Joseph Kennedy said in 1957; "he'll keep the Kennedys together, you can bet."[1]

Given the intensity of his belief that the good life finds its fullest expression in family life, it's odd that Bobby should have embraced, in his last years, an ideal that for much of Western history has been at odds with the ideal of family life. To the thinkers of old Greece the family was the great and unworthy rival of the community. The classical myths of community celebrated heroes who, like the first Brutus or the brothers Horatii, sacrificed their families in the name of the City. Plato went so far as to outlaw the family in the ideal state he described in *The Republic*. The tangled, fleshy coils of family were the stuff of tragic poetry, not of communitarian politics; for the Greeks the emergence of the polis represented the triumph of reason and order over the dark passions, the secret lusts, the furious blood feuds of the patriarchal family.

In practice, of course, great families have thrived in the communitarian world of the polis; from the Scipios and Metelluses of Rome to the Adamses and Roosevelts of our own republic, families have played as important a role in the political life of free communities as more formally public institutions like law courts and standing armies. And yet the Greeks were surely right to perceive an antagonism between the community and the family; the two cultures have for most of human history been utterly dissimilar. Until relatively recently women, the great generative force in families, were excluded from the political life of free communities, and the political culture of the Western democracies to this day bears the marks of their exclusion. Women have been queens and empresses for centuries, but not until our own age have they been prime ministers or even voters. Misogyny, a suspicion of women and the claims of family, a fear of the feminine: they are all to be found in the political tradition that descends from the Greek polis. And yet this overt sexism has rarely made a certain kind of Western political animal uncomfortable; it almost certainly, for example, did not trouble Jack Kennedy. American women, Kennedy once wrote, were "either prostitutes or housewives" and in either case did "not play much of a role" in the "cultural or intellectual life" of the country.[2] For him, as for so many men raised on the old classical notions of politics, women were not *meant* to participate in political life; they were, like the children it was their business to bear and raise, a diversion from the serious business of life, a diversion from the masculine avocation of politics. Pericles might while away an idle hour with Aspasia, but afterward he returned to the agora and resumed the manly business of leading Athens.

If men raised in the Western tradition of communitarian politics were not supposed to depend on women for the confidence they needed in order to be political players, Bobby was an exception to the rule. He very obviously *did* depend on women for that confidence; the celebrator of community required in his own life the constant affirming presence of the very sex the communitarians had for so long excluded from their counsels. Women were for Bobby much more than a temporary diversion, a source of merely social or sexual gratification, a necessary adjunct to the light and frivolous side of life. They were an indispensable bulwark of character. As a boy he had been too young to be a companion to his older brothers, to Jack and Joe Junior, and he had spent much of his time in the company of his sisters—so much so that Rose's mother worried that her grandson would become a "sissy."[3] In his teens Bobby developed something more than crushes on girls; he adoringly worshiped the unattainable female in the way that romantic minds sometimes do. The name of one of these Beatrices has even come down to us: she was called Ann Appleton. Doubtless there were others. Bobby's infatuations were in great contrast to Jack's more prosaic attitude toward women; the older brother rapidly penetrated whatever mystery and romance chivalry attributed to the fair sex, and is said to have lost his virginity to a whore. The older brother soon afterward embarked on a long line of somewhat passionless affairs, very different from the series of intense attachments that the younger brother was to form.

He married early: he was twenty-four when he married Ethel Skakel in Greenwich in 1950. (Jack, by contrast, was thirty-six when he married Jacqueline Bouvier in 1953.) Unlike Jack, Bobby did not hesitate to marry; he preferred, perhaps required, the care and attention of a wife, and he was no doubt grateful for a woman's ability to nurture self-confidence and self-respect in those she loved.[4] Ethel helped Bobby to break out of the lonely self-absorption that characterized his adolescence and early manhood; she was as responsible as anyone for the emergence, in the early fifties, of the extraordinarily talented and energetic statesman that Bobby, to the surprise of everyone who knew him, became. Lively, not complicated, and completely in love with him, Ethel drew her husband out of himself, and helped him become the self-confident operator who made even strong men jump, who made Jimmy Hoffa tremble and Lyndon Johnson wince.

His other relationships with women are more difficult to decipher. There was, of course, Marilyn Monroe; even Schlesinger conceded, in his oblique, literary way, that there was a bond between the two, that Bobby, "with his curiosity, his sympathy, his absolute directness of response to distress," "got through" the "glittering mist" that surrounded Monroe "as few did."[5] Jean Kennedy Smith supposedly wrote Monroe a letter in the early sixties in which she joked that "you and Bobby are the new item."[6] But what did the bond amount to? A casual friendship? A passing dalliance? A grand affair? The fragmentary glimpses that history affords are hardly dispositive. A dinner party at Pat and Peter Lawford's Santa Monica beach house in October 1961: Marilyn drank too much champagne, and Bobby and Ed Guthman, concerned for her safety, drove her home.[7] Another dinner party at the Lawford house in February 1962, where among guests who included Kim Novak, Natalie Wood, and Janet Leigh, Marilyn questioned Bobby about his civil rights program and may have taught him how to dance the twist.[8] A party at Arthur Krim's Manhattan penthouse in May 1962, on the evening that Marilyn sang "Happy Birthday" to the President at Madison Square Garden: Bobby dodged about the actress that night "like a moth around the flame," or so Adlai Stevenson remembered.[9] A log of telephone calls from the actress to the Attorney General's office at the Justice Department during the last melancholy summer of Monroe's life.[10] That is all; the rest is speculation, or gossip.[11]

His relationship with his sister-in-law Jacqueline is only slightly less difficult to interpret. He had, while his brother lived, been as solicitous of her as a brother-in-law could be; it was Bobby, after all, not Jack, who rushed to Jacqueline's bedside in Newport in 1956 when she was prematurely delivered of a baby that soon afterward died. (Jack was enjoying himself on a yacht in the Mediterranean and apparently overcame the urge to hurry home.) After the President's death the bond between the two deepened. They spent long hours together beside the fire in Averell Harriman's Georgetown drawing room. They flew to Antigua. (Ethel stayed home.) He was a frequent guest at her Fifth Avenue apartment. Their intimacy has been variously characterized as the chivalrous courtesy a man owed his brother's widow, as a spiritual tutorial in which a latter-day Diotima broadened her pupil's intellectual and moral horizons, even as something more purely Greek: an affair rooted in a tragic and doomed desire to honor a dead beloved brother and husband. Whatever the truth of their relationship, for Bobby it was almost certainly yet another exercise in the all-important business of confidence building. If he gave her the courage to face a new life, she gave him the confidence to read books and poetry and to discuss openly those questions, of life and death and love and suffering, that Kennedys tended to avoid.

And she led him to the Greeks. By putting *The Greek Way* into Bobby's hands, Jacqueline Kennedy introduced her brother-in-law to the tragic poetry that helped him make sense of his own family's sufferings—and put him on the road that led to his discovery of the Hellenic idea of community. The tragic poets of Athens, in celebrating the shame and suffering of the family, point their audience in the direction of a supposedly nobler ideal, that of the polis. The birth of tragedy is the death of family: the death of family as a high ideal, the highest social ideal a man can have. Like the early Greeks, the Kennedys, too, had made family the highest ideal; but now Bobby, an Aeschylus in his hands, was ready to look away from the messy complications of family, was ready to look, as Aeschylus had looked, to the community for salvation instead. The tragedies performed in the shadow of the Acropolis proclaimed the advent of a new dispensation; the soaring city, resplendent in marble, the embodiment of reason and justice, was, the audience was assured, altogether superior to the old ideal of bloodshed in the name of consanguinity. This transition from family politics to polis politics is usually taken to be a sign of progress, one of the West's great leaps forward: instead of being hacked to death by the Furies for murdering his mother, Orestes is, in the final play of Bobby's favorite tragic trilogy, lawfully tried by a tribunal of Athenian citizens. The polis, not the family, emerges victorious in the *Oresteia*. Athens is the real hero of Aeschylus' play, not the discredited House of Atreus. Bobby was himself a member of what Gore Vidal (perhaps only half in jest) called the Riverdale House of Atreus; and, like the fifth-century Greeks, he was ready to look beyond the ideal of family, was ready to embrace the cleaner, less complicated ethos of community.

Had he fallen into a trap? Had the poets led him astray? The blessings of the polis are obvious enough: our notions of law and order, democratic governance, etc., descend from it. Its curse is more subtle, is to be found in the vague and abstract ideal of community—a vapidly defined "common good" or "general will"—that it enshrines, a pleasing ideal that diverts us from the messier realities of life, the messier realities of the family. The enduring themes of family—the sacrifices we must make for our spouses, our children, our parents—are ignored: the great communitarian myth makers, from Plato and Livy to Rousseau and Marx, escape these questions by telling us instead about the sacrifices we must make for our community. The Kennedys were masters of the high rhetoric of community ("Ask not what your country can do for you . . . ," and all that). The problem with their rhetoric lay in its loftiness; many of our most pressing problems exist not at the exalted level of community, but at the humbler level of the family. Families, not communities, are the nurseries of productive citizens.

Why Bobby Couldn't Talk About Family

WHY DID BOBBY, in seeking a solution to America's problems in the sixties, avoid the problems of family? Why did he shrink from the eternal questions of the relations between men and women, their differing needs and desires, their struggle to accommodate these in the institution of marriage, in order that families might flourish? Why did he take refuge instead in a vapid politics of community?

In part because of the tendencies of his times. A politician courting certain liberal constituencies in that era could hardly afford to speak candidly about, say, the problems of the black family; those who tried found themselves accused of insensitivity—and worse. The sixties, too, witnessed the beginnings of a sexual revolution that altered the moral landscape of the West; a politician who proclaimed the importance of what are now called family values would have been perceived as disappointingly old-fashioned. And, of course, the troubled lives of Bobby's own relations prevented him from speaking out frankly on the question of family. He had, it is true, done a better job with his own marriage than any of his brothers had done with theirs, and yet it would still have been difficult for him to talk about the importance, say, of honoring one's marriage vows when such talk would have given reporters yet another excuse to mention the breakdown of Pat's marriage to Peter Lawford, or Steve Smith's philandering, or the loveless marriage of Ted and Joan Kennedy, or Jack Kennedy's satyriasis—or even Bobby's own reported interest in the pretty blondes who filled a number of positions on his staff.[12]

Marriage is by its nature a fragile institution, and the family, though it is the most fundamental, is also among the most delicate of social units. The marital strains experienced by the Kennedys in the 1960s were experienced by millions of others as well: it was for this reason that the Kennedys were in such an ideal position to talk about those strains, strains felt in the impoverished inner-city families that Mr. Moynihan's report described no less than in the prosperous suburban territory charted by Mr. Updike in *Couples* (published the year Bobby died). But any attempt by Bobby to talk about the fragility of families would have done more than cause the press to dredge up tabloid muck: it would have forced him to talk about a subject more taboo even than family.

Religion is, of course, the great bulwark of family. Family and religion were, Schlesinger said, the rocks upon which Bobby's own Irish forebears had built their new life in America.[13] Bobby, however, was reluctant to talk about religion in public, even though religion meant a great deal to him in his own private life. It is too bad. Without religion, the institution of marriage—the foundation of family life—is no longer the product of vows made solemnly before God; it is just another contract, less binding, even, than a mortgage obligation.

The Other Tradition

ONE BEGINS TO understand, then, why Bobby should have over-looked a tradition that, unlike the communitarian tradition of ancient Hellas, does form a part of our heritage and our traditions. One begins to understand why he should have overlooked those institutions that have always exerted a degree of influence in our communities, and have shown an unparalleled ability to deal compassionately with the individual human soul. The temper of the times was against it; for Bobby there could be no alliance between church and state in the war against poverty.

The potential inherent in the churches, the synagogues, and the mosques, with their deep roots in the community soil, with their traditions of compassion and charity, with their capacity to nourish not only the body, but also the soul, was, of course, always very great; it would be difficult to conceive of a more effective agency than religion for dispensing hope to the hopeless. Jonathan Kozol has shown us how much these places mean in the poorest neighborhoods in America. "In one of the most diseased and dangerous communities of any city in the Western world," Kozol wrote of the Mott Haven section of the Bronx, "the beautiful old stone church on St. Ann's Avenue is a gentle sanctuary from the terrors of the streets outside."[14] To go there, he says, is to be immediately aware of the "presence of small children." "They seem to be everywhere: in the garden, in the hallways, in the kitchen, in the chapel, on the stair."[15]

So-called faith-based rescue programs, programs that emphasize religious notions of love, compassion, and individual self-worth, have demonstrated a remarkable ability to help people without homes, jobs, or both, gain the kind of confidence in themselves that leads to the rebuilding of shattered lives.[16] These programs have rescued thousands of men and women from dependence, addiction, and despair and guided them to lives of self-reliance and self-respect.[17] Even without the benefit of federal subsidies—for the federal government has until recently refused to support "faith-based" programs—the churches, the synagogues, and the mosques have done more to *improve* the lives of the downtrodden (as opposed to merely perpetuating their miserable status quo) than a host of federal welfare programs. If these institutions, rather than the dreary welfare office, could have been made the focal point for the distribution of some part of the nation's public charity and compassion, who knows what the result might have been? For once the government might have done something to remedy the problems of poverty, homelessness, and unemployment that continue to plague the inner city without erecting a vast (and expensive) federal infrastructure to do so, for, of course, the bricks and mortar are already there. There are churches in every neighborhood in America, and synagogues and mosques in many of them. But the jealous tenets and petty animosities of the Enlightenment have been taken, in America, to their ultimate conclusions, their furthest extreme, and we have been led to believe that any cooperation between government and religion, whether in the education of children, the maintenance of public morals, or the feeding and clothing of the poor, will be fatal to the principles of our coldly secular state, and will inevitably set us on the road to the dictatorship of a theocracy.

The idea that government might usefully cooperate with religion, and provide the churches, the synagogues, the mosques, with a portion of those funds that now course through the byzantine channels of the federal welfare bureaucracy, would have been dismissed out of hand by even the most open-minded reformers of the sixties as a prima facie violation of the First Amendment. To be sure, government agencies have in the past helped to fund certain charitable programs sponsored by churches, but in order to qualify for these funds, such programs have typically been required to eliminate the very faith-based elements that account for their astonishing success.[18] A federally funded faith-based rescue program would almost certainly fail the Supreme Court's *Lemon* test, so called because of a 1971 case, *Lemon v. Kurtzman*, in which the Court held that government subsidies that "advance or inhibit" religion are unconstitutional.[19] Bobby, contemptuous though he eventually became of much of the conventional wisdom of his day, could not break with the liberal consensus on so delicate a point as this. Although the arguments against the cooperation between church and state in the war on poverty were singularly unpersuasive, any attempt by Bobby to move very far in that direction would have cost him critical support in his own party. He would have been crucified, not indeed upon the altar of the First Amendment, but upon the altar of that frigid, fanatical ideal of absolute secularism that the First Amendment has been twisted into meaning.[20]

The Cross or the Capitol

EMERSON DID NOT dwell on the problem of failure in American life. His friend Thoreau did; Thoreau did not shrink from exposing the quiet desperation that underlies so many apparently solid, placid, respectable American lives. Emerson shrank from the oppressive reality. The world of second mortgages, compound interest, the lost job, the unfulfilling career, the wrecked marriage: it was unreal to him. "But when you have chosen your part," Emerson said, "abide by it, and do not weakly try to reconcile yourself with the world." Fair enough. But what of those men and women who, though unreconciled to the world, fail in their attempt to stand up to it, and are crushed by the power of those "badges and names," those "large societies and dead institutions," that Emerson chastises us for too easily capitulating to? What comfort can Emerson give *them?* Their money back? An autographed copy of "Self-Reliance"? A subscription to Dale Carnegie's course? Melville was only the first critic to perceive how perilously close the apostle of self-confidence came to being just another riverboat confidence man.[21]

The great virtue of religion, of course, is not so much its ability to help men succeed, although, of course, it *can* help them succeed. The great virtue of religion lies in its ability to console men in the midst of failure, to permit them to function even in the midst of despair. Bobby, however, was curiously oblivious of the consoling powers of religion. If he was a devout Catholic, he was also a troubled one. He "did not talk much about religion," vanden Heuvel and Gwirtzman report.[22] He found his "primary solace in Greek impressions of character and fate," Schlesinger says.[23] He continued to be a practicing Catholic. But he was uneasy in his faith.[24]

Part of the problem was politics. Bobby believed that the Church was too conservative, that it was out of touch with contemporary life. Hugh Carey told him that the Church was a "problem" in Brooklyn, and Bobby at once accepted the revelation as true.[25] Bobby told Pope Paul VI that the Church was a "reactionary force" in Los Angeles.[26] He wondered "why the kids who came out of parochial school" were "so conservative."[27] Though he regularly attended Mass, and wore a St. Christopher medal round his neck, the ancient traditions of his faith seemed to mean little to him; he was always urging the Church to become more "contemporary" in its orientation.[28] He welcomed those Vatican II reforms that did so much to undermine a number of the Church's oldest traditions. Bobby, the sympathetic celebrant of the cult of the polis, saw much less practical or spiritual value in the creed that had vanquished paganism and erected the banner of the Cross on the ruins of the Capitol. The deep piety of his boyhood was gone; he had become a secular man, one who was instinctively attracted to Greek ideals of citizenship and patriotism. The City of Man appealed to him in a way that the City of God did not. A Catholic from habit, he was a Greek by inclination, and to the end of his life remained curiously blind to the transformative power of religion. When in 1966 he set about asking the Paleys and Dillons of the world for help in Bedford-Stuyvesant, he neglected to call the bishop of Brooklyn. The bishop "very badly wanted to help," according to a 1966 memorandum from Walinsky to Bobby. But he had not been asked to.[29]

I wonder whether there was not another reason why Bobby should have been ambivalent about the social virtues of religion. He had seen, in his mother's life, the ability of religion not only to console but also to detach, to isolate. Perhaps it had been in Rose's nature to incline toward solitude, to be always, in Red Fay's words, "out of the loop," a "very lonely person," one who spent many hours by herself walking on the beach or lost in prayerful reverie.[30] Perhaps her powerful husband, so adept at encouraging his children, had failed sufficiently to encourage her—failed to encourage her to develop those social impulses that had rather touchingly manifested themselves, when she was young, in her "Ace of Clubs," a social group dedicated to the social and intellectual improvement of its members.[31] Whatever the cause of Rose's tendency to solipsism, she found, in religion, an excuse for indulging it more fully than was healthy, found in it an excuse for evading the world rather than coming to terms with it. The variety of religious faith with which Bobby was most familiar was his mother's, and her example must at times have made him doubt whether the creed that dominated her life was indeed the ideal one to draw people out into the world and give them the strength to act confidently in it.

Bobby did not break with all the Enlightened dogmas of his age. It was achievement enough to have broken with some. Like Disraeli before him, he found in the pre-Enlightened past the inspiration for a modern politics of compassion, and he softened the dogmas of nineteenth-century liberal individualism by recognizing how necessary it was to preserve certain of the older traditions of the West. Disraeli (and the other partisans of the Young England movement, of which he was the most illustrious representative) had hoped that religion might serve as the basis for a modern politics of compassion; in his novel *Tancred* Disraeli declared that Englishmen must look upon the Church of England as the "main remedial agency" in the "present state" of crisis: only the Church, he said, could supply the "machinery" by which "results might be realised."[32] Bobby, of course, looked not to religion for results, but to community, to the ancient Hellenic tradition of the polis. Although that choice seems now to have been a mistaken one, it should not be permitted to detract from the man's larger achievement, that of demonstrating how pre-Enlightenment traditions could be made the inspiration for a post-Enlightenment politics.

16

━◦⟨◦⟩◦━

Early in 1967 there were rumors that Hanoi had changed its position on negotiations with the United States; that it had dropped its insistence that a series of improbable conditions be met before it would come to the bargaining table; and that it was now insisting upon a single condition, that the United States halt its aerial bombardment of targets in the north. Bobby, in Paris at the end of his European tour, heard as much from Etienne Manac'h, an official in the Ministère des Affaires étrangères who was in close communication with the North Vietnamese Mission at Paris. Bobby was accompanied to his meeting in the Quai d'Orsay by an American diplomat, John Gunther Dean, who concluded that the French official's source was important enough to warrant a cable to Washington. Upon returning to the embassy, Dean dispatched a report to his superiors at the State Department. By the time Bobby's airplane touched down in the United States, the story was out: the North Vietnamese had made an important peace overture through the unlikely channel of a French diplomat and an American Senator in Paris.[1]

President Johnson believed that any indication of America's eagerness for peace threatened to upset his prosecution of the war; in a meeting with Bobby a few days after the "peace feeler" story broke, he accused the Senator of having himself informed the newspapers of his conversations in the Quai d'Orsay. Bobby denied it; he said that the President's own State Department was responsible for the press reports. "It's not *my* State Department, goddamn it," the President replied. "It's *your* State Department."[2] A presidential tirade followed. "I'll destroy you and every one of your dove friends in six months," Johnson said. "You'll be dead politically in six months." *Time* magazine claimed that Bobby responded to Johnson's threats by calling the President a son of a bitch to his face. But this was apparently an exaggeration. Bobby did, however, tell the President that he did not have to "take" the kind of abuse to which the President was subjecting him.[3]

Was Bobby, as President Johnson maintained, a "dove" on the question of Vietnam? One might more accurately say that he was continuing to press, as he had pressed in the past, for a political solution to the conflict—a negotiated peace, a settlement along the lines of the one that Averell Harriman had negotiated for his brother in Laos half a decade before. At their February meeting Bobby urged the President to halt the bombing of targets in the north, agree to a series of cease-fire arrangements, and permit the presence in South Vietnam of international peacekeeping troops, which in time could replace the American forces stationed there. But he failed to persuade the President to adopt these proposals. ("There just isn't a chance in hell that I will do that," Johnson said, "not the slightest chance."[4]) Privately Bobby wondered whether there was any point in even trying to work constructively with the President. The two men had, Schlesinger said, "reached the end of the road."[5]

While continuing to advocate a political settlement, Bobby began to denounce the war with a passion and a zeal that had been absent from his earlier pronouncements. In the Senate he rose to condemn the "horror" of the war, and he asserted that every American was morally responsible for the chemicals that scarred Vietnamese children and the bombs that destroyed Vietnamese villages. He said that what Americans were "doing to the Vietnamese" was "not very different than [*sic*] what Hitler did to the Jews." Critics, among them Richard Nixon, accused him of "prolonging the war by encouraging the enemy" and denounced him for using Vietnam to further his own ambitions.[6] Bobby himself was undaunted.

The Less Courageous Act

THE MELANCHOLY SPRING of 1967 gave way to a hot and violent summer. Deadly riots in Newark were followed by still deadlier riots in Detroit, and there were violent clashes in the streets of Boston, New Haven, Cincinnati, Milwaukee, and Tampa. In a distressing turn of events, civil unrest occurred even in cities that had made extensive use of Great Society urban aid programs.[7] President Johnson responded to the crisis by appointing a commission to investigate the underlying causes of the violence. Governor Otto Kerner of Illinois was made chairman, and a number of Stimsonian respectables (John Lindsay, Cyrus Vance) were appointed to give it an air of credibility. Bobby doubted whether it would do any good.[8] The cities were crying out in pain, and so even were the suburbs. It was a time of "social hemorrhaging," Joan Didion wrote, "of commonplace reports of casual killings and misplaced children and abandoned homes and vandals who misspelled even the four-letter words they scrawled."[9] It was unlikely that yet another assemblage of wise men could do anything to remedy the deeper evils that had taken root in the country.

Although the events of the summer confirmed Bobby's view of the seriousness of the crisis of the ghetto, he did not pique himself on his prescience. The cities had ceased to be his principal concern. Adam Walinsky was wrong: the ghetto would not carry him to the heights. Never again in his career would Bobby display such boldness of conception, such originality of thought, such richness of imagination, such contempt for established opinion, as he did when he challenged the welfare state. But that act of rebellion, however courageous it might have been, did not bring him the glory he craved. It was the decidedly lesser act of opposing the war in Vietnam that made him into a hero and a presidential candidate.

The Pleasures of Empire

MORE THAN FIFTEEN years had passed since he and Jack Kennedy had visited Vietnam together. In 1951 the two brothers had made a grand tour of the Orient, and French Indochina had been among the last stops on their itinerary. The disaster of Dien Bien Phu was still in the future, and it was the corrupt and romantic Saigon of Graham Greene's *The Quiet American* that the young Kennedys encountered: ceiling fans and drinks at the Continental, vermouth cassis and gunfire in the night, silk-trousered figures moving with grace through the humid noon, and golden rice fields shimmering in the late-afternoon sun.[10] It was, for both of them, an introduction to the pleasures of empire. The faults of the American Empire have been copiously cataloged; its pleasures have never been properly documented. Which is odd: those pleasures had a good deal more to do with its success than any number of diplomatic cables and State Department white papers. Since Virgil's time men have complained at tedious length of the burdens of empire, but few who have stared empire in the face have had the presence of mind to refuse its pleasures. The hope of gain, the love of power, the feeling of self-importance, are only a part of the explanation of empire; the other part has always lain in the pleasure man takes in strange and exotic things.

Ever since Alexander went east in the name of glory and conquest, the imperial man has found pleasure not merely in the strangeness of Persepolis, or even in the release from the burdens of his own civilization that life in a remote capital and a distant province affords. He has derived pleasure, too, from the experience of being, in a strange place, an exotic being himself, a sahib, a great man among little people, a lord among the coolies: thus Lawrence in Arabia, Clive in India, Kurtz in central Africa. Sojourns in the world's backwaters have brought out the patrician instinct latent even in very egalitarian natures. In his mind the egalitarian man may be committed to the principles of the democratic civilization he represents, but in his heart the sahib loves the feeling of being superior to the simpler, less complicated, more primitive beings whose pressing poverty surrounds him. The most innocent traveler is sensible of the gulf that separates him from the mass of humanity that sends forth the men and women who make his bed, polish his shoes, and mix his drinks. The less innocent traveler is not only sensible of this gulf, he thrives on it.

Nowhere is the complicated allure of the exotic more evident than in the farthest reaches of the East, where in the humid and fragrant air a belief in the white man's burden merges easily and ineluctably into a belief in the white man's prerogative, and where in the tropical heat the essential rightness of democracy becomes indistinguishable from the essential rightness of a vermouth cassis at the Continental. In *Lord Jim* Conrad described how corrupting was the effect of the East on a certain type of European man. Such a man at first became attached "to the eternal peace of the Eastern sky and sea," to the "softness of the sky," to the "languor of the earth," to the "bewitching breath of the Eastern waters"; at last he became addicted to the simple "distinction of being white."[11] In *A Passage to India*, Forster depicted Englishmen who at Chandrapore were as "little gods" in their smooth-skinned whiteness; he described how painful it was for these pink-faced divinities to retire to little suburban villas in England, where they lived out their lives far removed from their former glory.[12] Nor was the hierarchical Englishman alone in being susceptible to the bewitching mixture of sensual charm and native subservience of the East; the egalitarian American was not less susceptible. Alden Pyle, the quiet American of Greene's story, annoys the jaded journalist Fowler precisely because he is so authoritarian a democrat; when Pyle speaks of liberty, he does so in the patronizing manner of one who has been bred up on principles of noblesse oblige. Joseph Alsop was in love not simply with Chinese silk and porcelain, but with the memory of a place where he had been more fully an aristocrat than he could ever be— than anyone could ever be—in the United States. Even the prosaic McNamara succumbed to the East's flattering charm; in an otherwise colorless memoir of the Vietnam era he dwelt uncharacteristically on the poetry of the place, on the whirring ceiling fans of the Presidential Palace and on the beauty of Madame Nhu, a woman who knew well enough how to charm the Western man by making him feel important, potent, desirable. A few years ago I chanced to read an unpublished manuscript by a man who as a young State Department officer in the early sixties had been posted to Saigon to assist the Ambassador. Like Alsop, McNamara, Pyle, and all the others, he had quite obviously become a victim, a victim of the most pathetic kind. I suppose even a more stoical soul than he was would have found it difficult *not* to be carried away by the pleasures of that vanished world, by the sensation of being a member of the charmed circle to which one's status as an American, a diplomat, and a white man gave one an automatic entrée. It was all plainly, ingenuously there: the games of tennis with the powerful, the unending round of garden parties and grand meals with the local elite, the diplomatic intrigue, the exhilarating sensation of participating in matters of high state, the obligatory affair with a beautiful Vietnamese woman, a femme fatale on the model of Madame Nhu. The manuscript made it abundantly clear that the burdens of empire had become indistinguishable from its pleasures, that the empire was about something more than power—that it was about a perverse form of joy.

Decline and Fall

SALLUST DATED THE corruption of the Roman republic from the time when Roman soldiers, in Greece on an errand of empire, began to admire the sculpture and art of the subject race. Perhaps some future Sallust will date the corruption of the American empire to the time when Joseph Alsop returned from the East in love with Chinese silk and the idea of a permanent American commitment to the peoples of the Asian mainland. It was heady stuff, to be thirty-odd years old and know that one's actions could alter the course of Chinese history. Alsop loved it. So did Jack Kennedy. The future President might have been less enamored of the idea of putting

American troops on the Asian mainland than Alsop, but he was just as addicted to the pleasures of making imperial policy.[13] Not long after he entered the Senate, Kennedy and Ted Sorensen, the young Nebraskan he had recently hired for his Senate office, were discussing their interests and ambitions. Would it be fun to be in the Cabinet? Which portfolio was the most desirable to hold? Sorensen thought "Justice, Labor, and Health-Education-Welfare" the most interesting positions. Jack Kennedy demurred; he "wouldn't have any interest in any of those" jobs. Only the State Department and the Defense Department, he told Sorensen haughtily, interested him.[14] They were more fun.

Although their father was, like Senator Taft, a critic of the insidious "imperialism of mind" that threatened to corrupt the American people, Jack and Bobby themselves believed in the empire. They believed in it in part, of course, because it promised to bring democracy and constitutional government to the dark places of the world. Bobby, traveling in Soviet Central Asia with Justice Douglas in the middle fifties, was, in his eagerness to promote the American way in hostile and uncomprehending lands, the spiritual twin of Alden Pyle. (Partway through the trip an exasperated Douglas told Bobby to keep his mouth shut and stop waving the flag.)[15] But the brothers believed in the empire, too, because the activity of empire is inherently exciting, challenging, fun. This, of course, is the reason why even those Presidents who run for office on solidly domestic platforms end up devoting so much of their time, after they are elected, to foreign affairs. In 1993 Richard Nixon predicted that President Clinton himself, a domestic politician if there ever was one, would discover this—or risk being forgotten by history. History "will not remember him for anything he does domestically," Nixon said of Clinton. "The economy will recover; it's all short-term and, let's face it, very boring."[16] In time even Sorensen came to prefer foreign affairs to "boring" domestic ones; the young man who, fresh from the progressive politics of Nebraska, had wanted to run HEW later embraced more global pursuits. After leaving the White House, Sorensen went to practice international law at Paul, Weiss in New York City. Arthur Schlesinger observed that even so decent a man as Hubert Humphrey, the embodiment of the virtues of Middle Western reform politics, was eventually corrupted by the pleasures of empire; Schlesinger recalled how disappointed he was by the "obvious delight" Humphrey had come to take "in hobnobbing with statesmen," in recounting his conversations with "the Pope, de Gaulle, Radhakrishnan, etc., etc."[17] In succumbing to the pleasures of empire, the Kennedys were not alone.

That pleasure was a motive force behind the creation of the American empire is demonstrated, I think, by the speed with which the Stimsonians abandoned it as soon as it ceased to be fun. It is not my purpose here to describe the policies that, had the Stimsonians persuaded their Presidents to pursue them, might have spared the United States the horror of war in Vietnam. Nor is it my purpose to criticize the Stimsonians for failing to heed the warnings that, if they had been heeded earlier, might at least have limited the scope of the disaster. (George Kennan, a tragic Cassandra in the Stimsonian citadel, expressed doubts about the way his theory of containment was being applied as early as 1947.[18]) What is distressing about the Stimsonians' involvement in Vietnam is not the role their policies played in creating the crisis—anyone can make a mistake—but rather the way they tried to walk away from it once the magnitude of their miscalculation became apparent. Dean Acheson, according to journalists Walter Isaacson and Evan Thomas, "preferred to think about Vietnam as little as possible."[19] Jack Mc-Cloy thought Vietnam a "distraction" from the problems of the European nations, which he said constituted "the Big Leagues."[20] Chip Bohlen was "quite content to have as little as possible to do with the Vietnam War."[21] Paul Nitze never bothered to formulate a coherent position on the war.[22] A critical part of their imperial strategy had become painful to them, and the Wise Men did their best to stay away from it, to confine themselves to more pleasant subjects.

Lyndon Johnson, to his credit, forced them to confront the unhappy progeny their geopolitical policies had spawned. The results were disappointing. When pressed for counsel, the Wise Men gave advice that was sadly lacking in perspicacity: they limited themselves to baseball analogies and locker-room pep talks, delivered with all the eloquence of a high school football coach. They vacillated, equivocated, talked themselves in and out of half a dozen positions. Here is McCloy in 1965, as described by Isaacson and Thomas:

> He spoke at length about how "impressed" he was with the "toughness of the situation." He doubted that merely "blunting the monsoon offensive" would bring Hanoi into a "negotiating mood." He predicted that the situation would remain "critical" for a long time. Yet after carefully laying out his doubts, he proclaimed that there was really no choice. America's credibility depended on her meeting her obligations and honoring her commitments. To Rusk and McNamara, he was adamant: "You've got to do it," he said. "You've got to go in."

Acheson had at least the presence of mind to give his advice bluntly and forcefully; the only problem with that advice was that it changed dramatically from one year to the next. In 1965 he told Johnson that the President was "wholly right on Vietnam" and "had no choice except to press on." By 1968 he was telling the President that he must get out immediately and bring home the troops within a matter of months.[23] The lordly Dean was obviously frustrated by the crisis his policies had helped to create, and at times the frustration showed. "You go tell the President," the normally unflappable patrician snapped in a moment of irritation, "and you can tell him in precisely these words, that he can take Vietnam and stick it up his ass."[24] Perhaps it would be too much to expect of the Stimsonians the kind of comprehensive moral and intellectual analysis of the problem of empire that Burke put forward in the eighteenth century when he tried to persuade successive British ministries to adopt more far-sighted policies toward Britain's colonies in America and India. But baseball analogies and talk of the President "sticking Vietnam up his ass"? These were the *Wise* Men?

The Stimsonians abandoned the bastard child that their passionate embrace of empire had produced with the same guiltless ease that characterized so many of their activities: they would make no shrift, confess no error, beg no forgiveness. In Georgetown drawing rooms where scarcely twenty years before the right people had gathered to celebrate the triumphant creation of a new imperial order, their counterparts in the middle sixties politely turned their backs on those who had the temerity to support the war in Vietnam. The role played by their own class and coterie in creating the policies that led to the disaster was conveniently forgotten, and the denizens of the salon turned their wrath not indeed upon themselves, but upon the convenient scapegoats in the White House.[25]

Bobby deserves credit for having taken upon himself, in a March 1967 speech in the Senate, a share of responsibility and blame for the decisions that led to the war. But his criticisms of the war itself, while they may have been just, cannot be called courageous. To criticize the war in 1967: it was the popular, the fashionable, the easy thing to do. The really courageous aspect of Bobby's statesmanship lay in his challenge not to the empire, but to the welfare state. By 1967 the American empire had ceased to be a vital force, a compelling ideal, in American life. It had ceased to be the kind of institution that young men and women grew up hoping one day to serve. Alden Pyle's counterparts in the 1960s did not go to Vietnam, as Pyle himself had done, to fight for democracy: they stayed home to *protest* the fight for democracy in Vietnam. The empire could not long endure in the face of such unpopularity as this, and it was only a matter of time before the processes of contraction began. But three decades were to pass before a serious attempt was made to reform the welfare state.

17

O~N A COLD DAY IN JANUARY 1968 HE WENT TO WALTER~ Lippmann's apartment in New York. Arthur Schlesinger accompanied him. Lippmann, now an old man, had long been an adviser and friend to eminent Stimsonian statesmen; in different periods of his life he had been on close terms with Theodore Roosevelt, Learned Hand, Felix Frankfurter, Dean Acheson, and George Kennan. And yet he was also among the most perceptive critics of the policies of the Stimsonians. Although as a young man he had been attracted to the dogmas of Fabian socialism, in the 1930s he emerged as one of the wisest and most thoughtful opponents not only of the New Deal itself, but also of the President who, "drunk with power," stood behind it.[1] After the war, casting about for a suitable term to describe the deteriorating relationship between the United States and the Soviet Union, he had come up with the phrase "the cold war," and in his newspaper columns had criticized the methods with which the United States had chosen to fight it.[2]

Now the great man's career was drawing to a close, and Bobby, looking for the kind of guidance that only long experience can give, sought him out for a talk. Should he run for President in 1968? Lippmann's reply was Delphic. Although he agreed that the reelection of Johnson would be a "catastrophe" for the nation, he stopped short of openly advising Bobby to run. When Bobby left Lippmann's apartment, he was strangely elated; perhaps his encounter with the ancient sage, a relic from another age, a man who had known Shaw and Freud and William James, had heightened his consciousness of the jealousness of time, of the elusiveness of historic destiny: one had to seize one's opportunities when one could. He would, he told Schlesinger, "wash" 1972 out of his thoughts altogether; he would concentrate his efforts on 1968.

But the euphoria subsided, and he was no closer to a decision. War councils and strategy sessions did little to help him make up his mind. "It's all so complicated," he told Jack Newfield. "I just don't know what to do."[3] His friends and advisers were divided. Ted Sorensen, Pierre Salinger, Fred Dutton, Bob McNamara, and Dick Daley all said that he would be foolish to run in 1968; Allard Lowenstein, Adam Walinsky, Arthur Schlesinger, and Dick Goodwin countered that it would be wrong not to. His wife and sisters wanted him to run; his brother Ted didn't. Joseph Alsop penned a column in which he warned Bobby to stay out of the race; Jack Newfield wrote in *The Village Voice* that the best part of his character would die if he did not challenge Lyndon Johnson.[4]

Eugene McCarthy was running. Bobby, fantasizing about the kind of campaign he wanted for himself, said that McCarthy should "run against the organization, against the Democratic establishment, against the big shots."[5] He didn't like McCarthy, thought him a lazy, self-indulgent man, a spiteful Senator who "felt he should have been the first Catholic President because he knew more St. Thomas Aquinas than my brother."[6] No doubt Bobby resented the fact that McCarthy had dared to do the very thing he himself hesitated to do. He *hated* to hesitate, and he knew that others hated him for his hesitation. A student at Brooklyn College confronted him with a cruel sign: "RFK: Hawk, Dove, or Chicken?"[7] At a cocktail party at El Morocco, the Greek actress Melina Mercouri "harangued him for ten solid minutes on the moral imperative of his running."[8] Afterward, dining at Le Pavillon, Bobby told his sisters that he "thought he would run."[9] A week later he changed his mind. At the end of January he told a National Press Club breakfast that he would not oppose President Johnson under any "foreseeable circumstances." Although the careful language left him a degree of room for maneuver, he had for all apparent purposes taken himself out of the running.

It was a spectacular miscalculation, for on the very day he announced his decision, the Tet offensive began. Targets across South Vietnam were attacked; the United States embassy in Saigon was fired upon. Ellsworth Bunker, the American Ambassador, was awakened in the middle of the night by his Marine guards, led to an armored personnel carrier, and taken through the streets of the capital to a more secure hiding place. Eugene McCarthy all at once became a credible opponent of Lyndon Johnson; it was even conceivable that he might defeat the President in the New Hampshire primary. In gloomy isolation Bobby lamented his decision to stay out of the race.[10] When on March 12, 1968, McCarthy won 42 percent of the New Hampshire vote, opponents of the war rejoiced. Bobby himself retreated moodily to the "21" Club to ponder the future.[11]

Eventually, of course, he did enter the race. The circumstances surrounding his decision to do so are full of perplexed uncertainty. Schlesinger and Newfield claim that he made up his mind *before* the results of the New Hampshire primary were known.[12] Schlesinger's own book, however, casts doubt upon this assertion.[13] In it Schlesinger quotes from a letter written by Bobby to Anthony Lewis the day *after* the New Hampshire primary, a letter in which Bobby confides that, although his "basic inclination was to try [to run] . . . everyone who I respect with the exception of Dick Goodwin and Arthur Schlesinger have been against my running." That he had not yet made a final decision is clear: "What should I do?" he at one point asks Lewis. "By the time you receive this letter," he concluded, "both of us will know." He remained hesitant about running even after the New Hampshire results revealed the extent of Johnson's vulnerability. The day before the primary he authorized Ted Sorensen to look into the possibility of a deal with Johnson. In exchange for Bobby's implicit promise to stay out of the race, Johnson would appoint an independent commission to examine American policy in Vietnam. Bobby, instead of frankly telling both Sorensen and the President that the time for commissions had passed, spent a day or two after the New Hampshire result puzzling over the proposal until word reached him that Johnson had rejected it.[14]

Campaigning Against the Welfare State

AT LAST THE announcement was made. A speech was quickly put together. Bobby delivered it in the caucus room of the Old Senate Office Building on Saturday, March 16, 1968. It was not a masterpiece; it was not even wholly consistent with the themes of his campaign. He was running, after all, *against* the imperial policies of the Stimsonians, yet he nevertheless dutifully recited the lines that Sorensen, who was now more than ever a Stimsonian manqué, fed him about the necessity of American leadership in the world. To the horror of Adam Walinsky and Jeff Greenfield, Bobby told the world that the presidential contest was about nothing less than America's "right to moral leadership on this planet."[15]

After the announcement he flew to New York to march in the St. Patrick's Day parade there. (As he walked up Fifth Avenue, he was booed and jeered by supporters of the war.) And then he went to Kansas, the first of more than a dozen states he visited in the ensuing weeks. The crowds that greeted him wherever he went were for the most part enthusiastic. In Kansas and in California they were more than that: they were roused by his presence to a pitch of feverish ecstasy.[16] To cheering audiences Bobby denounced President Johnson for "dividing the country." He accused the President of calling upon "the darker impulses of the American spirit."[17]

It was a tumultuous and terrible spring. At the end of March Johnson announced that he would not seek another term as President. A few days later, in early April, Martin Luther King, Jr., was murdered in Memphis. Bobby, shocked by the rioting that followed, speculated on the underlying causes of violence in America. "What has violence ever accomplished?" he asked. "What has it ever created?" The answer, of course, is that violence has accomplished many things, both good and bad. The American republic was founded in an act of violent revolution; the Thirteenth and Fourteenth Amendments to the Constitution, as vital a part of the nation's charter of liberty as any, were the product of four years of violent civil war. And yet there was a difference between these extraordinary, isolated acts of organized and, as it were, idealistic violence and the random, pointless violence that too often prevailed in the America of the 1960s. Bobby wondered whether this new and unprecedented violence was not in some way the product of the country's institutions; after King's death he dwelt at length upon "the violence of institutions," institutions that destroyed the dignity of individuals and broke "a man's spirit by denying him the chance to stand as a father and as a man among men."[18] His target was obvious enough: the institutions of the welfare state—institutions that forced fathers out of their homes and lured them away from productive work—were one cause of the unprecedented violence of the sixties.

In April he campaigned in Indiana. Now that Johnson was out of the race, the war was a less critical issue, and Bobby returned again to the question of the welfare state. In places like Indianapolis and Gary and along the Lincoln Trail—the route the young Lincoln and his family had traveled in search of fresh opportunity in the West—Bobby "spoke out repeatedly against the federal welfare formula" and declared that welfare itself was nothing more than a cynical "payoff."[19] "We can't have the federal government in here telling people what's good for them," he told an audience at Fort Wayne.[20] Ronald Reagan was amazed. "I get the feeling I've been writing some of his speeches," the future President said.[21] Richard Nixon said that "Bobby and I have been sounding pretty much alike" on major issues.[22] Journalists were skeptical of Bobby's performance; noting that he had begun "to sound like George Romney on law and order," *The New York Times* ran a story entitled "Kennedy: Meet the Conservative." If the national press was not sympathetic to Bobby's positions, Indiana Democrats were; on May 7, they gave him 42 percent of the primary vote.[23] A week later Bobby took 51.5 percent of the vote in Nebraska.[24] He was winning.

He was winning in part because he had rediscovered a familiar theme—the theme of the individual, the theme of Emerson and Lincoln. He was almost proud of the fact that he had "every establishment in America against him."[25] The vast anonymous bureaucracies of big business and big labor filled him with an obscure dread; he did not trust the complacent men who led them, and they did not trust him. Although he "wasn't anti-union," Fred Dutton said, he was "un-union."[26] He didn't believe that "middle-class labor leaders" had "any of the answers."[27] His own investigative work in the fifties had made him thoroughly familiar with corruption and waste in the labor movement, and the movement's leaders could never forgive him for having aired their dirty linen in public. George Meany "would barely speak" to Bobby, and the candidate was neither surprised nor upset when big labor sided overwhelmingly with Hubert Humphrey that year.[28]

He was no less skeptical of the bureaucratic fiefdoms of much of corporate America. In the old progressive view, big government was supposed to counterbalance the power of big business. In practice, however, big government, so far from acting as a counterweight to the power of the largest corporations, bolstered their power at the expense of smaller businesses and entrepreneurial enterprise. Before a series of regulatory, market, and tax reforms undermined the cozy reciprocity between congressmen and conglomerates, big business thrived on the great dollops of corporate welfare that its allies on Capitol Hill served up to it. Corporate pashas grew lazy and fat on lucrative government contracts and generous tax subsidies, and were in many instances insulated from the pressures of competition by irrational regulations.[29] The world, of course, has changed since then; the era of the giant conglomerate and the faceless organization man is over; entrepreneurs, freer than ever before to create jobs for others and make money for themselves, have forced the nation's biggest businesses to become leaner, more competitive, and more responsive enterprises than they were in the past. Bobby, I think, would have been pleased with these changes. When he declared that his purpose in the '68 campaign was "to show that the individual *does* count in a society where he actually appears to count less and less," it was not, as Schlesinger maintained, yet another indication that he "had become the tribune of the underclass."[30] It was, on the contrary, an indication of his antipathy to the soul-killing spirit of bureaucracy. A paternalistic *tribunus plebis*, eager to save the world with welfare payments and government programs, is precisely what Bobby was not. He wanted individuals to develop the confidence to help themselves.

California Republic

EUGENE MCCARTHY BEAT him in Oregon. After Oregon came California. For several frenzied days he campaigned as hard as he had ever campaigned, and then on Saturday, June 1, 1968, one of those clear cloudless days that he loved, he rested. He spent most of the day in his suite at the Fairmont Hotel, alternately preparing for his debate with McCarthy that evening and staring out the window, entranced by the spectacle of San Francisco shimmering in the sunshine.[31]

The debate itself was not a memorable one. At one point the two candidates argued about how best to solve the problem of the ghetto. McCarthy advocated moving people out of the inner city and resettling them in less troubled areas. Bobby said that this was a bad idea; he favored policies that encouraged people not to move out of their shattered communities, but to rebuild them. To "take ten thousand black people and move them into Orange County" was simply wrong, Bobby said. "To take these people out, put them in suburbs where they can't afford the housing, where their children can't keep up with the schools, and where they don't have the skills for the jobs, it is just going to be catastrophic."[32] He had been the underdog going into the debate; McCarthy was thought to be the superior debater. By holding his own against a man renowned for his wit and intellect, Bobby emerged the victor in the eyes of a majority of Californians.[33] Relieved and happy, he and Ethel dined at the Fairmont.[34]

On Sunday, June 2, he campaigned at Buchanan Field near

Concord, California, and in Orange County. In the early evening he took six of his children to Disneyland.[35] The next morning he woke to begin a final arduous day of speeches and motor tours. From Los Angeles he flew to San Francisco, where he toured Chinatown and spoke at Fisherman's Wharf. Then he traveled to Long Beach, addressed a rally there, and pressed on to Watts. By the time he spoke at the El Cortez Hotel in San Diego, his speeches were disjointed and his sentences nearly incoherent. Exhausted and sick to his stomach, he flew to Los Angeles and collapsed at John Frankenheimer's house on the beach at Malibu. He slept late into the morning of Tuesday, June 4, a cool, sunless, overcast day. The polls were open. Bobby lunched with Teddy White at Frankenheimer's and went swimming in the ocean. His son David nearly drowned in the Pacific surf, but Bobby managed to bring him safely out of the water. In the afternoon he fell asleep beside Frankenheimer's swimming pool; when he woke he learned that CBS had predicted that he would win the primary with close to 50 percent of the vote. He napped again, woke, dressed, and around half past six was driven to the Ambassador Hotel downtown. Frankenheimer was at the wheel, and as he sped along the Santa Monica Freeway, Bobby told him to slow down.[36] "Life is too short," the candidate said.[37]

At his suite on the fifth floor of the Ambassador he discussed the future of his campaign and made a number of telephone calls. His friends and advisers were with him. The ever loyal Dave Hackett compiled lists of convention delegates. Steve Smith, who with John Seigenthaler had masterminded the California victory, worked on organizational matters. Adam Walinsky, Ted Sorensen, Fred Dutton, and Milton Gwirtzman plotted strategy. Dick Goodwin spoke to Kenneth Galbraith and Allard Lowenstein by telephone; he told them that the time had come for them to switch their allegiance from McCarthy to Bobby. They seemed willing to do so. Bobby himself spoke to Mayor Daley in Chicago; Daley implied that if Bobby won in California, the Illinois delegation would support him at the convention. Bobby was no doubt pleased; he had earlier said that "Daley means the ball game." He was perhaps even more pleased when he learned that he had received a plurality of the vote in the South Dakota primary, which had also been held that day. South Dakota was the birthplace of Hubert Humphrey.

While the professionals worked in one room, his social friends— journalists, celebrities, assorted hangers-on—gathered in another. Jack Newfield, Pete Hamill, Jimmy Breslin, George Plimpton, John Glenn, Theodore White, John Bartlow Martin, Cesar Chavez— they were all there, talking, listening, drinking, looking at the television set. The atmosphere became "like a party," Newfield remembered. A "bar was set up in the corner" of the room, and most of those present were soon on their second or third drinks.[38] Just before midnight, after completing a series of radio and television interviews, Bobby went with a large entourage to the ballroom downstairs. Ethel was with him, and so were Rafer Johnson, Rosey Grier, and Bill Barry, who acted as his bodyguards. As he walked to the elevator, Bobby told Newfield that he would see him later at the Factory, a fashionable Los Angeles nightclub where the victory celebration was to be held. He made his way to the ballroom, and at the lectern he thanked those who had helped him to win. He said that Americans must work to end the divisions that sapped the republic's vitality and its strength. He declared that ours was a great nation and a compassionate nation.[39] He left the room and entered an adjoining pantry, where he shook the hand of a busboy named Juan Romero. He was then shot in the head, apparently by a young man named Sirhan Sirhan. He fell to the floor; the busboy placed a rosary in his hands.

Death and Burial

HE DIED AT a quarter to two in the morning of Thursday, June 6, 1968. President Johnson put a presidential aircraft at his family's disposal, and it was in this plane that Bobby's body was brought back to New York. The jet landed at La Guardia Airport on a hot summer's evening. The coffin was taken to Manhattan, to St. Patrick's Cathedral, and was there placed in the sanctuary. A vigil was maintained through the humid night. The next day a requiem Mass was said over the body. The archbishop presided in his episcopal seat, and the clergy wore vestments of violet. Leonard Bernstein conducted the music: a passage from the slow movement of Mahler's Fifth Symphony, a portion of Verdi's Requiem for Manzoni, César Frank's *Panis Angelicus*, "The Battle Hymn of the Republic." Edward Kennedy delivered the eulogy.

After Mass the casket was taken to Pennsylvania Station and put aboard a special train. Members of his family and many of his friends accompanied it on the journey south. Great crowds of people lined the railroad tracks and waited for hours in the hot sunshine to watch the train pass. Some carried roses, others signs. One read: "We have lost our last hope." Some wept; others made the sign of the cross; still others fell to their knees in prayer. There were many nuns. Inside the train, separated from the crowds by steel and glass, the passengers sat and talked, their conversation mingling the tragic with the mundane.[40]

The train arrived at Union Station at dusk. The coffin was placed in a hearse. The hearse made its way slowly through the twilight toward the river. At the Department of Justice the car halted for a moment, and then it moved on. It passed beneath the shadows of the Lincoln Memorial and crossed the Potomac into Arlington. His body was buried in the federal cemetery there, not far from the grave of his brother.

CONCLUSION

The End of Aristocracy

————◦◦◦————

Today the Stimsonians are largely gone, a vanished breed, as extinct, almost, as the dinosaurs. No one will mourn for them; they were the least colorful and most prosaic of political aristocracies; they lacked imagination. What a contrast to their counterparts across the ocean, the aristocrats whom they so adored and upon whom they vainly tried to model themselves. The British aristocracy was burnt upon a splendid pyre; Churchill preferred to immolate himself* rather than stoop to the subterfuges of FDR. It is true that Churchill had himself once sought a bureaucratic revenge on a nation that no longer had any use for his class. But he had later given this up and had left socialism and the welfare state to Mr. Attlee.[1] As told by its historian, David Cannadine, and its tragic and comic poet, Evelyn Waugh, the story of the decline and fall of the British aristocracy entertains and even (as the success of *Brideshead Revisited* on television demonstrated) moves us. But who will weep for Stimson?

The Stimsonians are gone; the somebodies of yesterday, Joseph Alsop observed, have by and large become the nobodies of today. The once august names still exist, but they are for the most part buried in the obscure pages of the *Social Register*, or in the payrolls of Wall Street firms that have grown so large as to have lost their

---

*In the 1945 general election.

once distinctive character as citadels of an elite. Bobby, of course, played a role in the demise of the Stimsonians, and yet even after a careful review of his actions during the period, it is difficult to say precisely what his role was. In recounting the final, tragical chapter of the Stimsonians' story—in reflecting upon the *infandum dolorem* of their fall, and upon their inglorious behavior in the catastrophe that forever ended their career as a governing class—in reviewing those dismal scenes, we cannot help but feel a certain disappointment with our protagonist's caution. He had embarked upon the difficult and dangerous path of the heretic, and had chosen the unenviable lot of the heresiarch: he had challenged the system of Roosevelt, and he had questioned the creed whose truths he had been brought up to believe. But the boldness he showed at certain times was diminished by the caution he displayed at others. In the same year in which he criticized the welfare state, he condemned President Johnson for failing to fund it adequately. He pointed out the shortcomings of the federal bureaucracy, and promptly called for its expansion. He praised private enterprise as the essential foundation of the country's greatness, and condemned businessmen and corporations as the disciples of Mammon. He celebrated the virtues of the free market, and denounced the cult of the GNP.[2] Was this ambivalence? Excessive prudence? An attempt to appease the liberals in his party? The kind of inconsistency we should expect from a politician?

He will always be a difficult man to understand, and I cannot pretend to have done more in this essay than identify a few threads in the complex pattern of his life. Although the qualities of Bobby's statesmanship that I have treated in this book have never gotten the attention they deserve, they were not the only qualities; indeed, they may not even have been the most important. But I believe that they are the qualities that are most likely to have a permanent value. They are the portion of his legacy that will survive, the piece of his politics that will endure, when other aspects of his career are forgotten. In spite of the sordidness of practical politics, in spite of the compromises, the equivocations, the embarrassments in which a statesman must necessarily involve himself if he is to succeed, it is still possible to discover, in the best and highest forms of statesmanship, the ideal to which the statesman's confused and often contradictory activity tends, the higher order to which it aspires, the coherent pattern that it tries to make good. Once that ideal is discovered, once that order is discerned, it becomes relatively easy to dismiss the false paths, the wrong turns, the dead ends, that inevitably mark a statesman's progress. It becomes relatively easy to separate that which is essential to the particular form of statesmanship in question from that which is irrelevant. Bobby's praise of Che Guevara (he called Guevara a "revolutionary hero") is one example of such an irrelevancy: it is impossible to assign his admiration of a Marxist bandit a sensible place in a coherent interpretation of his statesmanship. It is a piece in the jigsaw puzzle that does not fit. And we should not try to force it to fit; should instead cast it aside, discard it as merely a daydream, one that had little to do with Bobby's real meaning as a man and a politician. His admiration of Lincoln and Emerson, on the other hand, *can* be connected, in a convincing way, to the highest purposes of his statesmanship; and we are therefore justified in treating that admiration as forming an essential part of that statesmanship.

None of this, of course, explains why Bobby's statesmanship has been so often misunderstood, explains why so many people have insisted on looking upon a small number of his sillier gestures—his profession of sympathy for a misguided Marxist, his interest in the radical left, his encounters with Tom Hayden and the Jefferson Airplane—as the key to an understanding of his politics. Both he and his older brother said that he could not be understood in terms of conventional labels, that it was impossible to classify him as either a liberal or a conservative. But the habit of claiming him for the left persists. I suppose this is so partly because he was a rebel and a dissenter, and we all but instinctively associate rebels and dissenters with the left. But dissent is not the exclusive property of the left. There was in Bobby's rage at the insensitivity of modern institutions a quality reminiscent of John Ruskin, the English moralist and critic who condemned the world the Enlightenment had made, and yet it would be difficult to call Ruskin, a self-professed Tory of the "old school," a conventional figure of the left.

The great Romantic rebels against Enlightenment, the rebels who trusted the ideals of the Greeks and of medieval Christendom more than they trusted modern notions of progress and Enlightenment, cannot properly be claimed by either the right or the left. Those rebels may have been, like Burke, like Newman, like Scott, like Ruskin himself, deeply conservative in their general orientation, but conservatism is not an exclusively right-wing phenomenon any more than dissent is an exclusively left-wing one. When it is divorced from the superficial garb of progress, science, and Enlightenment in which it is so often dressed, a great portion of the radical thought of the eighteenth and nineteenth centuries can be seen to have been distinctly conservative in its ends; the radicals sought to conserve as much as they sought to destroy, sought to conserve the values of an older and, as they supposed, a better society than seemed likely to flourish under modern conditions. Even the nineteenth-century liberalism of Lincoln and Emerson was, in a curious way, conservative; it was a liberalism that sought to conserve the idea of the sacredness of the individual in a world where that idea is constantly under attack. Insofar as they were radicals, Lincoln's and Emerson's was a conservative radicalism, a radicalism that celebrated the power and potential of the free, unhindered individual. If one were forced to affix a label to Bobby, one could do worse than to describe him as a Tory radical, a Romantic conservative, in the tradition of Ruskin. Such a classification makes a good deal more sense than attempts to classify him as a progressive radical along the lines of Tom Hayden and Che Guevara, or as a progressive liberal in the style of Eleanor Roosevelt and Adlai Stevenson.

The Ambivalent Conservative

CONTEMPORARY OBSERVERS WERE on to Bobby's complexity. But after his death they conspired to forget the more original (and, to

some, the more troubling) aspects of his statesmanship; they succeeded in persuading themselves that they were burying a pious
liberal martyr. They remembered the progressive, nodded to the
radical, and promptly forgot the conservative. Bobby *was* a conservative, conservative not only in the modern sense that he believed
in the potential of free men and free markets, but in the older sense
that he believed in learning from, and building on, ancient intellectual and cultural traditions, traditions whose value had been sanctioned by time and custom, traditions that could help people to act
confidently in a complicated world. His use of tradition was very
different from, say, T. S. Eliot's. Eliot used tradition as a weapon:
he used it to criticize, to condemn, to condescend to an Enlightened
world he did not like. Bobby, on the contrary, accepted the modern,
market-oriented world in which he found himself, and he accepted
the theory of liberal individualism, the creed of Emerson and Lincoln, that underlay it. If he recognized the limits of the world that
free markets had brought into being, he never repudiated that
world. A tradition like the old Hellenic cult of community could,
he believed, give men the strength and the confidence to prosper
in it.

In reconciling his commitment to nineteenth-century theories
of liberal individualism with his belief in the importance of those
intellectual and cultural traditions that are the most valuable legacy
of the past, Bobby used the past, not ironically, like Eliot, or friv-
olously, like the postmodernists, but constructively and practically,
in a way that strengthened rather than undermined the first principles of his Enlightened nation. His approach to both the traditions
of the past and the principles of the Anglo-Scottish Enlightenment
was in great contrast to the approach of the Stimsonians who, under
cover of theories of economic planning and control derived largely
from the French Enlightenment and European socialism, sought to
revive traditional notions, like the feudal notion of noblesse oblige,
that have no place in a modern democratic society. The Stimsonians
sought to transfer much of the political power that belongs by right
to free and independent citizens to administrative and judicial bureaucracies that were largely insulated from electoral control.

Bobby condemned the welfare state. But he never made a clean break with it. He indeed helped to inspire two very different trends. One sees this in the subsequent careers of the two bright young men upon whom he so greatly relied for advice and counsel during his Senate years. Peter Edelman became an ardent defender of the welfare state; he married Marian Wright; he advocated a guaranteed minimum income; he resigned his position in the welfare state when President Clinton signed the welfare reform bill in 1996. Adam Walinsky traveled in a different direction. Obsessed with the growth of crime and the decline of public order in the United States, Walinsky, who has argued that "the federal welfare system began the destruction of black family life" that helped to bring about the "huge increase in violence" in the nation's cities, has spent the last fifteen years advocating the creation of a militant domestic version of the Peace Corps called the Police Corps, an organization that he hopes will enable America to put at least half a million new police officers on the streets by the end of the decade.[3] (Walinsky shrugs off suggestions that his efforts to deploy massive amounts of police power in America's cities would turn police officers into an urban "army of occupation"; the cities, he observes, are already occupied by "hostile bands of brigands"[4]).

In what direction would Bobby himself have traveled? We don't know. The right was suspicious of Bobby—but so was the left. The *Ramparts* journalist Robert Scheer thought Bobby particularly dangerous because he *seemed* like a radical but really wasn't one; he provided "the illusion of dissent without its substance." Bobby was, Scheer thought, a deeply orthodox figure, a believer in America's free-enterprise system, one who looked to it to solve many of the nation's problems.[5]

The End of the American Enlightenment and the Question of American Pain

HE WAS TORN between the Enlightened idea that a statesman ought to offer something new and better and his own realization that the intoxicating and medicinal properties of old wine are very often superior to those of more recent vintage. It has always been necessary for the successful American statesman to seem to be offering something new, something that promises to deliver his constituents from the evils of the moment, something that has about it the visionary gleam of miraculous progress—an escape from pain. Proposals for new deals, new frontiers, and new covenants—for new world orders and great new beginnings—for new heavens and new earths—have been so common in our history as to have made novelty itself un-novel. Bobby was himself much given to exploiting this American weakness for visionary poetry; he frequently invoked Shaw's belief that there are two kinds of men: some who see things as they are and ask "Why?" and others who dream of things that never were and ask "Why not?" Bobby was not above resorting to such a cheap lollipop as this; it was a kind of Kennedy signature, one that gave the impression that Americans were going on to grander things, a better world, a new republic, without disclosing exactly how this wonderful progress was to be achieved. *Friend, go up higher.* But really the most original, the most novel, aspect of Bobby's statesmanship was his willingness to see the usefulness of older, pre-Enlightened ideas (like the Hellenic idea of community) in mitigating the terror of a modern world governed only by the morals of the marketplace and vast impersonal bureaucracies. He was unembarrassed to admit how much we, the most modern of peoples, could benefit from the ancient traditions of our civilization. We might not be able to *escape* our pain, but the older creeds could at least teach us how to live with it.

His relevance today? He reminds liberals of the importance of remaining true to the nineteenth-century liberalism of Emerson and Lincoln; he teaches them that reforms should help to create self-reliance and self-respect in individuals, not undermine those qualities. Turn the safety "net" into a trampoline. And he reminds liberals not to overlook the value inherent in older strategies for dealing with pain. He reminds conservatives that any genuine conservatism must be allied to compassion, and that, in their devotion to the principles of a free market, conservatives should not forget their obligations to the less fortunate among us. He was an imperfect man, possessed of many grievous faults, and yet we may number him among the saints.

Sources

Below is a list of sources consulted, together with the abbreviations used in the notes.

PRIMARY SOURCES

BSDPO	*Bedford-Stuyvesant Development Project Overview: A Working Paper* (April 4, 1967), in Walinsky Papers, file 1.
Collected Speeches	*RFK: Collected Speeches*, ed. Edwin O. Guthman and C. Richard Allen (New York: Viking, 1993).
Edelman Papers	The Papers of Peter Edelman in the Kennedy Library.
The Fruitful Bough	*The Fruitful Bough*, ed. Edward M. Kennedy (privately printed, 1966).
Profiles in Courage	John F. Kennedy, *Profiles in Courage* (New York: Harper & Row, 1964; originally published 1956).
RFK Senate Papers	The Papers of Robert F. Kennedy (1965–1968) in the Kennedy Library.
Ribicoff Hearings	Hearings before the Subcommittee on Executive Reorganization of the Committee on Government Operations—United States Senate—89th Congress—2d Session—Federal Role in Urban Affairs—August 15–16, 1966.
Speeches	*Speeches of the Honorable Robert F. Kennedy, Attorney General: 1961–1964* (Washington, D.C.: U.S. Department of Justice).
To Seek a Newer World	Robert F. Kennedy, *To Seek a Newer World* (Garden City, N.Y.: Doubleday, 1967).
Walinsky papers	The Papers of Adam Walinsky in the Kennedy Library.

Sources

SECONDARY SOURCES

American Journey	Jean Stein and George Plimpton, *American Journey: The Times of Robert Kennedy* (New York: Harcourt Brace, 1970).
An American Drama	Peter Collier and David Horowitz, *The Kennedys: An American Drama* (New York: Warner Books, 1985; originally published 1984).
Apostle of Change	Douglas Ross, *Robert F. Kennedy: Apostle of Change* (New York: Trident, 1968).
As We Remember Her	Carl Sferrazza Anthony, *As We Remember Her: Jacqueline Kennedy Onassis in the Words of Her Family and Friends* (New York: HarperCollins, 1997).
The Best and the Brightest	David Halberstam, *The Best and the Brightest* (New York: Ballantine, 1993; originally published 1972).
The Brother Within	Robert E. Thompson and Hortense Myers, *Robert Kennedy: The Brother Within* (New York: MacMillan, 1962).
Cape Cod Years	Leo Damore, *The Cape Cod Years of John Fitzgerald Kennedy* (Englewood Cliffs, N.J.: Prentice-Hall, 1967).
Conversations	Benjamin C. Bradlee, *Conversations with Kennedy* (New York: Norton, 1984; originally published 1975).
Crisis Years	Michael R. Beschloss, *The Crisis Years: Kennedy and Khrushchev 1960–1963* (New York: HarperCollins, 1991).
The Dark Side of Camelot	Seymour Hersh, *The Dark Side of Camelot* (Boston: Little, Brown, 1997).
Death of a President	William Manchester, *The Death of a President: November 20–25, 1963* (New York: Harper & Row, 1988; originally published 1967).
Founding Father	Richard J. Whalen, *The Founding Father: The Story of Joseph P. Kennedy* (New York: New American Library, 1964).
The Heir Apparent	William V. Shannon, *The Heir Apparent: Robert Kennedy and the Struggle for Power* (New York: Macmillan, 1967).
Honorable Profession	*"An Honorable Profession": A Tribute to Robert F. Kennedy*, ed. Pierre Salinger, Edwin Guthman, Frank Mankiewicz, and John Seigenthaler (New York: Doubleday, 1993).
In His Own Words	Edwin O. Guthman and Jeffrey Shulman, *In His Own Words: The Unpublished Recollections of the Kennedy Years* (New York: Bantam, 1988).

Sources

I've Seen the Best of It	Joseph W. Aslop and Adam Platt, *"I've Seen the Best of It"*: *Memoirs* (New York: Norton, 1992).
The Last Campaign	Hays Gorey, *Robert Kennedy: The Last Campaign* (New York: Harcourt Brace, 1993).
Kennedy	Theodore C. Sorensen, *Kennedy* (New York: Harper & Row, 1965).
The Kennedy Imprisonment	Garry Wills, *The Kennedy Imprisonment* (Boston: Little, Brown, 1982).
Kennedy Justice	Victor S. Navasky, *Kennedy Justice* (New York: Atheneum, 1971).
The Kennedy Men	Nellie Bly, *The Kennedy Men: Three Generations of Sex, Scandal, and Secrets* (New York: Kensington Books, 1996).
Kennedy and Nixon	Christopher Matthews, *Kennedy and Nixon: The Rivalry That Shaped Postwar America* (New York: Simon & Schuster, 1996).
Kennedy and Roosevelt	Michael R. Beschloss, *Kennedy and Roosevelt: The Uneasy Alliance* (New York: Norton, 1980).
The Kennedy Women	Laurence Leamer, *The Kennedy Women: The Saga of an American Family* (New York: Ballantine, 1994).
Let the Word Go Forth	*"Let the Word Go Forth": The Speeches, Statements, and Writings of John F. Kennedy*, ed. Theodore C. Sorensen (New York: Delacorte, 1988).
Making of a Folk Hero	Lester David and Irene David, *Bobby Kennedy: The Making of a Folk Hero* (New York: Dodd, Mead, 1986).
The Making of the President 1960	Theodore H. White, *The Making of the President 1960* (New York: Atheneum, 1962).
The Making of the President 1968	Theodore H. White, *The Making of the President 1968* (New York: Atheneum, 1969).
A Memoir	Jack Newfield, *Robert Kennedy: A Memoir* (New York: Plume, 1988; originally published 1969).
Mutual Contempt	Jeff Shesol, *Mutual Contempt: Lyndon Johnson, Robert Kennedy, and the Feud that Defined a Decade* (New York: Norton, 1997).
The Myth and the Man	Victor Lasky, *Robert F. Kennedy: The Myth and the Man* (New York: Trident, 1968).
The New Politics	Penn Kimball, *Bobby Kennedy and the New Politics* (Englewood Cliffs, N.J.: Prentice-Hall, 1968).
One Brief Shining Moment	William Manchester, *One Brief Shining Moment: Remembering Kennedy* (Boston: Little, Brown, 1983).

Sources

On His Own	William vanden Heuvel and Milton Gwirtzman, *On His Own: RFK 1964–1968* (Garden City, N.Y.: Doubleday, 1970).
The Other Mrs. Kennedy	Jerry Oppenheimer, *The Other Mrs. Kennedy* (New York: St. Martin's, 1995; originally published 1994).
President Kennedy	Richard Reeves, *President Kennedy: Profiles of Power* (New York: Simon & Schuster, 1993).
P.S.	Pierre Salinger, *P.S.: A Memoir* (New York: St. Martin's, 1995).
A Question of Character	Thomas C. Reeves, *A Question of Character: A Life of John F. Kennedy* (Rocklin, Calif.: Prima, 1992; originally published 1991).
Reckless Youth	Nigel Hamilton, *J.F.K.: Reckless Youth* (New York: Random House, 1992).
Remembering America	Richard Goodwin, *Remembering America: A Voice from the Sixties* (Boston: Little, Brown, 1988).
R.F.K.	Ralph de Toledano, *R.F.K.: The Man Who Would Be President* (New York: G. P. Putnam's Sons, 1967).
Robert Kennedy	Arthur M. Schlessinger, Jr., *Robert Kennedy and His Times* (Boston: Houghton Mifflin, 1978).
Robert Kennedy in New York	Gerald Gardner, *Robert Kennedy in New York* (New York: Random House, 1965).
Senatorial Privilege	Leo Damore, *Senatorial Privilege: The Chappaquiddick Cover-up* (Washington, D.C.: Regnery Gateway, 1988).
Shadow Play	William Klaber and Philip H. Melanson, *Shadow Play: The Murder of Robert F. Kennedy* (New York: St. Martin's, 1997).
The Sins of the Father	Ronald Kessler, *The Sins of the Father: Joseph P. Kennedy and the Dynasty He Founded* (New York: Warner, 1996).
A Thousand Days	Arthur M. Schlesinger, *A Thousand Days; John F. Kennedy in the White House* (Boston: Houghton Mifflin, 1965).
Times to Remember	Rose Fitzgerald Kennedy, *Times to Remember* (Garden City, N.Y.: Doubleday, 1974).
Unfinished Odyssey	David Halberstam, *The Unfinished Odyssey of Robert Kennedy* (New York: Random House, 1968).
With Kennedy	Pierre Salinger, *With Kennedy* (Garden City, N.Y.: Doubleday, 1966).
A Woman Named Jackie	C. David Heymann, *A Woman Named Jackie: An Intimate Biography of Jacqueline Bouvier Kennedy Onassis* (New York: Birch Lane Press, 1994).

Sources

OTHER SOURCES

Abinger Harvest	E. M. Forster, *Abinger Harvest* (New York: Harcourt Brace, 1936).
ACL	Laurence H. Tribe, *American Constitutional Law*, 2d ed. (Mineola, N.Y.: Foundation Press, 1988).
The Age of Jackson	Arthur M. Schlesinger, Jr., *The Age of Jackson* (Boston: Little, Brown, 1945).
The Age of Reform	Richard Hofstadter, *The Age of Reform: From Bryan to F.D.R.* (New York: Vintage, 1955).
Amazing Grace	Jonathan Kozol, *Amazing Grace: The Lives of Children and the Conscience of a Nation* (New York: HarperPerennial, 1996; originally published 1995).
The American Adam	R. W. B. Lewis, *The American Adam: Innocence, Tragedy, and Tradition in the Nineteenth Century* (Chicago: University of Chicago Press, 1955).
American Establishment	Leonard Silk and Mark Silk, *The American Establishment* (New York: Basic Books, 1980).
The American Establishment and Other Reports	Richard Rovere, *The American Establishment and Other Reports, Opinions, and Speculations* (New York: Harcourt Brace, 1962).
American Nervousness	Tom Lutz, *American Nervousness 1903: An Anecdotal History* (Ithaca, N.Y.: Cornell University Press, 1991).
American Renaissance	F. O. Matthiessen, *American Renaissance: Art and Expression in the Age of Emerson and Whitman* (Oxford: Oxford University Press, 1968; originally published 1941).
An Artist's Story	George Biddle, *An Artist's Story* (New York: Harold Ober Associates, 1939)
Anti-Intellectualism	Richard Hofstadter, *Anti-Intellectualism in American Life* (New York: Knopf, 1963).
The Antitrust Paradox	Robert H. Bork, *The Antitrust Paradox: A Policy at War with Itself* (New York: Basic Books, 1978).
APT	Richard Hofstadter, *The American Political Tradition and the Men Who Made It* (New York: Vintage, 1974; originally published 1948).
Aspects of Aristocracy	David Cannadine, *Aspects of Aristocracy: Grandeur and Decline in Modern Britain* (New Haven, Conn.: Yale University Press, 1994).
Axël's Castle	Edmund Wilson, *Axël's Castle: Studies in the Imaginative Literature of 1870–1930* (New York: Norton, 1985; originally published 1931).

Sources

Boston Irish	Thomas H. O'Connor, *The Boston Irish: A Political History* (Boston: Back Bay Books, 1995).
Brideshead Revisted	Evelyn Waugh, *Brideshead Revisted* (New York: Everyman's Library, 1993; originally published 1944).
A Bright Shining Lie	Neil Sheehan, *A Bright Shining Lie: John Paul Vann and America in Vietnam* (New York: Vintage, 1989; originally published 1988).
Centenary Remembrance	Joseph Alsop, *FDR: 1882–1945: A Centenary Remembrance* (New York: Viking, 1982).
Churchill	Martin Gilbert, *Churchill: A Life* (New York: Henry Holt, 1991).
The City in History	Lewis Mumford, *The City in History: Its Origins, Its Transformations, and Its Prospects* (New York: Harcourt Brace, 1961).
Clark's *Leonardo*	Kenneth Clark, *Leonardo Da Vinci* (New York: Viking, 1988; originally published 1939).
Collected Poems	T.S. Eliot, *Collected Poems: 1909–1962* (New York: Harcourt Brace, 1963).
The Confidence-Man	Herman Melville, *The Confidence-Man: His Masquerade* (New York: Penguin, 1990; originally published 1857).
Controversy	William Manchester, *Controversy and Other Essays in Journalism* (Boston: Little, Brown, 1976).
Creation of the Republic	Gordon S. Wood, *The Creation of the American Republic: 1776–1787* (New York: Norton, 1972; originally published 1969).
Culture of Disbelief	Stephen L. Carter, *The Culture of Disbelief: How American Law and Politics Trivialize Religious Devotion* (New York: Anchor, 1994; originally published 1993).
Culture of Narcissism	Christopher Lasch, *The Culture of Narcissism: American Life in an Age of Diminishing Expectations* (New York: Norton, 1978).
Decline and Fall	Edward Gibbon, *The History of the Decline and Fall of the Roman Empire*, 7 vols., ed. J. B. Bury (London: Methuen, 1909–14; originally published 1776–88).
The Degradation of the Democratic Dogma	Henry Adams, *The Degradation of the Democratic Dogma*, ed. Brooks Adams (New York: Macmillan, 1919).
Democracy's Discontent	Michael J. Sandel, *Democracy's Discontent: America in Search of a Public Philosophy* (Cambridge: Harvard University Press, 1996).

Sources

Discourses   Niccolò Machiavelli, *The Discourses on the First Decade of Livy* (New York: Penguin, 1983).

Disraeli   Robert Blake, *Disraeli* (London: Methuen, 1969; originally published 1966).

Edie   Jean Stein, *Edie: An American Biography*, ed. George Plimpton (New York: Knopf, 1982).

Education   *Henry Adams: Novels, Mont Saint Michel, The Education*, ed. Ernest Samuels and Jaune N. Samuels (New York: Library of America, 1983).

Eichmann in   Hannah Arendt, *Eichmann in Jerusalem: A Report on the*
Jerusalem   *Banality of Evil* (New York: Penguin, 1994; originally published 1963).

Eliot's New Life   Lydall Gordon, *Eliot's New Life* (New York: Farrar, Straus & Giroux, 1988).

Emerson   John Richardson, *Emerson: The Mind on Fire* (Berkeley: University of California Press, 1995).

End of Reform   Alan Brinkley, *The End of Reform: New Deal Liberalism in Recession and War* (New York: Vintage, 1996; originally published 1995).

Essays and Lectures   *Ralph Waldo Emerson: Essays and Lectures*, ed. Joel Porte (New York: Library of America, 1983).

The Essential Holmes *The Essential Holmes: Selections from the Letters, Speeches, Judicial Opinions and Other Writings of Oliver Wendell Holmes, Jr.*, ed. Richard A. Posner (Chicago: University of Chicago Press, 1992).

The Fatal Conceit   F. A. von Hayek, *The Fatal Conceit: The Errors of Socialism*, ed. W. W. Bartley III (Chicago: University of Chicago Press, 1991).

FDR   Ted Morgan, *FDR: A Biography* (New York: Simon & Schuster, 1985).

The Fifties   David Halberstam, *The Fifties* (New York: Villard, 1993).

Fire in the Lake   Frances Fitzgerald, *Fire in the Lake: The Vietnamese and the Americans in Vietnam* (New York: Vintage, 1973).

FND   Edmund Wilson, *The Fifties: From Notebooks and Diaries of the Period* (New York: Farrar, Straus & Giroux, 1986).

Frankfurter Reminisces Harlan B. Phillips, *Felix Frankfurter Reminisces* (New York: Reynal, 1960).

The Good Society   Walter Lippman, *The Good Society* (Boston: Little, Brown, 1937).

Sources

The Great Gatsby	F. Scott Fitzgerald, *The Great Gatsby* (New York: Charles Scribner's Sons, 1962; originally published 1925).
The Greek Way	Edith Hamilton, *The Greek Way* (New York: Norton, 1993; originally published 1930).
Growing Up Absurd	Paul Goodman, *Growing Up Absurd: Problems of Youth in the Organized System* (New York: Random House, 1960).
Hereditary Patriotic Societies	Wallace E. Davies, *A History of American Veterans' and Hereditary Patriotic Societies, 1783–1900* (unpublished doctoral dissertation, Harvard university, 1944).
Herndon's *Lincoln*	William H. Herndon, *Life of Lincoln* (New York: Da Capo, 1983).
History of the United States	Henry Adams, *History of the United States of America during the Administrations of Thomas Jefferson* (New York: Library of America, 1986; originally published 1889–91).
The House of Morgan	Ron Chernow, *The House of Morgan: An American Dynasty and the Rise of Modern Finance* (New York: Atlantic Monthly Press, 1990).
Human	Friedrich Nietzsche, *Human, All Too Human: A Book for Free Spirits*, trans. R. J. Hollingdale (Cambridge: Cambridge University Press, 1986; originally published 1878).
Ideological Origins	Bernard Bailyn, *The Ideological Origins of the American Revolution* (Cambridge: Harvard University Press, 1967).
Individualism	David Riesman, *Individualism Reconsidered and Other Essays* (Glencoe, Ill.: Free Press, 1954).
In the Time of the Americans	David Fromkin, *In the Time of the Americans: FDR, Truman, Eisenhower, Marshall, MacArthur—The Generation That Changed America's Role in the World* (New York: Vintage, 1996; originally published 1995).
Joe Alsop's Cold War	Edwin M. Yoder, Jr., *Joe Alsop's Cold War: A Study of Journalistic Influence and Intrigue* (Chapel Hill, N.C.: University of North Carolina Press, 1995).
Journals	*Emerson in His Journals*, ed. Joel Porte (Cambridge: Harvard University Press, 1982).
Keats	*Selected Letters and Poems of John Keats*, ed. J. H. Walsh (London: Chatto and Windus, 1954).
Lawyer's Lawyer	William H. Harbaugh, *Lawyer's Lawyer: The Life of John W. Davis* (Charlottesville: University Press of Virginia, 1990; originally published 1973).
Lead Time	Garry Wills, *Lead Time: A Journalist's Education* (New York: Penguin, 1984; originally published 1983).

Sources

Learned Hand	Gerald Gunther, *Learned Hand: The Man and the Judge* (Cambridge: Harvard University Press, 1995; originally published 1994).
Letters of Machiavelli	*The Letters of Machiavelli: A Selection*, (ed. and trans. Allan Gilbert (Chicago: University of Chicago Press, 1961).
The Liberal Imagination	Lionell Trilling, *The Liberal Imagination: Essays on Literature and Society* (New York: Harcourt Brace, 1950).
The Liberal Persuasion	*The Liberal Persuasion: Arthur M. Schlesinger, Jr., and the Challenge of the American Past*, ed. John Patrick Diggins (Princeton, N.J.: Princeton University Press, 1997).
Liberal Tradition	Louis Hartz, *The Liberal Tradition in America: An Interpretation of American Political Thought Since the Revolution* (New York: Harcourt Brace, 1955).
Literary Criticism	*Henry James: Literary Criticism*, ed. Leon Edel and Mark Wilson (New York: Library of America, 1984).
The Lonely Crowd	David Riesman, Nathan Glazer, and Reuel Denny, *The Lonely Crowd: A Study of the Changing American Character* (New Haven, Conn.: Yale University Press, 1950).
Lord Jim	Joseph Conrad, *Lord Jim: A Tale* (New York: Everyman's Library, 1992; originally published 1900).
Lyndon Johnson	Doris Kearns Goodwin, *Lyndon Johnson and the American Dream* (New York: St. Martin's, 1991).
Machiavellian Moment	J. G. A. Pocock, *The Machiavellian Moment: Florentine Political Thought and the Atlantic Republican Tradition* (Princeton, N.J.: Princeton University Press, 1974).
Marilyn Monroe	Donald Spoto, *Marilyn Monroe: The Biography* (New York: Harper, 1994).
Melbourne	David Cecil, *Melbourne* (New York: Grosset & Dunlap, 1954; parts 1 and 2 were originally published as *The Young Melbourne* in 1939).
Memoirs	Edward Gibbon, *Memoirs of My Life* (New York: Penguin, 1984).
Mornings on Horseback	David McCullough, *Mornings on Horseback: The Story of an Extraordinary American Family, a Vanished Way of Life, and the Unique Child Who Became Theodore Roosevelt* (New York: Simon & Schuster, 1981).
New Dealer in the Cold War	Howard B. Schaffer, *Chester Bowles: New Dealer in the Cold War* (Cambridge: Harvard University Press, 1993).
Nixon off the Record	Monica Crowley, *Nixon off the Record: His Candid Commentary on People and Politics* (New York: Random House, 1996).

Sources

Old Money	Nelson Aldrich, *Old Money: The Mythology of America's Upper Class* (New York: Allworth Press, 1996).
On Active Service	McGeorge Bundy and Henry L. Stimson, *On Active Service in Peace and War* (New York: Harper & Brothers, 1947).
The Other America	Michael Harrington, *The Other America: Poverty in the United States* (New York: Macmillan, 1962).
Palimpsest	Gore Vidal, *Palimpsest: A Memoir* (New York: Penguin, 1996).
A Passage to India	E. M. Forster, *A Passage to India* (New York: Harcourt Brace, 1965; originally published 1924).
Patriotic Gore	Edmund Wilson, *Patriotic Gore: Studies in the Literature of the American Civil War* (Boston: Northeastern University Press, 1984; originally published 1924).
Personal Impressions	Isaiah Berlin, *Personal Impressions* (New York: Penguin, 1982; originally published 1980).
Philadelphia Gentlemen	E. Digby Baltzell, *Philadelphia Gentlemen: The Making of a National Upper Class* (New Brunswick, N.J.: Transaction, 1989; originally published 1958).
Portraits	Charles-Augustin Sainte-Beuve, *Portraits of the Seventeenth Century*, 2 vols. trans. Katharine P. Wormsley (New York: Frederick Ungar, 1964).
Poverty and Compassion	Gertrude Himmelfarb, *Poverty and Compassion: The Moral Imagination of the Late Victorians* (New York: Vintage, 1992; originally published 1991).
The Power Elite	C. Wright Mills, *The Power Elite* (Oxford: Oxford University Press, 1956).
Present at the Creation	Dean Acheson, *Present at the Creation: My Years in the State Department* (New York: Norton, 1969).
The Price of the Ticket	James Baldwin, *The Price of the Ticket: Collected Nonfiction 1948–1985* (New York: St. Martin's, 1985).
The Prince	Niccolò Machiavelli, *The Prince* (New York: Penguin, 1995).
Promised Land, Crusader State	Walter A. McDougall, *Promised Land, Crusader State: The American Encounter with the World since 1776* (Boston: Houghton Mifflin, 1997).
The Quiet American	Graham Greene, *The Quiet American* (New York: Penguin, 1974; originally published 1955).
Radical Son	David Horowitz, *Radical Son: A Journey through Our Times* (New York: Free Press, 1997).

Sources

Reagan's America — Garry Wills, *Reagan's America: Innocents at Home* (Garden City, N.Y.: Doubleday, 1987).

Real Lace — Stephen Birmingham, *Real Lace: America's Irish Rich* (New York: Harper & Row, 1973).

The Rector of Justin — Louis Auchincloss, *The Rector of Justin* (New York: Signet, 1965; originally published 1964).

Reflections — Edmund Burke, *Reflections on the Revolution in France and on the Proceedings in Certain Societies in London Relative to that Event: In a Letter Intended to Have Been Sent to a Gentleman in Paris*, ed. J. G. A. Pocock (Indianapolis, Ind.: Hackett, 1987; originally published 1790).

The Right Places — Stephen Birmingham, *The Right Places (For the Right People)* (Boston: Little, Brown, 1973; originally published 1968).

Rockefeller — Cary Reich, *The Life of Nelson A. Rockefeller: Worlds to Conquer, 1908–1958* (New York: Doubleday, 1996).

The Roman Revolution — Ronald Syme, *The Roman Revolution* (Oxford: Oxford University Press, 1960; originally published 1939).

Roosevelt and Frankfurter — *Roosevelt and Frankfurter: Their Correspondence 1928–1945*, annotated by Max Freedman (Boston: Little, Brown, 1967).

The Roosevelts — Peter Collier with David Horowitz, *The Roosevelts: An American Saga* (New York: Simon & Schuster, 1994).

The Sacred Wood — T. S. Eliot, *The Sacred Wood: Essays on Poetry and Criticism* (London: Methuen, 1920).

Securities Regulation — Louis Loss and Joel Seligman, *Securities Regulation*, 11 vols., 3d. ed. (Boston: Little, Brown, 1989).

Selected Essays — T. S. Eliot, *Selected Essays* (New York: Harcourt Brace, 1950).

The Shores of Light — Edmund Wilson, *The Shores of Light: A Literary Chronicle of the 1920s and 1930s* (Boston: Northeastern University Press, 1985; originally published 1952).

The Sixties — Edmund Wilson, *The Sixties: The Last Journal, 1960–1972* (New York: Farrar, Straus & Giroux, 1993).

The Sixties Reader — *The Sixties: The Art, Attitudes, Politics, and Media of Our Most Explosive Decade*, ed. Gerald Howard (New York: Marlowe, 1995; originally published 1982).

Slouching Towards Bethlehem — Joan Didion, *Slouching Towards Bethlehem* (New York: Penguin, 1974; originally published 1968).

Speeches and Writings — *Abraham Lincoln: Speeches and Writings*, 2 vols., ed. Don E. Fehrenbacher (New York: Library of America, 1989).

Sources

The Stevensons   Jean H. Baker, *The Stevensons: A Biography of an American Family* (New York: Norton, 1997; originally published 1996).

Thoreau   *Henry David Thoreau: A Week; Walden; Maine Woods; Cape Cod*, ed. Robert F. Sayre (New York: Library of America, 1985).

The Triple Thinkers   Edmund Wilson, *The Triple Thinkers and the Wound and the Bow* (Boston: Northeastern University Press, 1984).

Turmoil and Tradition   Elting E. Morison, *Turmoil and Tradition: A Study of the Life and Times of Henry L. Stimson* (Boston: Houghton Mifflin, 1960).

United States   Gore Vidal, *United States—Essays: 1952–1992* (New York: Random House, 1993).

Upstate   Edmund Wilson, *Upstate: Records and Recollections of Northern New York* (New York: Farrar, Straus & Giroux, 1971).

Vanity Fair   William Makepeace Thackeray, *Vanity Fair* (London: Heron, 1978; originally published 1847–48).

The Very Best Men   Evan Thomas, *The Very Best Men: Four Who Dared: The Early Years of the CIA* (New York: Simon & Schuster, 1995).

Views from the Circle   Trustees of Groton School, *Views from the Circle: Seventy-five Years of Groton School* (privately printed, 1960).

Walter Lippmann   Ronald Steel, *Walter Lippmann and the American Century* (Boston: Little, Brown, 1980).

Whittaker Chambers   Sam Tanenhaus, *Whittaker Chambers: A Biography* (New York: Random House, 1997).

The Wise Men   Walter Isaacson and Evan Thomas, *The Wise Men: Six Friends and the World They Made* (New York: Touchstone, 1988; originally published 1986).

Worlds to Conquer   Cary Reich, *The Life of Nelson A. Rockefeller—Worlds to Conquer: 1908–1958* (New York: Doubleday, 1996).

Writings of Chapman   *The Selected Writings of John Jay Chapman*, ed. Jacques Barzun (New York: Farrar, Straus & Cudahy, 1957).

Yeats   Richard Ellmann, *Yeats: The Man and the Masks* (New York: Norton, 1978; originally published 1948).

1968   Jules Witcover, *The Years the Dream Died: Revisiting 1968 in America* (New York: Warner, 1997).

1968 World Book Year   *The 1968 World Book Year Book: A Review of the Events of
Book   1967* (Chicago: Field Enterprises, 1968).

Notes

Introduction

1. B. Drummond Ayres, Jr., "Reagan Joins a Kennedy Remembrance," *The New York Times*, June 6, 1981, p. 9.

2. Close ties: See Wills, *Reagan's America*, pp. 261–78.

3. Ibid., pp. 261–78, 285. Stein and Lew Wasserman were among Reagan's most important California patrons; curiously enough, Stein's son-in-law, William vanden Heuvel, was an important protégé of Bobby's.

4. Bobby helped Ted win a Senate seat: Schlesinger, *Robert Kennedy*, p. 371.

5. Bly, *The Kennedy Men*, p. 229.

6. Ibid., pp. 203, 208, 209, 225.

7. The article was published in *The Washington Monthly* in December 1979.

8. Ayres, op. cit.

9. Ibid.

10. Ibid.

11. Reagan in Hollywood: Wills, *Reagan's America*, p. 143.

12. *American Journey*, p. 193.

13. Tribune of the underclass: Schlesinger, *Robert Kennedy*, pp. 778–800.

14. Reagan said: "And may I say I remember very vividly those last days of the California primary and the closeness that had developed in our views about the growing size and unresponsiveness of government." The *Times* sneered: "A bit of politics did creep into the ceremony. The President managed to mention smaller government, while Senator Kennedy talked of looking after the needs of the forgotten." Ayres, op. cit.

15. Wills, *The Kennedy Imprisonment*, p. 207.

16. Ibid., p. 211.

17. Wills's argument is nonsense for the reasons noted by Arthur Schlesinger in *Robert Kennedy*, pp. 801–2.

18. For an example of Bobby's contemporary value as a liberal icon, see Peter Edelman's March 1997 *Atlantic Monthly* article, in which Edelman deployed Bobby's ghost against President Clinton in order to condemn the President for signing landmark welfare legislation in 1996. Edelman, "The Worst Thing Bill Clinton Has Done," *The Atlantic Monthly*, March 1997, pp. 43–58.

19. Schlesinger's *Robert Kennedy* is 1,066 pages long.

20. Schlesinger, *Robert Kennedy*, p. 803.

21. Ibid.

22. Newfield, *A Memoir*, p. 12.

23. Ibid., p. 19.

24. Ibid., pp. 19, 46.

25. Bobby, quoting Lincoln, in *Collected Speeches*, p. 210.

26. Robert Kennedy, foreword to *Profiles in Courage*, pp. ix–x.

27. Hamilton, *Reckless Youth*, p. 110.

28. Bobby and the intellectuals: see Schlesinger, *Robert Kennedy*, pp. 964–65.

29. Kozol, *Amazing Grace, passim.*

CHAPTER I

1. The revolutionaries who begin as revolutionaries, who never for a moment feel sympathy for the system they wish to overthrow, produce the least constructive revolutions; having never entered into the life of the system they wish to destroy, they do not understand its weaknesses or its strengths, and are thus ill-equipped to reform it.

2. See Newfield, *A Memoir*, p. 44. But cf. Schlesinger's assertion that Bobby's "devotions never . . . carried him to the point of contemplating the priesthood." Schlesinger, *Robert Kennedy*, p. 17.

3. Joseph Kennedy's motion picture company: Whalen, *Founding Father*, pp. 63, 91; Kessler, *The Sins of the Father*, p. 52. Bootlegged liquor: Kessler, *The Sins of the Father*, p. 38.

4. Collier and Horowitz state that the Kennedys spent their first summer on the Cape in 1928. Collier and Horowitz, *The Kennedys*, p. 45. The authors would seem to have confused the year in which Joseph Kennedy bought the Malcolm cottage with the year the family first stayed in the house (as tenants). See Damore, *Cape Cod Years*, pp. 19–21. On Joseph Kennedy's early career, see Whalen, *Founding Father*, pp. 18–113; Birmingham, *Real Lace*, p. 176.

5. Damore, *Cape Cod Years*, p. 20.

6. Kennedy's claim that he lost $1 million on the project is Birmingham, *Real Lace*, p. 183.

7. On Silver King, see Whalen, *Founding Father*, p. 80.

8. Damore, *Cape Cod Years*, p. 156.

9. Bly, *The Kennedy Men*, p. 325.

10. Whalen, *Founding Father*, p. 59; Leamer, *The Kennedy Women*, pp. 169–70; Birmingham, *Real Lace*, p. 185.

11. See Alsop, *I've Seen the Best of It*, p. 410.

12. When in 1951 Joseph Kennedy spoke up at a meeting of Hyannis Port's Civic Association, he was interrupted by a woman who "told the chairman she had not come to listen to that 'Johnny-come-lately' make a speech." Damore, *Cape Cod Years*, p. v.

13. Quoted in Whalen, *Founding Father*, p. 59.

14. Ibid.

15. Birmingham, *Real Lace*, p. 185; Wills, *Kennedy Imprisonment*, p. 63.

16. FDR said to Henry Morgenthau: "Who would have thought the English could take into camp a red-haired Irishman." Wills, *The Kennedy Imprisonment*, p. 76.

17. Schlesinger, *Robert Kennedy*, p. 5.

18. Birmingham, *Real Lace*, p. 179.

19. Cf. Whalen, *Founding Father*, p. 91 (Hyannis "came to be the place the Kennedys meant when they spoke of 'home' ").

20. Kessler, *The Sins of the Father*, p. 74.

21. Collier and Horowitz, *The Kennedys*, p. 263.

22. Rovere, *The American Establishment and Other Reports*, pp. 11–15. See also Vidal, *Palimpsest*, pp. 357–58.

23. Alsop, *Centenary Remembrance*, p. 29.

24. Whalen, *Founding Father*, p. 103.

25. Ibid., pp. 338–48.

26. Harbaugh, *Lawyer's Lawyer*, pp. 451–52.

27. Though at ease with the patricians, Davis never embraced the theories of grand government that men like the Roosevelts espoused, and he remained, to the end of his life, an unreconstructed Jeffersonian Democrat. See ibid, pp. 336–82 (chapters 21–22).

28. On Joseph Kennedy's insistence that his sons attend elite secular schools, see Halberstam, *The Best and the Brightest*, pp. 98–99.

29. See Whalen, *Founding Father*, pp. 22–24, 26.

30. Aldrich, *Old Money*, p. 104.

31. Ibid., pp. 273–74.

32. In Johnson's book Stover played football at Yale; in high school at Lawrenceville he had been the captain of the football team.

33. See Matthews, *Kennedy and Nixon*, pp. 18, 184. By the time Nixon talked to Monica Crowley in the early nineties, his admiration of JFK was considerably less extravagant than it had been forty years before; Crowley

characterized Nixon's later, cooler attitude toward his old rival as "a curious blend of admiration, exasperation, esteem, and healthy rivalry." Crowley, *Nixon off the Record*, p. 29. Nixon insisted that, contrary to what others had written, he "never envied Kennedy." Ibid., p. 36

34. *American Journey*, pp. 171–72.

35. Schlesinger, *Robert Kennedy*, pp. 72–73.

36. Recognition signals: Alsop, *I've Seen the Best of It*, p. 23.

37. *American Journey*, p. 39.

38. Schlesinger, *Robert Kennedy*, p. 623.

39. White, *The Making of the President 1960*, p. 17.

40. Ibid., p. 18.

41. A quintessential Boston Catholic: Newfield, *A Memoir*, pp. 33, 45.

42. Bly, *The Kennedy Men*, p. 326; Damore, *Cape Cod Years*, p. 40; Damore, *Senatorial Privilege*, p. 111.

43. Damore, *Senatorial Privilege*, p. 95. Mother and Dad frowned upon excess: Schlesinger, *Robert Kennedy*, p. 120.

44. Damore, *Senatorial Privilege*, p. 73.

45. Ibid., pp. 73–74.

46. Ibid., p. 105.

47. Bly, *The Kennedy Men*, p. 179.

48. Damore, *Senatorial Privilege*, pp. 23–28.

CHAPTER 2

1. Cf. Hofstadter, *The Age of Reform*, pp. 131–73 (chapter 4). Although Hofstadter's account of what he calls "the status revolution" differs considerably from mine, I am nevertheless indebted to his suggestive essay.

2. See Baltzell, *Philadelphia Gentlemen*, p. xi.

3. O'Connor, *Boston Irish*, pp. 118–33.

4. Ibid.

5. Wilson, "John Jay Chapman: The Mute and the Open Strings," *The Triple Thinkers*, p. 150.

6. See Lutz, *American Nervousness, passim.*

7. Hofstadter, *The Age of Reform*, pp. 138–39, n. 6; Davies, *Hereditary Patriotic Societies*, vol. II, pp. 441ff.

8. Mills, *The Power Elite*, p. 55.

9. Kessler, *The Sins of the Father*, pp. 145–48.

10. Lutz, *American Nervousness*, p. 79.

11. Theodore Roosevelt a hero to Bobby: Newfield, *A Memoir*, p. 48.

12. Quoted in Hofstader, *APT*, p. 272.

13. Cf. Hofstadter, *The Age of Reform*, pp. 140–41.

14. Ibid., p. 136.

15. Adams, *Education*, p. 1176.

16. Morison, *Turmoil and Tradition*, p. 120.

17. In seeking a structure "superior to the energies of the corporation," the men of Theodore Roosevelt's and Henry Stimson's generation "turned instinctively to the state." Ibid., p. 122.

18. The patricians championed a strain of Enlightened thought, ultimately French in origin, that emphasized the importance of rational planning superintended by a central agency (such as an enlightened despot or an executive and legislative authority that expressed, in an enlightened way, the "general will" of the people). This strain of Enlightened thought must be distinguished from the Anglo-Scottish strain, which emphasized the importance of economic and political freedom in making human progress possible.

19. Wilson, *Upstate*, p. 12.

20. Jack Kennedy told Theodore Sorensen that "I've almost never seen him [Joseph P. Kennedy] read a serious book." Sorensen, *Kennedy*, p. 32.

21. Waugh, *Brideshead Revisited*, p. 98.

22. Ibid., pp. 159, 268.

23. Whalen, *Founding Father*, p. 71.

24. Cf. Sir Robert Vansittart, quoted in Schlesinger, *Robert Kennedy*, p. 32.

25. Ibid., p. 5.

26. On the regulation of capital markets and securities issuances by the federal government prior to the creation of the Securities and Exchange Commission, see Loss and Seligman, *Securities Regulation*, vol. I, pp. 152–285.

27. Abe Fortas, a protégé of William O. Douglas and Thurman Arnold, worked at both the AAA and the SEC before he became general counsel to the Bituminous Coal Division of the Department of the Interior.

28. Schlesinger, *Robert Kennedy*, p. 11.

29. Steel, *Walter Lippmann*, p. 24.

30. Whalen, *Founding Father*, pp. 112–13.

31. Schlesinger, *Robert Kennedy*, p. 15.

32. Whitney's watch chain: Chernow, *The House of Morgan*, p. 422.

33. See Hofstadter, *The Age of Reform*, p. 140.

34. Ibid., p. 146.

35. Cf. Alsop, *Centenary Remembrance*, p. 30.

36. See Hofstadter, *APT*, p. 416.

37. Hofstadter used the term "Mugwumps," not "Stimsonians." Hofstadter, *The Age of Reform*, pp. 91–93, 167 *et seq.*

38. Bundy and Stimson, *On Active Service*, p. 17.

39. Cf. McDougall, *Promised Land, Crusader State*, p. 182, where the author states that the "Point Four" passage of Truman's 1949 inaugural address "amounted to a promise to extend the New Deal and Fair Deal to the world."

40. On the New Deal's "commitment to retaining and expanding the institutions of the welfare state," see Brinkley, *End of Reform*, p. 7. On a number of occasions Franklin Roosevelt expressed misgivings about certain

features of the welfare state; at one point relatively early in his presidency he called the dole "a narcotic, a subtle destroyer of the human spirit." But the welfare state nonetheless remains an enduring part of his legacy.

CHAPTER 3

1. Schlesinger, *Robert Kennedy*, p. 44.

2. Other graduates of Groton include Averell Harriman, Dean Acheson, Sumner Welles, Joseph Alsop, McGeorge Bundy, William Bundy, Francis Biddle, Douglas Dillon, Richard Bissell, Tracy Barnes, John Bross, George Rublee, and Stanley Resor.

3. On Endicott Peabody's "indifference" to business and his preparation of boys for "the ministry and statesmanship," see Louis Auchincloss, "The Different Grotons," in *Views from the Circle*, p. 243. Cf. John Train, "Letter to a Classmate," in *Views from the Circle*, pp. 288–89 ("many graduates are made to feel that there is something *infra dig.* about being a builder or a professional man" as opposed to making "a career in government").

4. Schlesinger, *Robert Kennedy*, p. 42.

5. Brooks Adams, introduction to Henry Adams, *The Degradation of the Democratic Dogma*. Public office *did* tempt Henry Adams when he was a young man. Adams said of his friend, Secretary of State John Hay, that "he did what I set out to do, only I could never have done it." Brooks, *Indian Summer*, p. 271.

6. Quoted by Harry Sedgwick, in Stein, *Edie*, p. 33.

7. Walter S. Hinchman, "My Groton Years," in *Views from the Circle*, p. 158.

8. Ibid.

9. Gibbon, *Memoirs*, pp. 75–91.

10. Auchincloss, *The Rector of Justin*, p. 39.

11. See, e.g., Biddle, *An Artist's Story*. The relevant material is reprinted in an essay, "As I Remember Groton School," in *Views from the Circle*, pp. 111–28, especially p. 122.

12. Alsop, *I've Seen the Best of It*, p. 59.

13. Mary Bailey Gimbel, quoted in *American Journey*, p. 37.

14. Schlesinger, *Robert Kennedy*, p. 45.

15. Ibid., pp. 44–46.

16. Mary Bailey Gimbel, quoted in *American Journey*, p. 37.

17. See Schlesinger, *Robert Kennedy*, pp. 67–68.

18. Ibid., p. 66.

19. "hitting the honors": ibid., p. 53.

20. On Arthur Krock's efforts to transform Jack Kennedy's Harvard thesis into the book *Why England Slept*, see Wills, *The Kennedy Imprisonment*, pp. 130–31.

21. Hamilton, *Reckless Youth*, pp. 168–69.

22. See William W. Walton, quoted in *American Journey*, pp. 190–91.
23. Schlesinger, *Robert Kennedy*, p. 81.
24. On Yeats's dreaminess, see Ellmann, *Yeats*, pp. 83–84.
25. Forster, "Notes on English Character," in *Abinger Harvest*, p. 5.
26. Newfield, *A Memoir*, p. 29.

CHAPTER 4

1. U.S. Constitution, Article I, Sections 9 and 10.
2. Syme, *The Roman Revolution*, p. 7.
3. "Just our type": Halberstam, *The Best and the Brightest*, p. 50.
4. Schlesinger, *Robert Kennedy*, pp. 150–51; vanden Heuvel and Gwirtzman, *On His Own*, p. 179.
5. De Toledano, *R.F.K.*, p. 16.
6. *Life* magazine, special issue, "The Kennedys: The Third Generation," p. 40 (1997).
7. Schlesinger, *A Thousand Days*, p. 83; see also Wills, *The Kennedy Imprisonment*, pp. 15, 24, 29, 73–74, 83, 150.
8. Schlesinger, *Robert Kennedy*, p. 595.
9. Cecil, *Melbourne*, pp. 15, 17.
10. *American Journey*, p. 165.
11. Ibid., p. 163.
12. Visitors at Hickory Hill: ibid., pp. 162–63; Schlesinger, *Robert Kennedy*, p. 607.
13. *American Journey*, p. 163.
14. Ibid., pp. 160–65.
15. Vanden Heuvel and Gwirtzman, *On His Own*, p. 16.
16. Birmingham, *The Right Places*, pp. 118, 125; David and David, *Making of a Folk Hero*, p. 263.
17. Lasky, *The Myth and the Man*, p. 19.
18. Crowley, *Nixon off the Record*, p. 32.
19. Schlesinger, *Robert Kennedy*, p. 153.
20. Ibid.
21. Geoffrey C. Ward, "A Charmed Life—Almost" (review of Reich, *Worlds to Conquer*), in *The New York Times Book Review*, November 3, 1996, p. 10.
22. Cannadine, *Aspects of Aristocracy*, pp. 130–31.
23. David and David, *Making of a Folk Hero*, p. 264.
24. "bedint": Cannadine, *Aspects of Aristocracy*, pp. 210, 224.
25. Bobby wanted good relations with Hoover: see Schlesinger, *Robert Kennedy*, p. 254.
26. Ibid.
27. Ibid.
28. Ibid., p. 257.

29. Ibid.
30. Ibid.
31. Bobby put his feet up on his desk: see Thomas, *The Very Best Men*, p. 297.
32. Lasky, *The Myth and the Man*, p. 364.
33. La Donna Harris, quoted in *American Journey*, p. 160.
34. Lasky, *The Myth and the Man*, p. 312; cf. Vidal, *United States*, pp. 823–24.

CHAPTER 5

1. Thackeray, *Vanity Fair*, p. 105.
2. Vidal, *United States*, p. 1269.
3. Lincoln, speech at Cincinnati, Ohio, September 17, 1859, in Lincoln, *Speeches and Writings*, vol. II, p. 84.
4. Though it was tempting, Hofstadter said, to view the New Deal as a continuation of that which had gone before, he himself rejected this approach. See Hofstadter, *The Age of Reform*, pp. 302–4.
5. In his early study of FDR, "Franklin D. Roosevelt: The Patrician as Opportunist," Hofstadter spoke of the New Deal almost as a failure, an experiment that didn't work, a chapter in the nation's life that FDR himself, ever the "realist," was eager to close. See Hofstadter, *APT*, pp. 445–46. By the time he wrote *The Age of Reform*, Hofstadter had revised his view of the New Deal; though he still maintained that it was the result of "a chaos of experimentation" rather than conscious design, he was now prepared to assert that the New Deal radically altered the conditions of American life. See Hofstadter, *The Age of Reform*, pp. 307–8.
6. The National Industrial Recovery Act was intended, among other things, to "provide for the general welfare by promoting the organization of industry for the purpose of cooperative action among trade groups" and to "induce and maintain united action of labor and management under adequate governmental sanctions and supervision." *Statutes of the United States*, vol. 48, p. 195. Frederick H. Wood, counsel to the defendant in the Schechter case, called the act a "bold and unparalleled piece of legislation of the most sweeping and drastic character," which, if upheld, would mean that "dictatorship is surely here." See *A.L.A. Schechter Poultry Corp. et al. v. United States*, 295 U.S. 495, 501 (1935). Title I of the Act, as applied in the *Schechter* case, was held by the Supreme Court to be an unconstitutional delegation of power to the President and to exceed "the power of Congress to regulate interstate commerce." *Schechter Poultry*, 490 U.S. at 529 *et seq.* and 542 *et seq.*
7. Hofstadter, *The Age of Reform*, p. 308.
8. Ibid., pp. 308–9. FDR and Keynes: Hofstadter *APT*, p. 444; Hofstadter, *The Age of Reform*, p. 309.
9. Alsop, *I've Seen the Best of It*, p. 464.

10. See Alsop's contrast of the reaction of Washington insiders to Roosevelt's death with the reaction of insiders to Kennedy's, ibid.

11. Quoted in Wills, *The Kennedy Imprisonment*, p. 164.

12. Vidal, *United States*, p. 821.

13. Bradlee, *Conversations*, pp. 41, 233; Schlesinger, *Robert Kennedy*, pp. 6, 332–33.

14. Berlin, *Personal Impressions*, pp. 12–13.

15. Cf. Vidal, *United States*, p. 780.

16. Cf. Hofstadter, *APT*, p. 415.

17. Alsop, *Centenary Remembrance*, p. 30.

18. May even have left scars: ibid., p. 35.

19. Morgan, *FDR*, p. 12.

20. Alsop, *Centenary Remembrance*, p. 36.

21. "Well-born, polite, not gifted": Berlin, *Personal Impressions*, p. 30.

22. Gunther, *Learned Hand*, p. 456.

23. Ibid.

24. Berlin, *Personal Impressions*, p. 25.

25. Vidal, *United States*, p. 746.

26. Acheson, *Present at the Creation*, p. 740.

27. Kessler, *The Sins of the Father*, p. 147.

28. Steel, *Walter Lippmann*, p. 316.

29. Acheson, *Present at the Creation*, p. 740.

30. Schlesinger, *Robert Kennedy*, p. 24.

31. Sophomoric jokes: Morgan, *F.D.R.*, p. 507.

32. An example of flippant complacency: "The facts are," FDR said in 1920, "that I wrote Haiti's constitution myself, and, if I do say it, I think it is a pretty good constitution." Hofstadter, *APT*, p. 419.

33. Alsop, *I've Seen the Best of It*, p. 136.

34. Vidal, *United States*, p. 747.

35. Morgan, *FDR*, p. 453.

36. Vidal, *United States*, p. 746.

37. Address, Fordham University, New York, June 10, 1967, quoted in Hall, *Apostle of Change*, p. 12.

38. The passage quoted is from chapter 6 of *The Prince*.

39. See Morgan, *FDR*, p. 542.

40. Bradlee, *Conversations*, pp. 107–8.

41. Schlesinger, *Robert Kennedy*, p. 371.

42. See Spencer Abraham, "A Pro-Growth Tax Plan," *The Wall Street Journal*, May 20, 1996, p. A-18.

43. There is a great deal of scholarly debate as to whether the West really was the "cradle of individualism" that historians like Frederick Jackson Turner made it out to be. See Wills, *Reagan's America*, pp. 87–94. Individualism may have represented the aspiration rather than the reality.

44. See Wills, *The Kennedy Imprisonment*, p. 193.

45. Lasky, *The Myth and the Man*, p. 81.

CHAPTER 6

1. Halberstam, *The Best and the Brightest*, pp. 53–54.
2. Ibid., pp. 47–57.
3. Sorensen, *Kennedy*, p. 18.
4. Ibid.
5. Schlesinger, *A Thousand Days*, p. 78.
6. "Our Harvard . . . Senator": ibid., p. 15; "perfect manners": ibid., p. 600 (quoting Pierre Salinger); "Brahmin taste": ibid., p. 100; "a young Lord Salisbury": Schlesinger, ibid, p. 78.
7. On JFK's love of the poetry of Byron, see Collier and Horowitz, *An American Drama*, pp. 213–14.
8. De Toledano, *R.F.K.*, p. 18.
9. "Happy, jolly things": ibid.
10. Schlesinger, *Robert Kennedy*, p. 78.
11. Bradlee, *Conversations*, p. 230.
12. Jack Kennedy's love of the novels of Scott: Hamilton, *Reckless Youth*, p. 87. His love of Churchill's prose: Schlesinger, *A Thousand Days*, p. 84. His love of Burke's prose: Manchester, *Death of a President*, p. 372. His love of English aristocratic gossip: Bradlee, *Conversations*, p. 230.
13. Schlesinger, *A Thousand Days*, p. 523.
14. Schlesinger, *Robert Kennedy*, p. 96.
15. Ibid., p. 68.
16. Ibid., pp. 66, 68.
17. Ibid.
18. "Brooks Brothers beatnik": Bradlee, *Conversations*, p. 227; "confuse him with Dean Acheson": de Toledano, *R.F.K.*, p. 12.
19. De Toledano, *R.F.K.*, p. 33.
20. Schlesinger, *Robert Kennedy*, p. 124.
21. Ibid., p. 96.
22. Halberstam, *Unfinished Odyssey*, p. 137.
23. Halberstam, *The Best and the Brightest*, p. 24.
24. Ibid., p. 27.
25. Schlesinger, *Robert Kennedy*, pp. 84–85.
26. Ibid., p. 70.
27. Ibid., pp. 69, 418.
28. Ibid., p. 59.
29. Jack Kennedy on America's role as "chief defender of Western civilization": *Let the Word Go Forth*, p. 38. JFK's commitment to the welfare state is discussed in chapter 8.
30. Schlesinger, *A Thousand Days*, p. 14.
31. Schlesinger, *The Age of Jackson*, pp. 10, 11, 20, 35, 505, 515, 518, 521.
32. Ibid., p. 43.
33. Schlesinger, *Robert Kennedy*, pp. 82–83, 109.
34. Ibid., p. 109.

35. Lasky, *The Myth and the Man,* p. 306.
36. Schlesinger, *Robert Kennedy,* pp. 203–4.
37. See Halberstam, *The Fifties,* p. 729.
38. Halberstam, *The Best and the Brightest,* p. 35.
39. Yoder, *Joe Alsop's Cold War,* p. 91.
40. Ibid., pp. 9, 30.
41. Alsop said that Jack Kennedy and Phil Graham were his two "closest younger friends": Alsop, *I've Seen the Best of It,* p. 375.
42. The Sunday-night supper club: Thomas, *The Very Best Men,* pp. 27, 99, 103–105.
43. The Sunday-night supper club: ibid.
44. Harriman and Nixon: ibid., p. 27.
45. Alsop's parties: ibid., pp. 104–5; Yoder, *Joe Alsop's Cold War,* pp. 27–28.
46. Alsop and the KGB: Yoder, *Joe Alsop's Cold War,* pp. 153–58; Thomas, *The Very Best Men,* p. 106.
47. Stimson's attitude toward the New Deal is not easily categorized. Certainly he was committed to the strain of progressive thought out of which the New Deal and the welfare state arose. He was brought into public life by Theodore Roosevelt, he praised Roosevelt's "New Nationalism," and he supported the paternalist state that the "New Nationalism" envisioned. See Bundy and Stimson, *On Active Service,* p. 22: "Stimson wrote congratulating his friend and leader on the famous Osawatomie speech, the most terrifying of the lot" of "New Nationalism" speeches that TR delivered in 1910. (The Osawatomie speech was the embodiment of the "intensifying paternalistic nationalism" that TR had come to embrace. Hofstadter, *APT,* p. 301. In his blanket denunciation of industrial combinations, Roosevelt made no exception even for those combinations that create efficiency and thereby benefit consumers; he argued that "the way out" lay not in using the antitrust laws to prevent undesirable combinations, but rather in government *"completely controlling"* all industrial combinations "in the interest of the public welfare." In a subsequent statement Roosevelt elaborated his position and declared that Americans ought to "abandon definitely the *laissez-faire* theory of political economy, and fearlessly champion a system of increased Governmental control . . . the only way to meet a billion-dollar corporation is by invoking the protection of a hundred-billion dollar government," one that was no doubt to be staffed by Enlightened experts possessed of a wisdom vastly superior to that of the marketplace.) In their book Stimson and McGeorge Bundy made it clear that Stimson sympathized not with the populist solutions of Progressive politics (the direct election of Senators, the direct primary contest), but with the paternalist solutions. "The true remedy for American misgovernment," Stimson believed, "would lie, then, in exactly the opposite direction from that indicated by the advocates of direct democracy. The elected officials must have more power, not less." Bundy and Stimson, *On Active Service,* p. 58. Stimson believed that Congress should establish "an administrative bureau for the permanent, continuous, and

watchful oversight of corporate business engaged in interstate commerce." Bundy and Stimson, *On Active Service*, p. 47. In his perceptive biography of Stimson, Elting Morison observed that Stimson and his peers, in their quest for a solution to the nation's problems, "turned instinctively to the state. . . . [T]hey discussed the possibility of enlarging the sphere of government ownership, considered the wisdom of fixing prices by government action and even . . . examined tentatively the methods of what they called 'collectivization.' Before the War, none of these procedures was introduced in any systematic way though the power of the central government to regulate the economy was steadily increased." Morison, *Turmoil and Tradition*, pp. 122, 125.

Although he remained a Republican, Stimson had little sympathy for Ogden Mills's harshly antagonistic attitude toward FDR. See Morison, *Turmoil and Tradition*, p. 458. And if Stimson was critical of the heavy-handed approach to regulation embodied in legislation like the Securities Act of 1933, in time he reconciled himself to most of the New Deal policies, reconciled himself even to the TVA, the state-sponsored monopoly that six decades after its creation continues to thwart and bully competitors who seek to bring cheaper power to the South. See John J. Fialka, "New Deal Undone: Using Savvy Tactics, Bristol, Va., Unplugs from a Federal Utility: Town Cuts Its Electric Bill By Standing Up to TVA as Others Watch in Envy," *The Wall Street Journal*, May 27, 1997, p. A1. Although Stimson initially opposed the TVA, by 1947 he was "prepared to admit—perhaps even to claim—that which he had denied in 1935, that the principle of TVA, as an adventure in the effective use of national resources, was a direct outgrowth of the position he and other conservationists had taken back in 1912." Bundy and Stimson, *On Active Service*, pp. 43–44.

Stimson's contribution to the national security state and the American empire is less ambiguous than his relation to the New Deal. Although he himself retired from public life prior to the advent of the Cold War, the former governor general of the Philippines groomed many of the leading statesmen of the generation that built and administered the postwar American empire. He was their model, and many of them said that, throughout their public careers, they tried to approach problems the way Colonel Stimson would have approached them. McCloy, Lovett, Forrestal, and McGeorge Bundy were all directly influenced by Stimson's ideas; countless other statesmen were indirectly influenced by them.

48. Bissell preferred Kennedy: Thomas, *The Very Best Men*, pp. 238–40. On the "Groton clique" at the CIA, see Thomas, *The Very Best Men*, *passim*, but especially pp. 90–91, 108.

Notes

CHAPTER 7

1. Isaacson and Thomas, *The Wise Men*, p. 431. The martinis were passed around like water: Thomas, *The Very Best Men*, p. 103.
2. See Stein, *Edie*.
3. Baker, *The Stevensons*, pp. 154, 156–57.
4. Ibid., pp. 253–54, 261, 264, 271–75.
5. Ibid., p. 6.
6. Schlesinger, *Robert Kennedy*, p. 133.
7. Thomas, *The Very Best Men*, p. 287.
8. Schaffer, *Chester Bowles*, pp. 7, 9–11, 15–17.
9. Bowles incurs Taft's wrath: ibid., p. 17. Bowles refuses to campaign in Wisconsin: ibid., pp. 171–72; Halberstam, *The Best and the Brightest*, p. 17.
10. Ibid.
11. White, *The Making of the President 1960*, p. 140.
12. Ibid., pp. 140–41. See also: Halberstam, *Unfinished Odyssey*, p. 78; Schlesinger, *A Thousand Days*, pp. 15–16.
13. Halberstam, *The Best and the Brightest*, p. 8.
14. On the "power elite," see Mills, *The Power Elite*. On the "real" versus "paper" power structure, see Halberstam, *The Best and the Brightest*, p. 195.
15. See *The Oxford English Dictionary*.
16. Alsop, *Centenary Remembrance*, p. 29.
17. Isaacson and Thomas, *The Wise Men*, p. 116.
18. On Acheson's relationship to Brandeis and Frankfurter, see ibid., pp. 125–26, 464–65.
19. Ibid., *The Wise Men*, p. 78.
20. See McDougall, *Promised Land, Crusader State*, p. 169: "At home, the Cold War demanded peacetime conscription, high taxes, federal intervention in science, education, business, and labor (Truman broke strikes in the name of national security), not to mention domestic surveillance and loyalty oaths."
21. Sheehan, *A Bright Shining Lie*, p. 43.
22. On Truman's loyalty tests, see Wills, *Lead Time*, p. 53. On the dismissal of Service, see Halberstam, *The Best and the Brightest*, p. 114.
23. See Halberstam, *The Fifties*, p. 57.
24. Damore, *Cape Cod Years*, p. 137.
25. Halberstam, *The Fifties*, pp. 704, 729.
26. Halberstam, *The Best and the Brightest*, p. 9; Isaacson and Thomas, *The Wise Men*, pp. 594–96.
27. See Schlesinger, *Robert Kennedy*, p. 237.
28. On Bobby's civil rights work, see ibid., chapters 14–18.
29. Halberstam, *The Best and the Brightest*, p. 99. Cf. Judge Posner's assessment: "We tend to forget that the early 1960s was a period in which the political establishment was optimistic about the ability of elites, whether

secretive foreign policy and military officials or secretive judges, to shape events." Richard A. Posner, "In Memoriam: William J. Brennan, Jr.," *Harvard Law Review*, November 1997, vol. III, p. 13.

30. *Let the Word Go Forth*, p. 12.

31. Alsop, *I've Seen the Best of It,* p. 440.

32. See Syme, *The Roman Revolution*, pp. 78–79.

CHAPTER 8

1. Morgenthau, quoted in *American Journey*, p. 145; Manchester, *Death of a President*, pp. 146, 195; Schlesinger, *Robert Kennedy*, p. 607.

2. Morgenthau, quoted in *American Journey*, p. 145; Manchester, *Death of a President*, pp. 195–96; Schlesinger, *Robert Kennedy*, pp. 607–8.

3. Schlesinger, *Robert Kennedy*, p. 608; Manchester, *Death of a President*, p. 256. Manchester reports that Bobby's exact words were "He died." Manchester, *Death of a President*, p. 257.

4. Dean Markham picked up David Kennedy at his school. See Manchester, *Death of a President*, p. 259.

5. Ibid., pp. 387, 389–91; Schlesinger, *Robert Kennedy*, pp. 608–610.

6. Schlesinger, *Robert Kennedy*, p. 611.

7. Quoted in Wilson, *The Sixties*, p. 164. Cf. Leamer, *The Kennedy Women*, p. 526.

8. Alsop, *I've Seen the Best of It*, p. 464.

9. Ibid.

10. Ibid.

11. Bradlee, *Conversations*, p. 242.

12. Newfield, *A Memoir*, p. 30.

13. Ibid., p. 31.

14. Lasky, *The Myth and the Man*, p. 192; Newfield, *A Memoir*, p. 31.

15. Lasky, *The Myth and the Man*, p. 193.

16. Schlesinger, *Robert Kennedy*, pp. 612–13.

17. Ibid., p. 613.

18. Ibid., p. 618.

19. The effect of *The Greek Way* on Bobby was considerable. Many of the passages of poetry and prose that he quoted in his speeches are to be found in Miss Hamilton's book. Bobby was moved by the lines of Sophocles quoted on page 158 of *The Greek Way* (see Schlesinger, *Robert Kennedy*, p. 618) and was fond of quoting the lines of Aeschylus that appear on page 156 of the book (see ibid., p. 618). In one of his notebooks Bobby copied out these words from *The Greek Way*: "All things are to be called into question; there are no limits set to thought" (see ibid., p. 617; Hamilton, *The Greek Way*, p. 25). The quotation from *Romeo and Juliet* that Bobby used at the 1964 Democratic National Convention in Atlantic City was said by Schlesinger to have been suggested by Jacqueline Kennedy, but Bobby must

himself have been familiar with it from his reading of *The Greek Way* (see Schlesinger, *Robert Kennedy*, p. 64; Hamilton, *The Greek Way*, p. 50). The Emerson quotation that Bobby so often used—about truth and repose—is also found in *The Greek Way*. Ibid., p. 36. Both Bobby and Jack quoted Miss Hamilton's rendering of the Greek definition of happiness. See ibid, p. 24.

20. Ibid., p. 40.

21. Ibid., pp. 65–67.

22. Ibid., p. 66.

23. Newfield, *A Memoir*, p. 32.

24. See the first speech of the priest in Sophocles, *Oedipus the King*.

25. Lasky, *The Myth and the Man*, p. 305.

26. See Schlesinger, *Robert Kennedy*, p. 637 ("His brother's last wish had been a war against poverty"). Leaders who . . . failed to "press": ibid., p. 151.

27. Manchester, *Death of a President*, p. 378.

28. See Newfield, *A Memoir*, p. 28.

29. Morison, *Turmoil and Tradition*, p. 81.

30. Newfield, *A Memoir*, p. 161.

31. Lasky, *The Myth and the Man*, p. 200; Schlesinger, *Robert Kennedy*, p. 667.

32. Lasky, *The Myth and the Man*, p. 201; Schlesinger, *Robert Kennedy*, p. 667.

33. On Bobby's rudeness to Mrs. Roosevelt and former Senator Lehman, see Lasky, *The Myth and the Man*, p. 126; a similar version of the story is told by the Davids in *Making of a Folk Hero*, p. 6. On Bobby and Chester Bowles, see Newfield, *A Memoir*, p. 28. Bowles himself denied the story that Bobby jabbed his finger into Bowles's body when he told the elder statesman that "he should keep his mouth shut and remember that he was *for* the Bay of Pigs." Schaffer, *Chester Bowles*, p. 207.

34. Schlesinger, *Robert Kennedy*, p. 668.

35. Ibid.

36. Ibid., p. 594.

37. Lasky, *The Myth and the Man*, pp. 205, 216; David and David, *Making of a Folk Hero*, p. 253.

38. Lasky, *The Myth and the Man*, p. 219.

39. Schlesinger, *Robert Kennedy*, p. 667.

40. *American Journey*, pp. 179–80.

41. Schlesinger, *Robert Kennedy*, pp. 669–70.

42. Ibid., p. 670.

43. Newfield, *A Memoir*, p. 145.

44. Schlesinger, *Robert Kennedy*, p. 616.

45. Ibid.

46. Ibid., p. 877.

47. Newfield, *A Memoir*, p. 30.

48. Ibid.

49. Ibid.

50. Your brother's dead: Schlesinger, *Robert Kennedy*, p. 670.

51. Lasky, *The Myth and the Man*, pp. 225–26.

52. Ibid., p. 233.

53. Newfield, *A Memoir*, p. 38.

54. Goodwin, *Remembering America*, pp. 267–81.

55. On his desire to emulate his heroes, see ibid., pp. 217, 259 (LBJ wished to "out-Roosevelt Roosevelt").

56. Lasky, *The Myth and the Man*, p. 285.

57. Ibid., pp. 323, 340.

58. Ibid., p. 324.

59. Trilling, *The Liberal Imagination*, p. 93.

CHAPTER 9

1. *Collected Speeches*, p. 156.

2. Ibid., p. 157.

3. Schlesinger, *Robert Kennedy*, pp. 782–83.

4. Newfield, *A Memoir*, p. 40.

5. Schlesinger, *Robert Kennedy*, p. 882.

6. Vanden Heuvel and Gwirtzman, *On His Own*, p. 62; cf. Salinger, *P.S.*, pp. 187–88.

7. Salinger, *P.S.*, p. 188.

8. "The Senate's Distinguished Traditions," speech delivered in the Senate, May 1, 1957, in *Let the Word Go Forth*, pp. 43–49.

9. Gardner, *Robert Kennedy in New York*, p. 47.

10. "Blackened tunnels": Robert Kennedy, *To Seek a Newer World*, p. 56; terrible housing projects: *Collected Speeches*, p. 180; "brutalities": ibid., p. 156; dirt and stink: ibid., p. 160; "grotesque" violence: ibid., p. 195; "congestion," "filth," "danger and purposelessness": *To Seek a Newer World*, p. 19.

11. RFK Press Release, February 1, 1965, in RFK Senate Papers, file 11.

12. Lasky, *The Myth and the Man*, p. 241.

13. *Collected Speeches*, p. 157.

14. Ibid., pp. 159–60.

15. Ibid., p. 163.

16. Ibid.

17. Ibid., p. 162; vanden Heuvel and Gwirtzman, *On His Own*, p. 83.

18. Excerpts from the speeches were later published in *Collected Speeches*, pp. 165–76.

19. *To Seek a Newer World*, p. 20.

20. Ibid., p. 8. Bobby found in Edith Hamilton additional support for his growing dislike of bureaucracy and the dull standardization of mind it fostered. See *To Seek a Newer World*, pp. 7–8, 61–62. Bureaucracy, according to Bobby, made it impossible for human beings to live up to the Greek ideal of happiness—"the exercise of vital powers along the lines of excellence in

a life affording them scope"—that he had adopted as his own. *To Seek a Newer World*, p. 61; cf. Hamilton, *The Greek Way*, p. 24.

21. *Collected Speeches*, pp. 208–9.

22. See David Riesman, *The Lonely Crowd*; Sloan Wilson, *The Man in the Gray Flannel Suit*; Mills et al., *The Power Elite*; and W. H. Whyte, *The Organization Man*. On this point I am indebted to Halberstam, *The Fifties*, pp. 521–36.

23. *Collected Speeches*, p. 170.

24. Draft of a speech, RFK Senate Papers, file 120.

25. Address, Day Care Council of New York, May 8, 1967.

26. *Collected Speeches*, pp. 209–210 (emphasis added).

27. Cf. ibid., p. 171.

28. Ibid.

29. Ibid., p. 188. It was "absurd," Bobby said, "to think that the federal government can find all the answers or meet our needs in any significant fashion." Ross, *Apostle of Change*, p. 113.

30. Schlesinger, *Robert Kennedy*, p. 783.

31. *Collected Speeches*, p. 173.

32. Ibid., p. 190. That which "is given or granted can be taken away," that which "is begged can be refused," but that which "is earned is kept," that which "is self-made is unalienable," and that which "you do for yourselves and your children can never be taken away." Ibid, p. 188.

33. Ibid., p. 205.

34. Vanden Heuvel and Gwirtzman, *On His Own*, p. 80.

35. Quoted in Ross, *Apostle of Change*, p. 159.

36. "We cannot," Bobby declared, "expect people to become independent and self-supporting if we treat them as entirely dependent." Draft of a speech, in RFK Senate Papers, file 120.

37. See vanden Heuvel and Gwirtzman, *On His Own*, p. 90.

38. *Collected Speeches*, pp. 209–10.

CHAPTER 10

1. Fortune, Machiavelli wrote, "is a woman and if she is to be submissive it is necessary to beat and coerce her. . . . Always, being a woman, she favours young men, because they are less circumspect and more ardent, and because they command her with more audacity." *The Prince*, p. 80.

2. Sainte-Beuve, *Portraits*, p. 140.

3. White, *The Making of the President 1960*, p. 166 ("As Caesar, after he had conquered Gaul, used the Gallic cavalrymen to mop up Pompey in the ensuing civil wars of Rome, so now Kennedy was using the big-city bosses to mop up Stevenson").

4. Fitzgerald, *The Great Gatsby*, p. 66.

5. Ibid.

6. Ibid., pp. 99–100.

7. Quoted in vanden Heuvel and Gwirtzman, *On His Own*, p. 86; cf. Ross, *Apostle of Change*, p. 115.

8. Vanden Heuvel, *On His Own*, p. 86.

9. Quoted in Newfield, *A Memoir*, p. 73.

10. With the possible exceptions of Theodore Roosevelt, his father, and his older brother Jack.

11. Newfield, *A Memoir*, p. 26.

12. Ibid., pp. 26–27; Schlesinger, *Robert Kennedy*, p. 801.

13. Vanden Heuvel and Gwirtzman, *On His Own*, pp. 16–17.

14. Manchester, *Death of a President*, pp. 602–3.

15. Emerson, "Self-Reliance," in *Essays and Lectures*, p. 265.

16. Emerson, "The American Scholar," in ibid., p. 65.

17. Ibid.

18. Chapman, "Emerson," in *Writings of Chapman*, p. 163.

19. Emerson, "Self-Reliance," in *Essays and Lectures*, pp. 259–60.

20. Ibid., p. 276.

21. See Schlesinger, *Robert Kennedy*, p. 801.

22. Halberstam, *Unfinished Odyssey*, p. 9.

23. Emerson, "Self-Reliance," in *Essays and Lectures*, p. 263.

24. See Lincoln, letter to Thomas Lincoln and John D. Johnston, December 24, 1848, in *Speeches and Writings*, vol. 1, pp. 224–25.

25. RFK notes on testimony of Dr. Robert Coles during the Ribicoff Hearings, in RFK Senate Papers, file 18.

26. Adams, *History of the United States* (Jefferson's administration), p. 107.

27. James, *Hawthorne*, in *Literary Criticism*, pp. 351–52.

28. Wilson, *FND*, pp. 264–65.

29. William James rejected his brother Henry's faith in institutions and the traditions they perpetuate. At the time of the Dreyfus affair James wrote: "We 'intellectuals' in America must all work to keep our precious birthright of individualism, and freedom from these institutions [church, army, aristocracy, royalty]. *Every* great institution is perforce a means of corruption—whatever good it may also do. Only in the free personal relation is full ideality to be found." Quoted in Hofstadter, *Anti-intellectualism*, p. 39.

30. Burke, *Reflections*, p. 76.

31. It will not be thought surprising that T. S. Eliot disliked Emerson or that Henry James found him wanting. See James, *Literary Criticism*, pp. 268–70. Eliot rejected the democratic and individualist creed that grew out of the Puritanism of his own (and Emerson's) ancestors; he was received into the English church in 1927, and became the subject of an English king (as James had before him). For Eliot, Emerson's essays were "already an encumbrance," a burden, a moral and intellectual dead end. Matthiessen, *American Renaissance*, p. 193. Eliot found his calling not in the profession of his own genius and powers (self-reliance), but in the assimilation of these to a series of larger traditions and creeds (reliance on others). He wrote poetry

not merely with himself or even his own generation "in his bones," but with the feeling that "the whole of the literature of Europe from Homer" had a meaning and canonical significance. Eliot, *Selected Essays*, p. 4. A mature poet could not, in Eliot's view, rely on his own subjective self as the principal source of his poetry, even if such experience was always, at some level or other, present in his work. Gordon, *Eliot's New Life*, p. 2 (describing her "attempt to elicit the autobiographical element in Eliot's poetry by measuring the poetry against the life"). Far more important than the poet's own personality was what Eliot called "the historical sense," a sense that he believed "nearly indispensable to anyone who would continue to be a poet beyond his twenty-fifth year." Eliot was dismissive of the type of poet—and of the type of man—who had too little historical sense, too little "maturity," too excessive a reliance on his own individual self. Eliot, *The Sacred Wood*, p. 49. Eliot's conception of the "historical sense" helps, of course, to explain his own poetic technique; his own poetry is haunted, perhaps burdened, by the weight of the whole of "the literature of Europe from Homer." The notes Eliot appended to *The Waste Land* give the impression almost of a pastiche of Baudelaire, Dante, Webster, Shakespeare, Ovid, Virgil, Spenser, Marvell, Augustine, Kyd, and Frazer. See Eliot, *Collected Poems*, pp. 70–76. Edmund Wilson observed that in reading Eliot "we are sometimes visited by uneasy recollections of Ausonius, in the fourth century, composing Greek-and-Latin macaronics and piecing together poetic mosaics out of verses from Virgil." Wilson, *Axël's Castle*, p. 111. "Immature poets imitate," Eliot asserted. "Mature poets steal." Eliot, *The Sacred Wood*, p. 125.

32. Emerson, "Literary Ethics," in *Essays and Lectures*, p. 97.

33. Emerson, "Self-Reliance," in ibid., p. 259.

34. The popularity of the drug Prozac seems in large part attributable to the fact that a person who, prior to taking it, exhibited all the signs of insufficient self-confidence is said to be miraculously transformed by the drug into a person who displays all the characteristics of a highly self-confident person.

35. See LeMoyne Billings's remarks in *American Journey*, p. 37.

36. Newfield, *A Memoir*, p. 42; Mary Bailey Gimble, quoted in *American Journey*, p. 37.

37. Quoted in Schlesinger, *Robert Kennedy*, p. 33.

38. Ibid., p. 42.

39. *American Journey*, p. 37.

40. Trilling, "A Washington Memoir," p. 62.

41. Ibid.

42. Halberstam, *Unfinished Odyssey*, p. 127.

43. Newfield, *A Memoir*, p. 18; *American Journey*, p. 294.

44. Newfield, *A Memoir*, p. 18.

45. Ibid., p. 35; *American Journey*, p. 279.

46. Newfield, *A Memoir*, p. 35.

47. *American Journey*, p. 194; Newfield, *A Memoir*, p. 18.
48. Halberstam, *Unfinished Odyssey*, p. 96.
49. *Collected Speeches*, p. 208; cf. vanden Heuvel and Gwirtzman, *On His Own*, p. 86; Ross, *Apostle of Change*, p. 105; Schlesinger, *Robert Kennedy*, p. 804.
50. *Collected Speeches*, p. 172.

CHAPTER 11

1. Newfield, *A Memoir*, p. 95.
2. Vanden Heuvel and Gwirtzman, *On His Own*, pp. 91–92; Schlesinger, *Robert Kennedy*, pp. 785–86.
3. Schlesinger, *Robert Kennedy*, p. 786.
4. See letter, Bobby to McGeorge Bundy, in the Walinsky Papers, file 1.
5. See Newfield, *A Memoir*, pp. 95–102; Schlesinger, *Robert Kennedy*, pp. 787–88; vanden Heuvel and Gwirtzman, *On His Own*, pp. 92–93.
6. Newfield, *A Memoir*, p. 97; Schlesinger, *Robert Kennedy*, p. 788; Walinsky, memorandum to Bobby, undated, concerning the need for action in Bedford-Stuyvesant to be consistent with "the community's own expression of will and interest," in the Walinsky Papers, file 2.
7. See *Collected Speeches*, p. 188.
8. Bobby believed in the necessity of "cooperation with the private business community" in the attempt to create "self-sustaining economically viable enterprises" in the ghetto. See *Collected Speeches*, pp. 188, 190, 191.
9. Ibid., p. 172.
10. The use of tax incentive and forgiveness schemes to stimulate private investment in underdeveloped areas was pioneered in the so-called Bootstrap program for Puerto Rico in the 1940s. See John R. Newsom and Herbert Sturz, "A Proposal for Major Economic Aid to Harlem," August 12, 1964, in Walinsky Papers, file 2. As David Rockefeller observed in his testimony during the Ribicoff hearings on urban affairs, the tax code had also been used to encourage American investment in developing nations. See Bobby's memorandum re: Urban Housing Investment Act, circa 1967, in RFK Senate Papers, file 11. By January 1967 Edelman was at work on a scheme to use "the Internal Revenue Code to encourage private enterprise to go into the ghetto." See memorandum, Edelman to Bobby, January 25, 1967, in RFK Senate Papers, file 112; letter, Edelman to John R. Newsom, January 16, 1967, in RFK Senate Papers, file 112. On July 12, 1967, Bobby introduced a bill "to provide federal tax credits, accelerated depreciation schedules, and job-training programs as incentive for businessmen to locate industry in poverty centers." See Ross, *Apostle of Change*, pp. 155–57. President Johnson declined to support the bill. Schlesinger, *Robert Kennedy*, p. 789; Newfield, *A Memoir*, pp. 105–6.
11. Newfield, *A Memoir*, p. 105.

12. The letter is dated January 18, 1967, and can be found in the Walinsky Papers, file 1.

13. Ibid.

14. Ford Foundation Proposal, March 9, 1967, in RFK Senate Papers, file 11.

15. Ibid.

16. See Ross, *Apostle of Change*, p. 153.

17. Memorandum noting questions for Walter Reuther in connection with testimony in the Ribicoff hearings on urban affairs, December 1966, in RFK Senate Papers, file 18; cf. Walinsky, memorandum to Bobby, undated, concerning the need for action consistent with "the community's own expression of will and interest," in the Walinsky Papers, file 2.

18. Ford Foundation Proposal, March 9, 1967, pp. 19–20, in RFK Senate Papers, file 11. Bundy collaborated with Stimson in the writing of *On Active Service in Peace and War*, an account of Stimson's career.

19. Ford Foundation Proposal, March 9, 1967, p. 19, in RFK Senate Papers, file 11.

20. Ibid., p. 20.

21. See Tom Wolfe's essay "The Radical Chic."

22. See BSDPO, 7; memorandum, Thomas Johnston to Bobby, May 3, 1967, in RFK Senate Papers, file 11; Schlesinger, *Robert Kennedy*, p. 786.

23. Marian Wright Edelman, quoted in *American Journey*, p. 124; cf. ibid., p. 279. Schlesinger, *Robert Kennedy*, p. 794.

24. *American Journey*, p. 279.

25. Ibid., p. 124.

26. Ibid.; Schlesinger, *Robert Kennedy*, p. 795.

27. Vanden Heuvel and Gwirtzman, *On His Own*, p. 171.

28. Newfield, *A Memoir*, p. 82.

29. Like the Lord: see Matt. 19:14.

30. The quotations in this paragraph are taken from a memorandum from Walinsky to Bobby entitled "Program for the Fall," 1966, in the Walinsky Papers, file 2.

31. Newfield, *A Memoir*, p. 95.

CHAPTER 12

1. Baldwin, "Letter from a Region in My Mind," in Baldwin, *The Price of the Ticket*, p. 339.

2. Ibid.

3. Ibid., p. 376.

4. Schlesinger, *Robert Kennedy*, pp. 330–31.

5. "Martin Luther Queen": Vidal, *Palimpsest*, p. 360.

6. Schlesinger, *Robert Kennedy*, p. 331; *American Journey*, p. 119.

7. *American Journey*, p. 119.

8. Ibid., p. 122.

9. Ibid.

10. Ibid., p. 119.

11. Ibid., p. 120.

12. Ibid., pp. 119 20.

13. Ibid., p. 120.

14. Ibid., p. 121.

15. Ibid., p. 122; Schlesinger, *Robert Kennedy*, p. 334.

16. Cf. the definition of the verb "humiliate" in the *Oxford English Dictionary*.

17. Schlesinger, *Robert Kennedy*, p. 878.

18. *American Journey*, p. 259.

19. Ibid., p. 260.

20. Ibid.

21. Ibid., pp. 305–6; Schlesinger, *Robert Kennedy*, p. 908.

22. Schlesinger, *Robert Kennedy*, p. 908.

23. *American Journey*, pp. 305–6.

24. Schlesinger, *Robert Kennedy*, p. 909.

25. Cf. ibid.

26. "Did you touch him?" was a refrain heard wherever Bobby appeared. Lasky, *The Myth and the Man*, p. 335.

27. Newfield, *A Memoir*, p. 239.

28. *American Journey*, p. 282.

29. Ibid.

30. White, *The Making of the President 1968*, pp. 173–74.

31. Ibid., p. 174.

32. Ibid.

33. *American Journey*, pp. 295, 299–300.

34. Ibid., p. 295.

35. "I can't plan. Living every day is like Russian roulette." Newfield, *A Memoir*, p. 31; cf. Schlesinger, *Robert Kennedy*, p. 902; *American Journey*, p. 293.

36. Cf. Charles Quinn, quoted in *American Journey*, pp. 294–95. After I wrote these lines, I discovered that Ralph de Toledano made a similar point in *R.F.K.*, p. 304.

37. Newfield, *A Memoir*, p. 17.

38. Arthur Schlesinger said that when Bobby "went to an Indian reservation or saw poor white families in Appalachia, those children became his children. The food they were eating was the food he might be eating; the hovel in which they were living was his." *American Journey*, p. 277.

39. Newfield, *A Memoir*, p. 90.

40. *Keats*, p. 37 (March 13, 1819).

41. Quoted in Schlesinger, *A Thousand Days*, p. 95.

42. Cf. Newfield, *A Memoir*, pp. 59, 280.

43. Newfield described Bobby's presidential campaign as a "narcotic ritual." See Newfield, *A Memoir*, p. 252.

44. Schlesinger, *Robert Kennedy*, p. 809.

45. Vanden Heuvel and Gwirtzman, *On His Own*, p. 171; Schlesinger, *Robert Kennedy*, p. 697.

46. Schlesinger, *Robert Kennedy*, p. 785.

47. Peter Edelman, quoted in *American Journey*, p. 278.

48. Emerson, "Friendship," in *Essays and Lectures*, p. 353.

49. Ibid., p. 342.

50. Herndon's *Lincoln*, p. 344.

51. Ibid., p. 474.

52. Ibid., p. 250.

53. Ibid., p. 483.

54. Nietzsche, *Human*, p. 125.

55. See *The Taming of the Shrew*, Act I, Scenes I and II.

56. Schlesinger, *Robert Kennedy*, p. 15.

57. Navasky, *Kennedy Justice*, p. 502.

58. Schlesinger, *A Thousand Days*, p. 79.

59. Joseph Kennedy did not "leave a stone unturned to encourage his boys," Franklin Roosevelt's eldest son said. He "was a great father." Schlesinger, *Robert Kennedy*, p. 18.

60. E. Kennedy, *The Fruitful Bough*.

61. Sorensen, *Kennedy*, p. 31.

62. Ibid.

63. Alsop, *I've Seen the Best of It*, pp. 408–9. See also Leamer, *The Kennedy Women*, p. 405.

64. Alsop, *I've Seen the Best of It*, pp. 408–9.

65. Schlesinger, *Robert Kennedy*, pp. 18–19.

66. See, e.g., Schlesinger, *Robert Kennedy*, p. 20.

67. Matthews, *Kennedy and Nixon*, p. 65.

68. Ibid., p. 149.

69. Ibid.

70. Ibid.

71. Reeves, *President Kennedy*, p. 76; Beschloss, *Crisis Years*, pp. 107–8.

72. Newfield, *A Memoir*, p. 59.

73. Bright sunshine lifted Bobby's spirits: ibid., p. 225.

74. Vanden Heuvel and Gwirtzman, *On His Own*, pp. 376–77.

75. Hersh, *The Dark Side of Camelot*, p. 15.

76. Sorensen, *Kennedy*, p. 38.

77. Richardson, *Emerson*, p. 181.

78. Beschloss, *Crisis Years*, p. 123.

79. Schlesinger, *Robert Kennedy*, p. 600.

80. Ibid., p. 857.

81. Wills, *The Kennedy Imprisonment*, pp. 93–94.

Notes

82. Halberstam, *Unfinished Odyssey*, p. 110.
83. Schlesinger, *Robert Kennedy*, p. 591.
84. Ibid.
85. Horowitz, *Radical Son*, p. 353.
86. Ibid.
87. See Wills, *The Kennedy Imprisonment*, p. 139.
88. Sallust, *Bellum Catalinae*, LIV.
89. See, e.g., Vidal, *United States*, p. 817.
90. On Joan Kennedy, see Wills, *The Kennedy Imprisonment*, pp. 39–40, 48–52.
91. Gibbon, *Decline and Fall*, vol. 3, p. 185. Theodosius' humiliation was part of an act of penance.
92. Matt. 4:24.
93. See Himmelfarb, *Poverty and Compassion*, pp. 219–34.
94. Statement of the Honorable Robert F. Kennedy, Attorney General of the United States, before the Subcommittee on Education of the U.S. House of Representatives, Committee on Education and Labor, H.R. 7178, July 12, 1961, in *Speeches*.
95. Ibid.
96. Ibid.
97. Walinsky, memorandum entitled "Précis and Summary," circa 1964, in Walinsky Papers, file 43. Cf. Walinsky's ms., "Poverty: Through the Looking Glass," in the Walinsky Papers, file 43.

CHAPTER 13

1. Ross, *Apostle of Change*, p. 510.
2. Dedication of swimming pool: vanden Heuvel and Gwirtzman, *On His Own*, p. 92.
3. Quoted in Lasky, *The Myth and the Man*, p. 315.
4. Schlesinger, *Robert Kennedy*, p. 759.
5. Lasky, *The Myth and the Man*, pp. 346–47.
6. Manchester, *Controversy*, p. 59.
7. Lasky, *The Myth and the Man*, p. 372.
8. Ibid., p. 308.
9. Ibid., pp. 368, 373.
10. Manchester, *Controversy*, pp. 75–76.
11. Lasky, *The Myth and the Man*, p. 375.
12. Ibid.
13. Vanden Heuvel and Gwirtzman, *On His Own*, p. 228.
14. Lasky, *The Myth and the Man*, pp. 376–82.
15. Ibid.; vanden Heuvel and Gwirtzman, *On His Own*, pp. 227–39.
16. Quoted in Schlesinger, *Robert Kennedy*, p. 593.
17. Ibid., p. xi.

18. Newfield, *A Memoir*, p. 10.

19. Such vestiges of nineteenth-century individualism as could be found in twentieth-century America were cheap and degraded versions of the original creed—or so individualism's critics maintained. See Lasch, *Culture of Narcissism*, pp. 9–13.

20. Lewis, *The American Adam*, *passim*.

21. Thoreau, *Walden*, in *Thoreau*, p. 348.

22. Cf. Burke, *Reflections*, p. 41.

23. Quoted in Ross, *Apostle of Change*, p. 32.

24. Memorandum, Robert Burke Johnson to Thomas Johnson, "First Report on Bedford-Stuyvesant Project," January 10, 1967, in the Walinsky Papers, file 1.

25. Vanden Heuvel and Gwirtzman, *On His Own*, p. 91.

26. *Collected Speeches*, p. 177.

27. Ribicoff Hearings, p. 28.

28. Ibid.

29. Ibid.

30. *To Seek a Newer World*, p. 20.

31. Ribicoff Hearings, p. 28.

32. Address, Day Care Council of New York, May 8, 1967, quoted in Ross, *Apostle of Change*, p. 112.

33. Ibid., pp. 112, 131. The observation that suburbs do not constitute true communities can also be found in *To Seek a Newer World*, p. 56.

34. Address, Day Care Council of New York, May 8, 1967, quoted in Ross, *Apostle of Change*, pp. 112, 131.

35. Ibid., p. 112.

36. Ribicoff Hearings, pp. 33, 37.

37. Speech in Bedford-Stuyvesant, October 10, 1966, quoted in Ross, *Apostle of Change*, p. 154.

38. Ribicoff Hearings, pp. 33, 37.

39. Ibid.

40. Ibid.

41. See memorandum, Robert Burke Johnson to Thomas Johnston, "First Report on Bedford-Stuyvesant Project," January 10, 1967, in the Walinsky Papers, file 1; BSDPO, pp. 5, 15; Ford Foundation Proposal, March 9, 1967, in RFK Senate Papers, file 11.

42. Memorandum entitled "Industrial Development—Job Creation Program: Proposed Minimum Revision," circa 1967, p. 1, in the Walinsky Papers, file 1. See also *The New York Times*, June 25, 1967, p. 1 ("Brooklyn Ghetto Given $7 Million"). The "special impact" legislation took the form of amendments to the Economic Opportunity Act of 1964. See memorandum entitled "Industrial Development," op. cit.

43. Memorandum, Walinsky to Thomas Johnston, undated, in the Walinsky Papers, file 11.

44. Draft of letter, Bobby to McGeorge Bundy, p. 2, in the Walinsky

Papers, file 1; Ross, *Apostle of Change*, p. 117. See also memorandum, Herbert S. Channick to Adam Walinsky, undated, in the Walinsky Papers, file 2.

45. See Daniel P. Moynihan, "The Crisis in Welfare: The View from New York," p. 5, unpublished ms. in RFK Senate Papers, file 118 ("the closed shop has been outlawed by Federal law, but the building-trades unions continue to maintain one de facto").

46. Memorandum, Thomas Johnston to Bobby, May 3, 1967, p. 3, in RFK Senate Papers, file 11.

47. Handwritten notes (Walinsky's?) apparently passed to Bobby during the Ribicoff hearings, in RFK Senate Papers, file 18; notes for questions for Walter Reuther, December 5, 1966, in RFK Senate Papers, file 18.

48. Memorandum from Walinsky to Bobby entitled "Program for the Fall," 1966, in the Walinsky Papers, file 2.

49. Ibid.

50. Ibid.

51. Ibid.

52. Ribicoff Hearings, pp. 45–46.

53. Memorandum, Edelman to Bobby, in RFK Senate Papers, file 18.

54. Newfield, *A Memoir*, pp. 95–96.

55. *Collected Speeches*, p. 186; Newfield, *A Memoir*, p. 96.

56. *Collected Speeches*, p. 186; Schlesinger, *Robert Kennedy*, p. 788.

57. *Collected Speeches*, p. 186.

58. *The New York Times*, June 25, 1967, p. 1 ("Brooklyn Ghetto Given $7 Million"); *Collected Speeches*, p. 190.

59. Vanden Heuvel and Gwirtzman, *On His Own*, p. 94.

CHAPTER 14

1. Machiavelli, *Discourses*, p. 267.

2. Clark's *Leonardo*, p. 192.

3. *To Seek a Newer World*, p. 56.

4. Ibid., p. 57.

5. See Wilson's essay on John Jay Chapman in *The Triple Thinkers* (especially pp. 149–50); Wilson's essays on Lee and Holmes in *Patriotic Gore*; Wilson, *FND*, p. 183; and Wilson, *The Shores of Light*, p. 528.

6. Ross, *Apostle of Change*, p. 111. See also Mumford, *The City in History*, and Hamilton, *The Greek Way*, pp. 72, 136.

7. Quoted in *The New York Times*, January 21, 1997, p. A14.

8. The more closely we investigate the *real* history of the classical city-state, as opposed to the ideal history the dreamers have given us, the less likely we are to accept the communitarian thesis. The classical Athenian polis for which Michael Sandel, among others, pines, a city "whose conditions of life afforded [its citizens] the leisure, learning, and commonality to deliberate

well about public concerns," was, even in the glorious fifth century of Pericles and Phidias, very far from being a civic paradise. In Thucydides' account of the period we discover a political life fully as ugly as our own; we find there the same relentless desire for power and mastery, the same unending clash of interest against interest, the same ceaseless aggrandizement of self and untiring devotion to merely personal felicity, that characterize our own American politics today. The citizens of fifth-century Athens, for all their careful deliberation, for all their exquisite sense of "commonality," acquired an empire and ruled it tyrannically; acted in reckless disregard of the principles of human decency and their city's long-term interests; and committed acts whose barbarity was exceeded only by their folly. The Athenians sent the innocent Miltiades, the architect of victory at Marathon, to die a horrible death in a dank dungeon, and forced Socrates, among the greatest of their city's men, to drink the cup of hemlock. The various treacheries, ostracisms, judicial murders, and mass executions sanctioned by the citizens of Athens in the golden apogee of their power and glory, and the disastrous civil war in which their deliberative politics culminated, ought to give even the most ardent communitarian pause.

9. See Machiavelli's letter to Vettori, December 10, 1513, in *Letters of Machiavelli*, p. 142. Rousseau's tendencies toward fantasy and dreaminess are evident in a number of his works, including the *Confessions* and the *Reveries of a Solitary Walker*.

10. At the heart of the communitarian idea is the belief that people should extend the same sympathy and affection that they instinctively feel for their families and friends to the larger spheres of the neighborhood and the city. One contemporary advocate of communitarian ideas, Suzanna Sherry, has argued that citizens should "behave toward their country and its citizens as they do toward their families: proud, protective, and willing to make sacrifices." Suzanna Sherry, "Responsible Republicanism: Educating for Citizenship," *University of Chicago Law Review*, vol. 62, p. 162 (1995). But it is not only unrealistic to ask people to love a crowd in the same way that they love those with whom they are intimately connected through blood or friendship, it is also deeply subversive of sound economic order. An observation of Hayek's is illuminating. Were we, he says, "to apply the unmodified, uncurbed, rules of the micro-cosmos (i.e., of the small band or troop, or of, say, our families) to the macro-cosmos (our wider civilization), as our instincts and sentimental yearnings often make us wish to do," we would "destroy" that wider civilization. Aristotle, the preeminent philosopher of the polis, was unable to see that an extended market order—a "macrocosmos" in which the profit-driven commercial trading he denounced played a critical role in the efficient allocation of resources—had a good deal more to do with the greatness of fifth-century Athens—a "microcosmos"—than the practice of public virtue that he extolled. See Hayek, *The Fatal Conceit*, pp. 18–19, 43–47, 80–81.

11. Bobby's admiration for Tacitus: Newfield, *A Memoir*, p. 48.

12. For Eichmann and the Freemasons, see Arendt, *Eichmann in Jerusalem*, p. 32.

CHAPTER 15

1. Schlesinger, *Robert Kennedy*, p. 97.

2. Either prostitutes or housewives: Leamer, *The Kennedy Women*, p. 461.

3. Rose Kennedy, *Times to Remember*, pp. 102–3.

4. Eunice thought Bobby "anxious for approval and love, and therefore when he got a lot of that, which I think he did when he married Ethel, he blossomed." Schlesinger, *Robert Kennedy*, p. 89.

5. Ibid., p. 591.

6. Oppenheimer, *The Other Mrs. Kennedy*, p. 317.

7. Spoto, *Marilyn Monroe*, p. 601.

8. Details of the February 1962 party: ibid., pp. 601–2; Oppenheimer, *The Other Mrs. Kennedy*, pp. 311–12. Oppenheimer states that Bobby and Guthman drove Monroe home from the February 1962 party; Spoto states that the drive followed the October 1961 party.

9. Schlesinger, *Robert Kennedy*, p. 590.

10. Spoto, *Marilyn Monroe*, pp. 664–65.

11. See ibid., pp. 600–5.

12. See Oppenheimer, *The Other Mrs. Kennedy*, pp. 322–23.

13. Schlesinger, *Robert Kennedy*, pp. 3–4.

14. Kozol, *Amazing Grace*, p. 6.

15. Ibid.

16. See Lee Schmookler, "Rescuing the Homeless," *The Wall Street Journal*, August 13, 1996, p. A12.

17. Ibid.

18. Dana Milbank, "In God's Name: Michigan Now Relies on Churches to Help People Leave Welfare," *The Wall Street Journal*, March 17, 1997, p. A1.

19. Carter, *Culture of Disbelief*, pp. 109–15, 120–23.

20. Out of an excessive fear that government might create an "established" religion—a state church like the Church of England—the Supreme Court has given us, in the last few decades, a jurisprudence that misreads the First Amendment and effectively prohibits the government from supporting promising means of rescuing people from despair, even when those means would tend neither to establish a church nor to infringe upon the free exercise of religion. (The First Amendment states that "Congress shall make no law respecting an establishment of religion, or prohibiting the free excercise thereof . . .") In the Supreme Court's view, however, even the most indirect support of religion *in general*—as opposed to particular religions—is a violation of the Establishment Clause. The Court invented this consti-

tutional prohibition out of thin air; the First Amendment itself says nothing about government support for religion in general. If the Establishment Clause requires the government to be scrupulously neutral between faith and faith, it nowhere requires the government to be neutral between religion, agnosticism, and atheism. The constitutional case law of the last few decades is at odds with the country's shaping traditions; the federal government has *never* been neutral on the question of the value of religion in general (as opposed to the value of particular religious faiths). American history is full of examples of government "support" for religion, from chaplains and prayers in the legislature and the armed forces to the federal holiday of Christmas. When the other day I went to mail some letters, I could not help but note the irony, perhaps the tragedy, of a constitutional regime in which the post office is permitted to print stamps depicting the Blessed Virgin and play "Silent Night" in public places but in which federal aid to "faith-based" programs that save people's lives is forbidden. There are, however, indications that this hostility toward religion is beginning to wane. In an influential book, *The Culture of Disbelief*, constitutional scholar Stephen Carter took issue with those who would make the Establishment Clause a "guarantor of public secularism." Carter argued that if the Founders' vision of a "wall" between church and state is to be made "compatible with the structure and needs of modern society," a "few doors" need to be carved into the wall. Congress, emboldened by the change in public sentiment, recently passed a law guaranteeing "that a church has a right to compete for state contracts to perform welfare services without compromising 'definition, development, practice and expression of its religious beliefs.' " The state of Michigan has gone so far as to instruct "its welfare officials to start 'reaching out to . . . faith-based organizations for help' in guiding people off public assistance and back into the mainstream." It's not clear, however, that this new approach will survive scrutiny in the courts.

21. Cf. the character of Mark Winsome in Melville, *The Confidence-Man*, pp. 223–44 (chapters 36–39).

22. Vanden Heuvel and Gwirtzman, *On His Own*, p. 23.

23. Schlesinger, *Robert Kennedy*, p. 619.

24. Vanden Heuvel and Gwirtzman, *On His Own*, p. 23.

25. Newfield, *A Memoir*, p. 25.

26. Schlesinger, *Robert Kennedy*, p. 781.

27. Newfield, *A Memoir*, p. 25.

28. Vanden Heuvel and Gwirtzman, *On His Own*, pp. 23–24.

29. Memorandum, Walinsky to Bobby, "Tasks Immediately Ahead in Bedford-Stuyvesant," 1966, p. 3, in the Walinsky Papers, file 2.

30. On solipsistic, "emotionally distant" Rose, see Leamer, *The Kennedy Women*, pp. 134, 136, 191, 375.

31. Ibid., pp. 113–14.

32. Quoted in Blake, *Disraeli*, pp. 201, 208.

Notes

CHAPTER 16

1. The meeting with Etienne Manac'h is described in Schlesinger, *Robert Kennedy*, pp. 766–69, and vanden Huevel and Gwirtzman, *On His Own*, pp. 236–39.

2. Schlesinger, *Robert Kennedy*, p. 768; vanden Heuvel and Gwirtzman, *On His Own*, p. 238.

3. *Time* exaggerated: Schlesinger, *Robert Kennedy*, p. 768.

4. Ibid.

5. See ibid., p. 769.

6. Ibid., p. 774.

7. See the *1968 World Book Year Book*, p. 266.

8. See Schlesinger, *Robert Kennedy*, p. 846. Bobby changed his mind after the Kerner Commission issued a first-rate report.

9. Didion, *Slouching Towards Bethlehem*, p. 78.

10. Greene, *The Quiet American*, p. 25.

11. Conrad, *Lord Jim*, pp. 12–13.

12. Forster, *A Passage to India*, p. 27.

13. On JFK's skeptical attitude toward an American presence on the Asian mainland, see Schlesinger, *Robert Kennedy*, p. 701.

14. Sorensen, *Kennedy*, pp. 17–18.

15. Schlesinger, *Robert Kennedy*, p. 124.

16. Crowley, *Nixon off the Record*, p. 173.

17. Schlesinger, *Robert Kennedy*, p. 775.

18. Isaacson and Thomas, *The Wise Men*, pp. 422, 446.

19. Ibid., p. 648.

20. Ibid., p. 647.

21. Ibid., p. 671.

22. Ibid., pp. 670–71.

23. Ibid., pp. 652, 693–95, 702.

24. Ibid., p. 687.

25. One must make an exception for Joseph Alsop, who continued to support the Vietnam War even after it became unpopular in Georgetown; he refused to abandon his principles in the name of changing political fashions.

CHAPTER 17

1. Lippmann and the Fabians: Steel, *Walter Lippmann*, pp. 23–49; "drunk with power": ibid., p. 319. Lippmann as a perceptive critic of the New Deal: ibid., pp. 318, 322–26. See also Lippmann's book *The Good Society*.

2. Steel, *Walter Lippmann*, pp. 433–49. Lippmann was also an early and astute critic of America's policies in Vietnam; in 1964 he wrote that the

military outlook there was "dismal beyond words." Newfield, *A Memoir*, p. 119.

3. Newfield, *A Memoir*, p. 196.

4. Schlesinger, *Robert Kennedy*, p. 836; Newfield, *A Memoir*, pp. 195–96.

5. Schlesinger, *Robert Kennedy*, p. 832.

6. Newfield, *A Memoir*, p. 191.

7. Schlesinger, *Robert Kennedy*, p. 836.

8. Newfield, *A Memoir*, p. 202.

9. Ibid., p. 203.

10. Ibid., p. 204.

11. See Schlesinger, *Robert Kennedy*, pp. 848–49; Newfield, *A Memoir*, p. 218.

12. Schlesinger, *Robert Kennedy*, p. 854; Newfield, *A Memoir*, p. 211.

13. Schlesinger wrote that although to many "it looked as if [Bobby] were deciding to enter only after McCarthy had shown the way in New Hampshire," the reality was that "he had reached that decision a week or more earlier." Schlesinger, *Robert Kennedy*, p. 854. Schlesinger's eagerness to demonstrate that Bobby had decided to run even before the results of New Hampshire were known is understandable; by coming late to the race, Bobby appeared to be an opportunist and a coward, a politician who had been unwilling to act until another man had revealed the extent of the danger, a weakling who, in Murray Kempton's words, came "down from the hills to shoot the wounded." See Schlesinger, *Robert Kennedy*, p. 861. It is true that Bobby had, before New Hampshire voted, sent his brother Ted to tell McCarthy that he was going to run; but this doesn't demonstrate that Bobby had irrevocably made up his mind. If Johnson had trounced McCarthy in New Hampshire, Bobby would have been perfectly free to walk away from the contest. It is telling that Bobby himself said that he decided to run for President only *after* the New Hampshire primary, when he learned that Johnson had rejected the idea of a Vietnam commission and was commited to achieving a military victory in Indochina. See Schlesinger, *Robert Kennedy*, p. 854.

14. Newfield, *A Memoir*, pp. 216–17.

15. Schlesinger, *Robert Kennedy*, p. 855.

16. Newfield, *A Memoir*, pp. 231–41.

17. Schlesinger, *Robert Kennedy*, p. 863.

18. Ibid., p. 877. Cf. Bobby's statement that "the welfare system itself has created many of [America's] fatherless families." Press release, May 19, 1968, in *Collected Speeches*, p. 385.

19. Lasky, *The Myth and the Man*, p. 405. The Lincoln Trail: vanden Heuvel and Gwirtzman, *On His Own*, p. 344.

20. Can't have the federal government telling people what's good for them: Newfield, *A Memoir*, p. 36, quoting Warren Weaver, Jr., "Kennedy: Meet the Conservative," *The New York Times*, April 28, 1968, The Week in Review, Section 4, p. 1.

21. Lasky, *The Myth and the Man*, p. 405; Gladwin Hill, "Reagan Derides Kennedy Stands," *The New York Times*, May 21, 1968, p. 29.

22. Ibid.

23. Schlesinger, *Robert Kennedy*, p. 883.

24. Ibid., p. 889.

25. Ibid., p. 872.

26. Newfield, *A Memoir*, p. 81.

27. Ibid.

28. Meany "would barely speak" to Bobby: ibid. On big labor siding with Humphrey, see Schlesinger, *Robert Kennedy*, p. 884.

29. Irrational regulations (such as those that used to govern the airline industry): See Bork, *The Antitrust Paradox;* pp. 183–84. The biggest businesses were also better able to bear the costs of regulatory overkill in areas like the environment than their smaller competitors, were better able to withstand the onslaught of litigation that various product liability laws created, and found it easier to raise money in heavily regulated capital markets.

30. The individual does matter: Schlesinger, *Robert Kennedy*, p. 872.

31. Vanden Heuvel and Gwirtzman, *On His Own*, pp. 376–77.

32. Schlesinger, *Robert Kennedy*, p. 911.

33. On this point I follow Newfield's analysis; see Newfield, *A Memoir*, p. 282.

34. Bobby after the debate: details are from Schlesinger, *Robert Kennedy*, p. 912.

35. Sunday, June 2, 1968: Newfield, *A Memoir*, pp. 283–84.

36. Details of Monday, June 3, 1968, and Tuesday, June 4, 1968, are drawn primarily from Newfield, *A Memoir*, pp. 282 *et seq.* and Schlesinger, *Robert Kennedy*, pp. 900 *et seq.*

37. Schlesinger, *Robert Kennedy*, p. 913.

38. Newfield, *A Memoir*, p. 290.

39. *Collected Speeches*, pp. 401–2.

40. *American Journey*, p. 60.

CONCLUSION

1. Churchill's father, Lord Randolph Churchill, pioneered the idea of "Tory Democracy," a democratic political order in which aristocrats and patrician "experts" would play the largest part. David Cannadine observed that Winston's own early efforts "on behalf of the poor—regulating wages and conditions in the mines and the sweated trades, and setting up labour exchanges and unemployment insurance—were essentially authoritarian and paternalistic in their benevolence." Cannadine, *Aspects of Aristocracy*, p. 156. As late as 1930 Churchill advocated the creation of the very type of regulatory and administrative state that Roosevelt himself set about constructing during his presidency; speaking at Oxford in 1930 Churchill called for the

establishment of a new "economic sub-parliament" composed of persons "possessing special qualifications in economic matters." Cannadine, *Aspects of Aristocracy*, p. 158. Churchill's desperate capitulations to the welfare state mentality in the 1945 general election must not be permitted to obscure his belief that those who thought like Mr. Attlee and the other architects of Britain's postwar welfare state committed themselves to an equal distribution of miseries, while those who championed a system of free enterprise, as he did, favored an unequal distribution of blessings.

2. Bobby supported welfare state programs even as he criticized the welfare state. See Lasky, *The Myth and the Man*, pp. 284–85, 323, 324, 340.

3. Adam Walinsky, "America Is Under Siege: The Crisis of Public Order," *The Greensboro News & Record*, August 27, 1995; Lars-Erik Nelsonn, "Domestic War Shortchanged by Congress," *The Star-Ledger* (Newark, N.J.), June 22, 1995. See also Walinsky's essay in the July 1995 number of *The Atlantic Monthly*.

4. Nelsonn, op. cit.

5. Schlesinger, *Robert Kennedy*, p. 805.

Index

Index

Index

Index

Index

Stimsonian statesmen, 22, 44–84, 141
  administrative state and, xx, 46, 53, 69, 80, 212
  backgrounds of, 26, 58, 76
  Bobby's break with, xx, 103–109, 124–27
  defined, 26
  demise of, 52–53, 83–84, 208–10
  factions, 68–69
  free market economy and, 20, 21, 125
  Johnson and, 99
  lack of intellectual and imaginative excellence among, 34
  lack of political base, 73
  national security state and, xx, 27–28, 63, 68, 78–79, 83, 92
  paternalistic view of government, 21, 44–46, 52–53, 212
  pleasures of the empire and, 191–95
  practical achievements of, 34, 57
  problem of individual self-confidence and, 113–14
  public service and, 53–54, 58, 62
  reverence of English aristocracy, 37
  schooling of, 26, 30–34, 37, 58, 78
  spiritual life and, 91
  Stimsonian establishment, 74, 76–78
  twentieth-century liberalism and, 27, 100
  welfare state and, xx, 21, 26, 46, 53, 69, 80, 83, 92
  see also names of individuals
Stover at Yale (Johnson), 10
Styron, William, 13
Suffering, human, 91
  Bobby's compassion for, xxi, 132–33, 139–43, 145, 154
  the paternalistic state and, 21
Sunday-night supper club, 68, 70
Sunday Telegraph, 42
Supreme Court, 37, 82, 144
  Lemon test, 184–85
  New Deal and, 46

Swanson, Gloria, 4, 7, 22
Syme, Ronald, 36

Tacitus, 173
Taft, Robert A., 72, 79, 194
Tampa, Florida, 190
Tancred (Disraeli), 187
Taylor, Elizabeth, 159
Taylor, Telford, 24
Teamsters Union, 40
"Teddy's Women Problem/ Women's Teddy Problem," xvi
Thomas, Evan, 195, 196
Thoreau, Henry David, 161, 185
Time, 189
Tocqueville, Alexis de, 117
Tory Party, 84, 211
To Seek a Newer World (Kennedy), 105, 171
"Tradition and the Individual Talent," 119
Tree, Ronald, 70
Trilling, Diana, 123–24
Trilling, Lionel, 100
Truman, Harry S, 52, 62, 79
Truman Doctrine, 62
Tuchman, Barbara, 96
Turkey, 62

United Nations, 81
University of Virginia Law School, 34, 65
Updike, John, 182
Urban riots of 1967, 190

Vance, Cyrus, 81, 190
vanden Heuvel, William, 167, 186
Victura, 14
Vidal, Gore, 38, 50, 95, 180
Vietnam, 191
Vietnam War, 150, 195–97
  Bobby and, 156, 186–91, 197
  Dien Bien Phu, 191
  Tet offensive, 200
Village Voice, The, 199

About the Author

Michael Knox Beran was born in Dallas, Texas, in 1966. He graduated from Groton School in 1984 and holds degrees from Columbia and Cambridge Universities as well as from Yale Law School. A lawyer, he lives in Westchester County, New York, with his wife, Mary.